LEADERSHIP PARENTING

EMPOWER YOUR CHILD'S SOCIAL SUCCESS

MOTHER GOPI GITA

Difference Press

Washington, DC, USA

Published 2022

Editing: Madeline Kosten

Cover Design: Jennifer Stimson

Author's photos courtesy of Radha Young

Artist of saint and swan illustrations: Padma Walsh

Artist of diverse children illustration and two saints illustration: Neelmadhav Naik

Artist of henna illustration: Mother Gopi Gita

ADVANCE PRAISE

"In her excellent book, *Leadership Parenting*, Mother Gopi Gita shares her vast and invaluable experience as a very successful mother and teacher. Written in reader-friendly prose, yet comprehensive and profound, this book offers all those concerned with parenting a reliable, realistic, optimistic guide that will enhance the lives of all concerned. I offer sincere thanks to Gopi Gita for this extraordinary contribution."

— DR. HOWARD J. RESNICK, *HRDAYANANDA DAS GOSWAMI*, PHD IN SANSKRIT AND INDIAN STUDIES, HARVARD UNIVERSITY, SENIOR SPIRITUAL LEADER OF ISKCON

"Here is a powerhouse book of tools for any mother or father looking to completely revolutionize their parenting! Mother Gopi Gita will personally take you by the hand through every moment with your child, and guide you to bring out their highest potential. It's rare to find such classic bhakti parenting principles coupled with lifelong experiences in such an accessible format. I highly recommend it to all parents looking to step up their child's leadership skills."

— BRIAN TIBBITS, *INDRADYUMNA SWAMI*, CEO, FESTIVAL OF INDIA, DIRECTOR, VIVA KULTURA, AUTHOR, INTERNATIONAL MONK, GURU

"Powerful, practical, and solid advice on parenting with confidence. I especially found the new and unique cultural stories helpful in conveying time-honored lessons for parents and children."

— SETH W. SPELLMAN, *SESA DAS*, MINISTER OF EDUCATION, INTERNATIONAL SOCIETY OF KRISHNA CONSCIOUSNESS

"I highly recommend Leadership Parenting for all parents, those who are contemplating having children, and those who are guiding children. In an engaging way, utilizing her own experience, Mother Gopi Gita walks the reader through a coherent, simple, step-by-step process to facilitate the maximization of a child's potential."

— BRUCE JACOBS, *BIR KRISHNA GOSWAMI*, AUTHOR, INTERNATIONAL MONK, GURU

"*Leadership Parenting* is a fun read. One feels as if Gopi Gita is sitting right there, chatting, sharing, and demonstrating her wide-ranging insight and decades of experience regarding raising children successfully. Her book is full of such a variety of wisdom and practical tools, that even incorporating just a few points in this book into your relationship with your children will add value to your life and theirs. Even if one is already very experienced and educated in how to raise children, there are so many gems in this book that every reader is likely to find something rare and useful to add to their knowledge and skills. Gopi Gita is expert at taking all these gems and showing us how they form patterns for easy recall and application."

— DR. EDITH BEST, *URMILA DEVI DASI*, PHD IN EDUCATION, AUTHOR, INTERNATIONAL PARENT & EDUCATOR COACH

"The information in this book, *Leadership Parenting: Empower Your Child's Social Success*, just works. With age-old leadership strategies from the bhakti culture, Mother Gopi Gita teaches parents to highlight the best qualities in their children. And with mindfulness and connection techniques, she introduces the revered practice of mantra meditation to energize all our relationships. Every parent should read this book."

— GLENN TETON, *GIRIRAJ SWAMI*, ISKCON GURU, MONK, AND AUTHOR

"In Mother Gopi Gita's book *Leadership Parenting* we may have the first manual for raising children. It dives deeply into many ways children have been reared over the years and points out how these have affected our children's lives. We learn how positive reinforcement, without overindulgence or exaggerated praise, can move our children to be the best they can be. Finding the child's strengths and allowing them to express their inner natures allows them to take on the challenges the world sets before them.

"The style in which the book is presented, with the focus on the bhakti tradition, leads us through a wonderful journey. This ancient bhakti tradition is steeped in a loving process, where we not only flourish materially but also find our inner spiritual voice, guiding us to our ultimate goal of truly understanding our real self.

"I hope you gain as much as I have from this book and share its wisdom with whomever you can."

— ROBERT J. MABIN, *RTADHVAJA SWAMI*, BOARD OF DIRECTORS FOR BANA, & NACPO

"This is a beautiful and timely book. As we rebuild our lives after the isolation and confusion of the pandemic, it helps us reimagine the word 'empowerment' in social and collaborative ways. It reminds us that leadership awareness begins at home and can be found in every child. As we draw it out of them, we find it in ourselves. Supported by Mother Gopi Gita's own life experience as a mother and a teacher, and connected to wisdom truths from the East, this is a handbook you will come back to again and again."

— CATHERINE AND BRIAN BLOCH, *ANANDA DEVI AND VRAJA VIHARI DAS*, DIRECTOR, ISKCON OF D.C., OMBUDSMAN, UNITED STATES DEPARTMENT OF THE INTERIOR

CONTENTS

Foreword xi
Introduction xv

Part I
MEET UP

1. You Are Not Alone 3
2. The Brain Tumor 17
3. Climb with Me 27

Part II
DISCOVER

4. Why Does My Child Feel So Broken? 41
5. Why Have I Been Chosen? 69

Part III
CONNECT

6. How Can They Connect with Others? 87
7. How Can They Be Understood? 111

Part IV
PRACTICE

8. How Can They Accept Boundaries? 137

Part V
ACCOMPLISH

9. What If They Make Mistakes? 175
10. When Can I Take a Break? 201

Part VI
LEAD

11. Where Is Their Place? 223
12. How Can They Feel For Others? 255
13. What about the Conflicts? 277
14. The Garden of Harmony, Sri Mayapur 299
15. You Got This 315

For the Bhakti Yogis 319
Acknowledgments 325
About the Author 335
Other Books by Difference Press 337
Gift for the Reader 339

DEDICATION

To my dear husband, Rupa M,
Thank you for showing me how to parent with bhakti love, and being the sugar to my spice, despite the struggle. You are my rock.

* * *

To my older boy, Vraja,
Thank you for giving me sound leadership guidance and showing me effortless success. You are the reason I breathe.

* * *

To my younger boy, Nitai,
Thank you for showing me the meaning of determination in purpose and sharing your glittery laughter when I want to cry. You are the reason I wake up and smile.

* * *

To my sister, Gaura Mani

Thank you for reading my first journals and listening for hours when we were kids. You are my motivation and shining star.

To my dad and mom, Vishvambhar Das and Mother Vrindavaneshvari

Thank you for introducing me to the Inner Parents and saints as soon as I was born. I am privileged to be your daughter. You are the embodiment of leadership parents.

To my grandfather, Srila Prabhupada

Thank you for accepting me, encouraging me, believing in me and always pushing me past my comfort zone. You are my destination.

To my children around the world

You deserve to be seen, heard, and loved. Let every adult in your life know how to empower you. You are my masters and I love you to the ends of this earth. I can't wait to meet you through your parents.

FOREWORD

Mother Gopi Gita works a kind of magic with children. I've seen it on the playground in occasional visits to her school, as when a first grader went running to her in tears with a scraped elbow. He left shortly thereafter with dry eyes and newfound strength. Or when a slightly older child wanted an adult to make the other girls treat her fairly. After stopping to speak with Mother Gopi Gita at a playground picnic table, the student went back to the group with whatever nugget of wisdom the magician had shared, all of a sudden able to intervene for herself, without adult help. And I've seen that same magic at work in a classroom of students who – after greetings and a few words – showed a quiet, new focus for their morning activity.

My early work as a classroom teacher – and later as a teacher trainer and educational consultant – has taken me to scores of schools throughout North America, and rarely have I been in a school where an entire staff shared a common vision for children's growth to the extent that reigns among Gopi and her colleagues. The aura is one that says, "children are in good hands here."

Unlike the "tricks" of magicians, however, Gopi's magic is for sharing, and she wants to share it with you. For her, it's not really magic; she simply calls it "tools." As you will hear her say, there is nothing magic about what the parent does. The beauty is all in the child's transformation – when life situations that have not been working (for the child, or the parent's satisfaction) can be "re-tooled" into life situations that fill children's needs and open their hearts to meaning, purpose, and accomplishment. She wants to share these tools because she, like so many of the parents she has worked with, has seen their transformative power.

What looks like the ability to peer into children's souls and tap into all the positives that lie within is really the practiced skills of connecting with children and helping them feel like they belong, of recognizing their ability to be agents for good and helping them achieve what they are capable of.

There are several things I like about *Leadership Parenting,* and a few more that I absolutely love. First and foremost on my "love" list is the fact that this book is not written by a know-it-all talking down to an audience. This book is written from one parent to another, by a parent who grew up with her own challenges and difficulties and who admits to making her own mistakes, both earlier in life and as she began the endeavor of raising her own children. She may not have encountered all parenting problems, but she does understand the struggles that parents face, just as she understands the heartbreaks, fears, and doubts that confront all parents as they do their best, yet still too often feel like failures. Happily for us, Gopi was not only a quick learner; she has also been a careful gatherer and organizer of the myriad of strategies that have come her way over her years of interacting with children of a variety of ages, in a variety of settings.

What I love about this book even more than its parent-to-parent style, however, is the supportive, joyful optimism that bursts forth from nearly every page. Gopi's message is immediate and unmistakable. She knows what you are capable of. If you will allow me to paraphrase what I read as her message:

"You, dear reader, are a leader, and the seeds of leadership lie also within your child. Yes, things are hard; yes, there are problems. But I will take you by the hand, and we will do this together. Your child's beauty will shine forth as you master the tools that await you in the pages to come. I will be your guide. But you will be the magic worker in your child's life."

The "toolbox" Gopi offers reflects deep wisdom, but when understood, it all makes so much sense. She weaves her many suggestions together with rich examples, mostly from her own experience with young people at school or with her own two sons at home. Woven throughout, also, are the beautiful threads of the bhakti philosophy that has guided Gopi throughout her life. Bhakti is an ancient philosophy about the origins and sharing of love; though ancient, it is so much in line with twenty-first century child psychology.

When Gopi calls you "dear reader," she does so with absolute sincerity. With similar sincerity, I say that you, dear reader of Gopi's collected wisdom, are in for a treat.

Leadership Parenting is a support-filled, positive – even life-changing – opportunity to open new possibilities, both for your child and for the relationship the two of you share. No, it's not really magic. It just feels like magic because your ability to see your child with new eyes and to act in ways that open your child's potential will be transformative.

You are indeed in good hands.

— DAVID STREIGHT, RESIDENT SCHOLAR, HEART OF CHARACTER, WWW.HEARTOFCHARACTER.ORG

Author's note: David Streight is Resident Scholar at Heart of Character, a non-profit association dedicated to helping educators foster greater intrinsic motivation in their students and in their schools. He is an author, coauthor, and editor of a number of books, including *Breaking into the Heart of Character* (2013) and *Structure and Guts of Character*

Education (2015). His earlier teaching career was most noted for helping high school students explore the nature and power of love, where he pushed them to focus on what exactly love is, on how best to give it, and how best to get it. He can be reached at dstreight@heartofcharacter.org

INTRODUCTION

WHY LEADERSHIP PARENTING?

"Why 'leadership parenting?' Why not 'follower-ship parenting?' Don't we have plenty of *'leaders'* already?" A friend questioned me jokingly when he heard about the book I'd been writing.

"I'll have to write a follow-up book to yours on 'follower-ship parenting' for all the followers your leaders are going to need." He continued sarcastically. "Maybe you have authority issues," I retorted.

Jokes aside, he has a point. This world already has too many "leaders" who just boss others around.

BEING BOSSY

His comments brought me back to when I was a six-year-old. I overheard a group of my friends discussing whether they would invite me to a party. "She's too bossy," I remember distinctly hearing. *Bossy*. I tasted the word, deciding how I felt about it. What did it mean? *I have to be bossy because things need to be done right!* I thought. At least being called bossy was better than not being noticed at all. *Bossy is a good thing,* my little brain decided.

A few years later, my mom bought Adele Faber's *How to Talk So Your Kids Will Listen*. One night I read it cover to cover. I was fascinated. Unfortunately for my mom, I would interrupt her instructions, "But Mommy, the book says you're supposed to...." Yup. I was that annoying. My poor mom.

Twenty years later, I visited my best friend who had a child the same age as mine. From the goodness of my heart, I decided to write a thirty-page document full of parenting advice directly meant for her. How graciously she accepted. "Hey, Gopi, I understand your intention, but telling your friend how to parent is plain rude." Our friendship didn't last long after that. My bossiness had struck again.

Because efficiency, competence, and success were important to me, I was placed into management positions. I led teams, organized events, and educated children and parents. Once, when I directed a drama with over sixty players, I inadvertently snubbed the costume designer. She had spent weeks gathering the right outfits, only to be summarily dismissed by me – they weren't good enough. When I saw her crying backstage, I questioned myself. Was my leadership style affecting the spirit of team members? I started noticing that while I was hitting objectives and was "successful" from an external point of view, my teams never lasted. Because I hadn't nurtured them, teams fell apart.

It took me over two decades to truly understand leadership. A major catalyst was working with young children. Because children are so authentic, results of interactions with them are visible immediately. I was able to see the difference between bossing and leading.

One summer, we had opened an at-home catering business. My four-year-old helped out. Using detailed drawings, he was able to help out with packing, labeling, and greeting customers. His efficiency was parallel to none. Something that surprised me was his eagerness to serve. This was such a contrast to adults I had worked with. I noted that a desire to serve was a key ingredient for success, and kids have plenty of it.

That was only the beginning. Later that year, I became a full-time elementary school teacher at a private school in Dallas, spending my days with young children. How eager they also were to serve. Just by working with them every day, my understanding of leadership blossomed.

When I became Vice Principal, I upped my leadership skills. The principal had a little notebook: every item she wrote in it would be completed. Though clearly, she was very efficient, what surprised me was how she made collaborative decisions. Even for stressful, time-sensitive situations, she would hold off until she knew that key stakeholders were a part of the solution. This was my second lesson. Collaborative decisions were an integral part of leadership.

These two principles – service and collaborative decisions – these are key ingredients to leadership success.

NOT BORN, *MADE*

I have also learned that leaders are not born; they are made. Anyone, with careful nurturing, can become a leader. I heard the most profound definition of leadership at St. Mark's School of Texas in Dallas. With crisp uniforms and excellent presentation skills, high-schoolers led our tour across the state-of-the-art campus, sheltering students up to twelfth grade.

After the tour, in front of several hundred attendees, Colin Igor, the Head of the Upper School, summarized leadership: "Leadership is about helping every member of the community achieve a common goal."

Let's think about that – not my goal, not your goal, but a common goal. Helping every member of the community. It brought me back to my own definition: service and collaborative decisions.

Serving others with collaborative decision-making isn't easy. It requires humility, and humility is the exact opposite of bossing others around.

I shared this definition with my sarcastic friend, the one traumatized by leaders. Leadership parenting is for those who are ready to empower their children to become leaders – by serving others and reaching common goals.

Leadership parents are those who are gathering teams, working with volunteers, managing staff. Leadership parents are also the ones who may stay back after the event, because everyone else is tired, and clean up. Leadership parents are the ones who spend that extra hour on the phone hearing the disgruntled employee who's having a difficult time. Leadership parents help their companies and their communities and have a deep need to serve.

In this book, you will hear about two saints Gaura and Nitai, the patron saints of love and learning. They exemplified leadership and promoted the path of bhakti yoga – where leadership is seen as a collaborative endeavor with service and humility at its core. I have analyzed their teachings and carefully crafted parenting strategies for you. After working with leaders, parents, educators, and children for over two decades, I've adapted ancient spiritual philosophy into simple techniques that can be implemented immediately with your child.

Though these strategies are simple, they are not easy. They take self-reflection, commitment, and perseverance. You will need to be ready to reevaluate your mindset. If you have read this far, and are a parent in leadership, I know you're up for the challenge.

We'll start off with where you're at now. You have a child who isn't all that comfortable in social environments. Together, we'll get your child to a happy, productive space, and they will be able to step into leadership.

Let's get started.

PART I

MEET UP

1

YOU ARE NOT ALONE

"Having children makes you no more a parent than having a piano makes you a pianist."

— MICHAEL LEVINE

A MOM IN PAIN

It was Labor Day weekend, 2021. I was conducting workshops in Manhattan, right in the middle of the pandemic. It was my first airplane trip in over a year and a half. Masks covered faces, gyms required vaccination cards, people distanced themselves. The evening before my return flight, I got a phone call from a client in New Jersey. Because I serve as an educational consultant and a parent coach for an international society, I travel frequently – but the pandemic put that on hold. I had been working online with this mom for a few months.

When I answered, she frantically shared that she was at the hospital because her five-year-old daughter had hit her head. Her husband was out of town, and she was alone. Without a moment's hesitation, I took the hour journey to where they were. Having spent many of my own days in hospital spaces, I knew Mom should have someone by her side. As I left, I grabbed my "kids toolkit" with coloring pages, stickers, markers, and scissors. I always travel with this toolkit, just in case I'm around a child who needs to be attended to.

She was surprised at my arrival. After all, I was on vacation and didn't know her that well. Gratefully, tearfully, she shared how distraught her daughter was. There had been serious friend issues at school. She cried every day, latched onto "friends," who then hurt her when they needed space. Like a swinging pendulum – rushing toward a friend, getting hurt, jumping back, feeling the pain of rejection and loneliness, her daughter had been crying every evening. Distraught Mom felt the fall was related. Hours had passed at the hospital, and she remained stuck on uncomfortable waiting room chairs. Her feelings came pouring out. I could understand what she was going through.

She's not the only one who keenly feels the struggle of a child's sadness because of friend issues. It's all been heightened during the pandemic; with young kids meeting each other through screens for more than a year, key development stages have been missed.

Recently, a dad from California shared that his six-year-old son is so hyper when friends come over. He never wants them to leave. If they even hint at going home, the boy cries and cries. "My other kids didn't act like this. What's wrong?"

Another mom, from Michigan, is in tears when I speak to her. "I dread parent-teacher conferences. I just know they're going to tell me that my daughter's being mean to her friends. She can be so cruel. When she's upset, she doesn't care what the other kids are feeling. I've tried everything! We have put up a kindness wall; we watch videos; we have bought a bunch of books to read to help. But it's not working! What am I doing wrong?"

It's not just limited to the United States. Parents around the world struggle with this. A couple in London shared: "I get a pit in my stomach every time a parent approaches me at pick-up. I know they blame my kid for their own kid's issues. My son and the other boys fight so much, but they can't stay away from each other. I've literally lost my appetite over it – how can I fix this?"

MEETING YOU

You are reading this book because you are experiencing something similar. Your child is hurting in their social environment: they can't make friends, or they can't keep them and be happy. Parents in leadership like you, feel the most worried; you just can't imagine your child unable to navigate social interactions. Relationships are important to you; others' needs are important to you; your image is important to you. You're not accustomed to your child being unable to manage their social space. You've tried plenty of solutions; you've googled it, you've asked parents, you've read books, you may even have gone for counseling with your child. But nothing has worked. Now you've picked up my book.

Guess what. I've got you. The fact that you've picked up my book is not a coincidence. I will walk you through this, as I've done with so many others. When you see my little backpack of strategies, you will literally be looking for opportunities to use them.

THE DEVELOPMENTAL FACTS

Children aged three to six are transitioning from egocentrism to empathy. Egocentrism is seeing the world from their own point of view, a key stage for a young child. As their social experiences increase, they learn how to see the world from another's point of view. This includes sharing, understanding feelings, and taking others' perspectives. Psychologists, such as Piaget and Vygotsky, have researched important methods for guiding our children from one stage to the next.

Children who may have missed social milestones, who may be neurodivergent, or who may just not be equipped with these tools will struggle more with this transition from egocentrism to empathy. The pandemic has borne a whole generation of children who've socially distanced, which means it's going to take them more time to make the transition. It's to be expected and it's not your fault. It will be okay.

"I QUIT" MOMENTS

There are scenarios when your child is falling apart and crying over friendships, and you have no idea what to do. These scenarios bring you right into moments of wanting to run away. I call them "I Quit Moments." Does this sound familiar? "Omg, I can't do this anymore! Nothing I'm doing is helping! I need to run away or yell!"

HERE ARE some scenarios that breed I Quit moments:

- When you're so grateful that your child has a playdate, but only ten minutes later you hear fighting. "I'm never going to come over again!" After the playdate, the mom of your kid's friend calls to complain about your kid.

- When you pick your kid up from school and they complain about the other kids: "He stole my pencil. He told me I'm a liar. He's calling me bad names." You say, "Okay, so stay away from them." But guess who your kid is playing with the next day? The same one who stole their pencil and called them names.

- When you start fantasizing about either going over to that trouble-maker's house and yelling at him or his parents. Of course, you know you can't do that, so you want to secretly whisk the kid over to Antarctica where he can bother the penguins and not your child. Or worse still, you fantasize about going to Antarctica yourself, because surely hanging out with a bunch of cute, waddling penguins is better than dealing with this stuff, *every single day.*

- When your child gets quiet and withdrawn and rarely shares. After prodding, you find out they're being tormented by mean kids and don't know how to stand up for themselves. You email the teacher, talk to the principal, but nothing happens, nothing changes. The pit in your tummy grows oversized. You want to just quit.

We parents quit in so many ways: turn on the T.V., pour that drink, do that socially irresponsible thing. Maybe you just don't tell anyone or go for a "work trip" to get away from it all. We're quitting to hide the internal chaos ... the chaos of not knowing the answer to this underlying question:

"If I have finally stepped into empowering others, leading/ guiding/ mentoring teams, why can't I empower my own little one in my own home? Is there something wrong with them? With me? Why don't they *know* how to navigate it?

FIVE MISCONCEPTIONS

In addition to the social dysfunction your child is facing, many parents have five parenting misconceptions that exacerbate the I Quit moments. These ideas are insidiously pervasive, and ruin one's ability to parent.

Misconception #1: I need to be with my child all the time.

You do not need to spend every waking moment with your children to be a good parent. I wish someone had told me this a long time ago. I put so much pressure on myself to engage my children constantly and be by their side. Thousands of years ago, in the age of bhakti leadership in Ancient India, kings and queens had a variety of support: nurses, bathers, dressers, cooks, servers, tutors, and more. Children were nurtured by many hands. "It takes a village." Even as recently as a hundred years ago, children were raised with support from the extended family. Of course, children do need our time, and the more the merrier – but it does not mean that you, as a working parent in leadership, with a ton of other responsibilities, need to carry this burden of guilt when you're not with your child.

Life is busy – don't add this extra bit to it. It's better to recharge yourself and spend quality time when recharged. It beats being completely depleted and frustrated when you're around them. I will work with you to powerpack the time that you have with them. Take a deep breath and release that guilt.

Misconception #2: I need to listen to other parents' opinions and use their techniques.

No one's opinion matters but yours and your co-parent's. If all you see is the judgment of parents around you, guess what, not one of those people are dealing with the challenges you are facing.

Each person is created uniquely. There is no perfect strategy that will work for everyone. Don't listen to someone who pretends there is. You know that know-it-all mom who seems to have everything under control and forces her opinion on you – ignore her. She's the one with four kids under age five, and just has to share her "wisdom" with everyone she knows. It's perfectly okay if her techniques don't work for you. Just nod, thank her, and move on.

All those parents who gossip about others – ignore them as well. Most likely, they're bored. Why do their opinions matter so much to you? They may not even be talking about you. Stay focused on your goal – raising your child to be a leader. Give up the drama and gossip, and you do you, boo.

If your child sees you being authentically you, and not worrying about what other people will say, that in and of itself, will boost their confidence incredibly. We parents grow and learn with our children – each one being so amazingly unique. What works for some may not work for you. I'll teach you to observe and respond to ever-changing dynamics. I'll teach you to hear your inner voice and know the right thing to do. There will be no judgment.

Misconception #3: In order to raise my child right, I should be doing it all.

This is another impossible standard. Teach them manners, give them spinach and other vegetables, make sure they have good grades and do their homework with them, cook healthy meals for them (all that spinach and veggies and oh yeah, it needs to be organic too), get them fancy clothing to keep up with their friends, take them to the doctor, piano teacher, ballet class, soccer, martial arts class, art class, and oh yeah, make sure they have friends, and do the PTA expectations, and go to work, and get some sleep while you're at it. Oh, and add on some meditation and mindfulness (which you'll end up falling asleep to) and eff it all, "I'm not going to do any of it. Here, have some microwave popcorn for dinner, won't you? Because honestly, *I can't do all of this.*"

Guess what, literally no one is expecting that. Only choose the very important stuff and say a very big *no* to everything else. Just let it go. Your sanity and your confidence in yourself are so much more important. Then, when your child starts wigging out, you're peaceful enough to manage it. I will help narrow down the to-dos so you can focus on the stuff that's high priority for you. If it's not organic, so be it.

Misconception #4: If my kid cries, I'm a failure.

This one's a big one. When your beautiful little one throws a tantrum right in front of everyone at school pick up, don't you wish you could cry as well? It's near impossible to not take your child crying personally. It makes us feel like a total failure when our children are upset – like our job is to raise porcelain dolls with no emotion and if negative emotion comes, something is wrong with our parenting skills. But hey, it's totally okay if your child cries every now and then. I know it can be heartbreaking, but tears have such a purpose. Allow them the space to feel. I'll teach you important perspectives on mistakes, crying, and the struggle.

Misconception #5: I should already know how to parent perfectly.

I'm about to break the bubble of perfection that you've placed on parenting. First of all, parenting isn't natural. How does society expect that raising a human being, in a perfectly messed-up world, with the many human complexities around us, will be natural?

Secondly, no one is perfect. Those perfect moms, dressed to the tee, juggling everything in their life without a snitch or a glitch and four kids carefully poised around them – guess what? They're faking it. Yup, read that again. They're imposters. FYI. Or they're horribly screwing up their kids and their kids will be gracing therapist couches for decades. Or nannies and grandmas are raising their kids and they put on a hell of a show. (I'm sorry if you're one of those perfect moms and I'm offending you. If so, you wouldn't be reading this book. You picked it up by mistake and now you can put it down. I wasn't talking to you, so please mind your own business.)

My point is that parenting doesn't come naturally to anyone, and perfect parenting is a myth. Nothing is perfect in this world.

Somehow or other, we've been expected by society to know how to perfectly parent in every moment.

Just to become a car mechanic: that means memorizing the location of an engine, using nuts and bolts and gadgets, learning how to use the *jacky thingy* to lift up a car, learning what a fuel injector is, and what to do when smoke is flying out of the car – but literally just becoming a car mechanic, takes at least four years of school. More complicated goals like becoming an electrical engineer takes high school plus college, eight years of school. Even learning how to teach yoga is a 200-hour set of courses.

But parenting? Which college courses teach you how to raise a kid? Not an engine. Not a mechanical structure. A living, breathing, changing, dynamic human being who has different needs every three seconds as a baby, every minute as a one-year-old, and every three hours as a five-year-old. Where in the world did society give us the pressure that we are supposed to know what we're doing? Parenting is absolutely not natural. Let's be clear about that.

Unfortunately, the society we're in has the least amount of education for parents. Yeah, maybe a Lamaze class or two when we were pregnant where we pretended to simulate the pain of childbirth, and maybe in Home Ec. in seventh grade when you carried a crying doll around. But nothing prepares you for the challenges you face today. No mandatory courses, no degrees, no nothing.

WHOLLY, COMPLETELY, TOTALLY UNPREPARED

Perhaps you did educate yourself, like me. Not only did I read Adele Faber's amazing book at age nine, but I also studied child psychology straight out of high school and amassed a bunch of certifications before I had kids. I bought a stack twenty-books-high when I was pregnant, and even found out that Dr. Sears (parenting guru of the 2000s) had his office ten miles from where we lived in Laguna Beach. I schmoozed my way in so he could be my kid's pediatrician *before the baby was even born.* But even though I had books, certifications, and the best doctor ever, still *nothing prepared me for every single day with my child.*

You do not have to do it alone. Just as you get a guide when you take an art class, or golf, or any new position at work, you need a guide for your parenting. You do not need to do it alone and you *shouldn't* do it alone.

For the duration of this book, and if you become my client, I promise to be that guide.

FROM "I QUIT" TO "I GOT YOU"

I will help you fix those misconceptions. You will be stepping from I Quit to I Got You.

My classroom is filled with adorable little children. When a friend gets hurt, they rush to get the First Aid box from my drawer. They love looking at all the Band-Aid varieties – long skinny ones, butterfly ones, round circle ones, colored ones. They play doctor under my watchful eye. They love helping their friend feel better.

You're going to feel the same. You're going to feel so good when your child has a "heart-boo-boo" because you're going to have a little backpack of techniques to make it better. In every chapter, you'll learn a few new ones to deal with specific scenarios. Whenever the I Quit arises, because you will know how to solve it, you'll feel this powerful "I Got You!"

I GOT YOU

Once, my three-year-old was jumping on the bed. I would sing that song – you know, the one that's supposed to *discourage* kids from jumping on the bed about the monkeys that fell off one by one because they bumped their head.

So, I'm in middle of singing that and saying, "hey please get off the bed, you'll get hurt."

Sure enough, he jumped too close to the windowsill and cut his eyelid. There was so much blood; his white t-shirt, the blue bed sheet, the Thomas the choo-choo train blanket; all of it was quickly covered with blood. I had never seen so much blood.

I felt panic – I Quit moment feelings – *what am I going to do? OMG, I can't handle this. Oh no, this is too freaky*. My son was screaming bloody murder.

Somehow, when our kids are in pain, we figure it out. I grabbed an ice pack and his big brother called 911. Luckily, I had the brilliant idea to give him a popsicle. It quieted him immediately.

So, there we were. I will never forget that moment. My three-year-old sitting on my lap, a popsicle in his mouth, the blood literally pouring out from the corner of his eye, and the paramedics on the way. There were a few whole minutes of total silence. All three of us, just sitting there, wide-eyed, looking at each other. Nothing but the sound of the younger one sucking on his popsicle, sucking his pain away. Total peace.

It was so intense, and so hilarious at the same time, that I suddenly started cracking up. My older son started laughing too. The little one, with the popsicle firmly in his mouth started giggling too. We were a mess of blood, pressure, gauze, and pain, and we were laughing our heads off with the paramedics on the way.

In that moment, I knew one thing: "I Got You." The ice pack was on his face. He had the popsicle. The paramedics were taking him to the hospital. It was going to be fixed. We were all okay. This was just a problem and problems happen every day. He was in my arms and I had him covered.

Of course, no, technically we were not all okay; it was a massive gash, blood was pouring everywhere, and he needed surgery and stitches. *Would he even be able to see?* But the I Got You feeling wasn't from the what ifs. It was because I knew what to do to handle them. I had the tools, I was confident, he felt that confidence, and we were even all laughing.

I want you to step into that I Got You space, dear friend. The world will never stop with its problems, and having kids blows that up a million-fold. You've chosen this book today. Not only do I Got You – I want you to feel that same feeling with your child. I'm going to help you get there.

Imagine your child wrapped in your arms, feeling your safety, just happily sucking on a popsicle even when everything is falling apart around them. Imagine even when they're not with you, when others are cruel, and it hurts, they will be fine because they will feel your presence around them like a blanket of love.

If you're in leadership, you can do this. You know deep inside that you can do it.

LIVING THE DREAM

I know, it sounds like a dream. But today, this dream is my reality. Day after day, I see and hear children, parents, teachers expressing the incredible feeling of social empowerment. They're using my toolkit and how blessed it all is.

A little boy has been sad. He feels his friends don't care about him and don't understand him. I talk to his parents. We make a plan. Only three days later, he's skipping away, hand-in-hand with them. He's got confidence, he's got the words, he's happy! My heart swells with pride.

I give another mom the plan. Her girl was always fighting. Now she's only cried once that month – it's working. Mom is feeling so excited about the change. My heart beams.

Even ten years ago, these tools worked. A gentle young lady struggled daily with friends. After working with her parents for only three months, it was solved. Today she leads a team of volunteer youths who are working on a documentary for their church.

Another teenager fought incessantly when he was in first grade. He was the bully. I worked with his dad. Today, he leads the rowing club.

My own son has had the same painful experience of social discomfort. Today, he mentors over fifty students in youth leadership classes online, preparing each of them to identify problems in their communities, work with friends and teams, and solve them.

This dream-come-true will become your reality as well.

Step into the next chapter where I will share my own parenting journey with my boys and how I found answers.

2

THE BRAIN TUMOR

"There are three levels of pain for a parent: Pain, Excruciating Pain, and Stepping on a Lego."

MY HOSPITAL TIME

Pain is searing through my arms like a hot flash that burns the insides. I feel even the burn of red blood cells coursing through my veins.

I'm sitting on a cold, hard vinyl cushion on a hospital bench at the Dallas Children's Hospital. The light blue walls have larges circles and squares, painted in primary colors. My fifteen-year-old son is undergoing surgery: brain surgery.

Only three days earlier, doctors told us he had a brain tumor. Nothing feels real. Things are moving too fast for us to even process, and in this moment, all I feel is searing pain, like waves of heat coursing through my body.

I know this pain enters because my child is in pain. His discomfort is exponentially magnified in my psyche; my very being is biologically made for his protection, and now I sense impending danger. The surgeons are cutting through the soft malleable tissues, moving around all those jiggly brain parts, with their cold, mechanical instruments. Even the surgeon, though one of the top neurosurgeons in Dallas, felt cold and brisk to me when she explained the procedures.

The surgery is to last six hours. I have a phone in my hand. It's supposed to ring every hour with updates from the surgical team. Children's Hospital boasts nationally ranked staff, top medical care and customer service – but all I can think of are the what-ifs. *What if her hand slips and cuts where it's not supposed to? What if he can't talk to us or understand what we're saying? What if he never wakes up?* The twelve-page legal document of what-ifs we had to sign before they started covered many scenarios. They were cutting into the Wernicke and Broca areas of the brain, the area of communication.

As the first hour passes, I greet many who are here with us. My sister has canceled all her engagements – she's a world-renowned international singer and flew in from India on the first flight out. Our Mati (mother-in-law) is walking the halls with my husband who's crying here and there. She faints at some point. The pressure is too much. A dear Swami sits on the seats with us. Other friends from our community start pouring in. They have shared in our joys and now they share in our pain. I'm keenly aware of their thoughts: *Is she doing okay? How is she getting through this?* Their worried eyes question. I want to smile at them, I want to crack jokes and relieve their pain. *It's okay everyone, it'll be fine, these surgeons do this routinely.* But I'm unable. The surgery was described as an eight-out-of-ten difficulty level. Usually many turn to me for comfort, for nourishment, and yet today, I don't know where my strength is. I'm just me. A mom. Worried about her kid. What to do.

The time inches by, like a caterpillar crawling up a branch. No, even slower. Have you ever watched a snail cross a wet sidewalk? Like that. I close my eyes and meditate. I am determined to reach that space where answers lie. I have nothing better to do anyways.

I withdraw from the physical space I'm in. I'm going to relieve the anguish, the burning in my limbs, and the stress of seeing others around me worried. I'm going to pray, harder than I've ever prayed and let this damned surgery be successful, let my boy come back to my arms and let this stupid nightmare be over.

Why did my child have to suffer? Why did it affect me so much? How will he get through this? How will I get through this? What brought us here? What's the point of it all?

In that silent space, in the middle of a bustling hospital, in those six hours, I find many answers within. I'll sprinkle these answers through this book for you to use when you're worried about your child. I know these answers will help you. I journeyed through fifteen years of his life, of my own childhood, looking through different memories to find answers to our predicament.

A YOUNG SCHOLAR

First, I remember just months before, how successful he had been. He is the light of my life. Highly intelligent, he has already started amassing college credits, and is part of the Dual Credit program (high school and college at the same time) at the private school I run. Papers in our local news and international news have shared: "Young scholar enters college at fourteen."

He's gotten rave reviews from his professors. "He showed great leadership skills that were invaluable. Students continually turned to him for guidance and sought him out as someone with beneficial knowledge," wrote Ms. Mitzi Morris George, his Psychology professor.

His success cemented my own identity and belonging in a spiritual community where learning and character are highly valued. Having taken on the risky venture of leading a character-based school, I felt such a need to prove that spirituality can go hand in hand with academic success. I saw his success as proof of my own hard work and goals. I had already begun guiding many other parents who wished for their children to be fully developed in academic achievement, leadership, and service. "Learn, Lead, Serve" was the motto we used to represent our school.

Suddenly, however, our life had come to a grinding halt. One crisp Monday morning in February, he complained of being nauseous. When he started throwing up, we all thought it was a stomach bug. At the end of my workday, I went to check on him. "I don't know what's going on, Mommy, but I can't read," he stated matter-of-factly.

"What!?" *How could he be so peaceful!* I grabbed his nearby text from college and saw indeed that he was sounding out the words like a preschooler. We all raced to the hospital. A variety of CT scans and X-rays later, they held up a scan of his brain. It had a big white spot – a two-inch circle – amidst all the gray matter. The nurses' eyes got all big and the verdict came in: it's a brain tumor. It has burst and is causing issues in his Wernicke and Broca areas.

A surgery was scheduled where they would try to remove the tumor to gather more information. So here we are.

Again, my mind fills with anguish as I think about the cold tools inside my boy's head. *No, no, don't get distracted by the pain. Go deeper.* Yes, I see this had to do with my own social belonging and worth – using my son's success to cement my own identity.

Maybe there shouldn't be that pressure on him? Maybe I should have my own identity separate from my child's accomplishments? I can take those lessons. What other messages are here for me?

A VICTIM

As I close my eyes again, I remember other very painful moments as a mom.

I see him as a five-year-old, playing in the backyard with a bunch of friends one evening. We had gone to a party, and the kids were playing on the trampoline, or so I thought. As I lingered, I listened to their words. What I thought was playing was exactly the opposite.

My memory is him standing in the middle of the trampoline with the other kids pointing and jeering at him. "You're so fat you can't even jump on that trampoline!" "You shouldn't even be on it, why try?" "You're a total fat dummy!"

Today, he tells me my memory is over-exaggerated and it didn't happen quite that dramatically. But I will never forget the words they spoke to him. He was a gentle, quiet soul, and never had spoken ill of others. He didn't deserve that from his so-called friends.

I just couldn't tolerate hearing anymore. I don't remember what I even said, just that I grabbed my boy off the trampoline and yelled like never before. I was a teacher and not supposed to lose my composure around children. Now I was being the bullying adult. Quickly realizing that other parents were around and I might be overreacting, I brought him to the car. I tried to understand why his "friends" were talking to him like that, and was he okay? I remember being unable to sort through it rationally. My child was in danger, and I was scrambling to protect him. I remember venting and feeling chaotically upset about it. I needed to empower my child so he would never experience that again! *How did I fail as a parent so bad? How could I consciously place him in that kind of danger? To be publicly humiliated like that! Fie on all my degrees and certificates, my stack of parenting books, my vast knowledge. I can't even figure out how to manage my child's social happiness.*

These memories popped in my mind as I continued down my quest for answers. I had been able to change the storyline for him, as I nurtured him through social comfort. Today, even college professors were noting his ability to lead and make friends.

But why did it bother me so intensely? *Why are these yucky memories coming in as I'm seeking a safe space? What more am I supposed to learn?*

LONG LETTERS

Now I see my own reflection, a little girl who loves friends, and yet struggles with them. I remember every single friend from elementary school and the underlying feeling of unease that accompanied the relationship. If I disagreed with one of them and didn't resolve it, what would happen the next day? Would I still be loved and accepted? When I made my friends upset, I overdid the apology, writing four- to five-page letters, drawing hearts and paisleys and butterflies. The need to belong was such a strong need for me. Was something wrong with me? No one else wrote these long letters. So much uneasiness.

I try to shake off these memories. The unease of my childhood and of his childhood mixes with the unease of the surgery he's undergoing; I don't want to feel it. *Please help me understand: what is the purpose of all of this? What am I supposed to learn?*

Go deeper. Deeper I pray, meditate and journey, looking for answers.

Finally, I find my safe space. I'm a little girl cuddled up in my bed, my blankets tucked all around me. It's the wee hours of early morning, and the night is dark and quiet. My dad's powerful, singing voice floats over to me from the front room.

A BACKGROUND OF LEADERSHIP

My dad was a brahmin priest, a missionary. Although he came to America in 1970 and founded a chain of thriving dental clinics in Chicago and Detroit, he began seriously meditating and increasing his priestly duties. He was born in a brahmin family in India, with high standards of service and leadership expected of him. His ancestry traces back to the brahmins who guided the kings of ancient Gujarat. As the eldest of his family, he was the first to cross the seas with a medical degree, and the first to take spiritual ministry alongside his dental practices. Even in his twenties, he was highly respected. His mother was the first woman in her state to get a college degree, and had opened a Montessori school back in the mid-1900s.

My mom also had an education background. Her father, the head "*pramukkha*" or council leader for five cities, was the principal of the first school in the area, with over 6,000 students. She was a teacher in that school after graduating with a bachelor's in Education.

The expectations were high for me, their eldest daughter. Not only was leadership in my blood, my birth right, it was instilled in me at every age. Serving others, fostering humility and accomplishing grand tasks that helped humanity – these were all integral values from birth.

But leadership, as I shared previously, is not born, but made. It's a perplexing dichotomy of being in charge and yet being a servant. It takes time and hard work to discover how to lead. I had put in that time, learned what I needed to purify in order to develop humility and a service attitude. I had accomplished so much. I thought I had learned to integrate the two identities – being a servant and yet being in charge. But here in this hospital seat, I became keenly aware that everyone and everything is equalized. Did my heritage, learning or experiences even matter if my son is at death's door? As I was navigating these thoughts, the pain poked through my consciousness again.

Why would my son, already a leader in his space, already guiding his peers, having figured out so many social interactions, having been raised to the pinnacle of success for a student, why did he have to get a tumor in his brain and stop reading? Will he be made fun of again? Will he be seen as a dumb, incapable, idiot? Will his brain come back to normal function? Will he be unable to speak properly, unable to walk? Will he be socially inept, socially discarded, and most importantly, will he live? Where is the plan in all this?!

SAFE MANTRA SPACE

Okay, Gopi, back to the search. Find your safe space. I see myself cuddled up with my blanket, my dad's voice singing. It's 3:37 a.m. to be exact; I can see the red numbers on the alarm clock on my nightstand.

My dad always woke before dawn. He would meditate each morning in front of our shrine of Deities. His main worship was to the patron saints Gaura and Nitai.

His meditation was reciting mantras (affirmations and prayers) meant for the early morning to fortify his day of service and work. These mantras were sung in ancient Sanskrit and were rich, full of *raagas* – deep classical tunes, melodious and powerful. The mantras would ride his voice over to where I slept, puncturing through my slumber. Their energy would enter my heart, nudging me, *get up dear one, it's time to rise.* Every day our family attended the first morning service at the temple before sunrise, but I would usually grumble. *I wish he wouldn't sing so loudly so I could sleep.* I would pull my pillow over my head trying to but inevitably would lose the battle, mantras vs sleep. So, I would lay there, and listen. The mantras became dear friends and by the time I was a teenager, I woke up with him, before the temple service, and spent time with these beautiful mantras as well.

Today, as I sit with my back erect, on this hospital bench, with my eyes tightly closed, as I'm trying to sift through all the painful moments of life, as I'm trying to find a safe space for me and my child who's undergoing the worst of the worst experiences right now ... those divine mantras come to me. I hear my dad's voice. I hear the Sanskrit words. I remember the meanings of the affirmations. I find lessons and strength.

One-by-one they appeared in my consciousness. They drifted through the guck of pain. They were a soothing balm. They peered through the curtain of bad memories of being a mom, of all my boys' issues, of all the troublesome crap we had to sort through when we ourselves didn't know what we were really doing with our kids. They blew those memories away and they placed themselves firmly in the forefront of my mind.

You are safe. You have come this far. You are exactly where you need to be. Your child is safe. There is a plan. This is just the beginning. We are with you. Trust us. We will carry you through this.

In that safety, I saw saints Gaura and Nitai, with their arms outstretched bringing golden light to my heart. Now I felt like I was floating on a cloud. My pain lifted. I felt safe. I felt like my child was safe. I felt like there was a plan. I deeply felt there were answers. I knew my life and his life was a journey in discovering those answers and I felt almost euphoric to find out what it would be. Even if he was not to wake up, yes, it would be the most intense trauma ever, but I knew – he was eternal and there was a plan for him. Whatever it may be, I accepted it.

Tears started to well up in my eyes. They do now even as I write this. They came to me at a time I needed them the most. They showed my safety, my purpose.

Many answers came to me in those hours after the mantras had appeared. They appeared in the form of memories, of encounters, of learning from whomever I was in touch with. Those answers I will share with you in this book.

As I opened my eyes, my meditation had lifted. Yes, the pain of my child's danger was still there, but now I was a little distant from it. The limbs still felt heat, the mind still a little anxious; but the deep fear was gone. There was a plan.

I looked over at the bench besides me. My sister was talking to another mom and dad. Their three-year-old daughter had inadvertently placed a bead up her nose. Super deep, it had entered the brain space. She was also in brain surgery – at only three! I could now truly understand their pain, like never before.

PARENT PAIN IS EVERYWHERE

Suddenly I realized parents' pain. All around me were moms and dads feeling this exact excruciating pain I was feeling. I would never wish this pain on anyone, not even my worst enemy. But throughout this hospital, along the corridors, I saw moms crying, dads crumpled over. I thought, *how many corridors must there be? How many hospitals must there be? How many cities and states and countries must have parents experiencing this pain I'm going through?*

Now I was wide awake, completely aware of the collective pain of parents. It was everywhere. I was fortunate to find answers in the mantras. And I decided in those moments, that this was my purpose. The very purpose of my life. I had to help relieve this pain.

So in this book, dear parents, I will share my answers with you. You have come to me wanting to know how to empower your child's social environment. I will share with you what I've learned before and after that surgery, from every parent, educator and child I've had the honor to work with.

I'm here with you. I know your pain. I have probably felt exactly as you feel at some point in this life or known someone who's experienced what you're going through. We will walk hand-in-hand together.

In the next chapter, I'll show you our trek. Let's get started.

3

CLIMB WITH ME

"A leader is one who knows the way, shows the way and goes the way."

— JOHN MAXWELL

EMPOWERMENT LEVELS

Raising a human being who can get along with and support other human beings is no ordinary task. You've already got a leg up; you have experience doing this with adults. You know how to fulfill the needs of others. But a five-year-old's needs can be so elusive. They can make you question everything you know. Do you have what it takes to empower them?

For us to get to where you need to go, we will climb together. This trek will be like walking up to the Himalayas, the region of the Gods, where powerful saints practice their meditation, and hone their skills, before they return to the world of mankind. There will be eleven levels with instructions and techniques. They are simple; many are common parenting strategies, but it will not be easy. At the end of the trek, we will arrive at the summit, the Garden of Harmony, known as Mayapur. It is where empowered children, who are leaders, reside.

Are you ready to empower your beautiful little child to be a fully grown leader in the making? Are you ready to change your mindset with mantras, and to implement strategies that will not be easy to do? Are you ready to climb with me?

Here are the different levels of EMPOWERMENT:

- **E** – **E**nvision Your Dream Child
- **M** - **M**eet Your Inner Parents
- **P** - **P**reserve Their Hearts
- **O** - **O**ffer Your L.O.V.E Boost
- **W** - **W**orship Their Work
- **E** - **E**mbrace Their Mistakes
- **R** - **R**est, as a Spiritual Practice
- **M** - **M**agnify their Purpose
- **E** – **E**ncourage Their Empathy
- **N** – **N**eutralize Their Conflicts
- **T** – **T**ransform Their Leadership Skills

THE SUMMIT: THE GARDEN OF HARMONY

When we reach the Garden of Harmony, Mayapur, we will enter an enchanting playground, where happy children are fully absorbed in collaborative productive spaces. Here, the trees are wish-fulfilling trees. Every step is a dance, and every word a poem, with lyrics that reach deep within and empower hearts. Swans float by in pairs on rippling, bluish ponds. Soft red, yellow, and pink lotus flowers open to drink the golden light of the sun. Green parrots chirp amongst the trees. Tigers play with deer, snakes play with birds, as there is no animosity or envy in this garden. All the children support one another.

They know how to share love, how to settle disputes, and how to reach goals together. They work to formulate the plans for mankind for the next fifty years.

When you enter, you will recognize your child. You'll know not to disturb their harmonious space. Actually, dear friend, the secret is that your child is already there. But climbing the trek with me through the levels of EMPOWERMENT will give you the eyes to see them as they already are, happily playing and creating in the Garden of Harmony, Mayapur.

THE PATRON SAINTS

Saints Gaura and Nitai reside in this garden. As the patron saints of love and learning, they empower children with their spiritual grace. Coming from the land of Gaudadesh, they traveled all over South Asia in the fifteenth and sixteenth centuries, ushering in a golden age to counteract the effects of the Age of Quarrel that we are in currently. They are the antidote to quarrel, isolation, and loneliness. Their very ethos was to empower social success and leadership through humility. They empowered millions of followers with this message. In 1965, their preeminent follower Swami Prabhupada brought this message to America and established the path of bhakti yoga as an international society. Gaura Nitai, as they are called, envisioned a house in which the whole world can live, without discrimination, and with empowered generations serving around the world. The divine collaboration they taught is known as "*sankirtan*" and is what your child will experience in the last chapters.

I'll be sprinkling in short historical accounts of their activities, showing how they taught the strategies in this book through their actions. Remembering them will help settle discomforts in yours and your child's hearts.

AFFIRMATIONS

At each level, you will learn affirmations (known as *mantras*) to help in your quest. Mantras are spiritual sound vibrations filled with divine potencies that communicate to a space beyond the gross material sphere. They are Sanskrit words invested with meaning, and I will share the English equivalent as well. Mantra literally means "to free the mind." Basically, what the mantra does is place you in deep mindfulness and self-reflection, settling you for the day. As part of your spiritual practice, you can recite these for a few minutes a day, gradually increasing the time and quantity. They will level up your ability to implement all the strategies you learn, as they give you a heightened sense of connection to your child and those your child is interacting with. Each section of this book has an underlying quality that you will need for when things get difficult. This quality can be energized through the Sanskrit sound introduced.

The strategies in this book are just as useful for those who are not accustomed to mantra affirmations, and should you choose, you can skip the mantra practice at the end of each chapter. The implemented strategies will still be powerful and get your child to social empowerment.

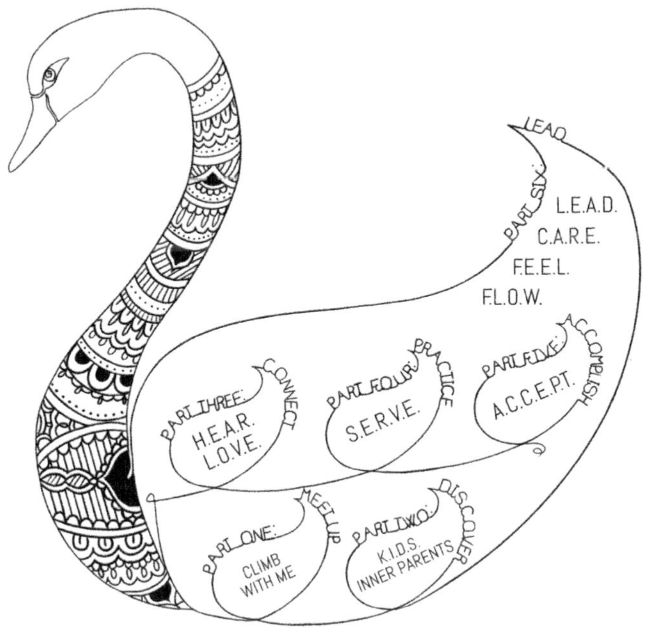

PART ONE: MEET UP

We have already met. I'm ready to go on this journey with you. Here is what is ahead.

PART TWO: DISCOVER

First, we discover the identities of you and your child: who are you both? You'll doubt your ability to get to where you need to go and you'll doubt whether or not I can take you there. You'll muster faith with the mantra meditation and step into the first level. *(shraddha)*

Level 1: E – Envision Your Dream Child

The first identity we establish is "your dream child," a leadership personality who has the very best "soul qualities" you wish for. In Chapter 4, you will view your child with a different lens, K.I.D.S., and uncover their three core needs.

Level 2: M – Meet the Inner Parents

Here you fortify your identity, choose your parent personality type, and see yourself as chosen. You will meet your very own Inner Parents in Chapter 5. You'll learn to connect with them and see that you are never alone in this parenting journey.

PART THREE: CONNECT

Here, you learn to fulfill your child's first set of core needs: connection and belonging (*sambandha*). You will need the quality of enthusiasm for the two levels here.

Level 3: P – Preserve Their Hearts

The fastest way to connect is through the heart. In Chapter 6, you'll learn to hear their feelings with the process H.E.A.R. Once they're heard, they can support the hearts of their friends.

Level 4: O – Offer Your L.O.V.E Boost

The other side of hearing is speaking, and in Chapter 7, you'll practice which words to say and which to avoid. You'll learn to strengthen every interaction with them with the L.O.V.E. process. This will, in turn, give them the ability to strengthen their interactions with others.

PART FOUR: PRACTICE

You'll already see positive differences in your child. In Part 4, you will fulfill the second set of core needs: free will and agency (*abhidheya*). You'll need determination for this level.

Level 5: W – Worship Their Work

When a child knows their place, they lessen their social conflicts. In Chapter 8, you'll transform their work and play into service, with the S.E.R.V.E. process. You will also learn to enforce consequences and boundaries with compassion.

PART FIVE: ACCOMPLISH

Now your child's third set of core needs, achievement and completion (*prayojana*) can be empowered. You'll need patience to get to the end.

Level 6: E – Embrace Their Mistakes

In Chapter 9, you'll learn how to accept your child's mistakes and turn their weaknesses into their strengths with the process A.C.C.E.P.T.

Level 7: R – Rest as a Spiritual Practice

The climb is arduous. With the R.E.S.T. process, you'll learn the importance of your rest and see which obstacles make it difficult to follow the processes in the book. Your frequent breaks are vital to help your child fulfill their final needs of achievement and completion.

PART SIX: LEAD

These are more advanced levels - a synthesis of everything you've been doing so far with your child. All three core needs are engaged in flow (*samadhi*). Humility is required to step back and allow the Inner Parents to guide you.

Level 8: M – Magnify Their Purpose

In Chapter 11, you will learn to discover their purpose (*dharma*) and engage them in the F.L.O.W. process. What motivates them? Where are they really absorbed? You will find the answers here.

Level 9: E – Encourage Their Empathy

A child who feels a sense of purpose now has the social confidence to support another child. With the F.E.E.L. process, you'll learn three ingredients to empathy and learn to encourage those in Chapter 12.

Level 10: N – Neutralize Their Conflicts

With empathy, your child can step into collaborative spaces (*sankirtan*). This means there will be plenty of conflicts. You'll learn ways to deal with those natural conflicts with the C.A.R.E. process. You're at gate of EMPOWERMENT.

Level 11: T – Transform Their Leadership Skills

Finally, you enter the Garden of Harmony, Mayapur. Your child's social issues have evaporated. With the process L.E.A.D., you'll learn how to showcase their leadership skills.

Take a minute here. Just imagine sitting in that Garden of Harmony and watching your child in action. Imagine them gathering friends from all over, an international society of children playing together in this garden, planning to solve the world's problems together. Imagine them knowing the language to use when there's conflict (which undoubtedly there will be) and running off with a sense of purpose, contentment, and laughter. What does it look like to you? What is your child doing? Dear reader, how do you feel right now?

IS IT REALISTIC?

Does it seem too perfect to be true? I can say with 100 percent confidence that if you climb the levels with me, you will absolutely find amazing leadership experiences with your child. I know this because I have walked this same path all by myself and with many others. I have experienced the ups and downs on the journey – the fear of slipping, the need to rest. I have journeyed to that Garden of Harmony, Mayapur, and I've seen the very magic of leadership parenting in action with hundreds of parents who have found these same results. I'm so excited to be your guide throughout this journey and I honestly can't wait until your eyes light up with the same excitement to see your child in full leadership. Do let me know throughout this process; I'm literally here for you, every step of the way.

As I write this, I hear my son online with our leadership classes. Whenever we have a Zoom class, we have breakout rooms where students can choose to join who they want as their mentor. The majority of kids have chosen to jump into his breakout room (not mine and not the other adults on the teaching team!). He's guiding their final Action Learning Projects (ALPs). In their ALPs they are to develop a team of six others, guide them toward a group objective, and work through all the principles we've taught in the leadership course. One girl in Sacramento asks about how to communicate with a team member who's not getting their work done and my son helps her. Another student is concerned that the leader of the community center she's developing a program for doesn't see eye-to-eye with her and she feels discriminated against. He guides her in how to communicate directly to that leader, "I can be on the call if you want." I'm amazed. Is this the same boy who went through brain surgery, who was being made fun of by his friends on that trampoline and who I was so worried about?

So many children we've worked with throughout the past fifteen years are thriving in leadership roles in their communities. If they get the right support as a five-year-old, they will step into an amazing paradigm when they're fifteen, and they will hit the ground running when they're adults! I'm living this dream today; every single day I see the magic of social empowerment in children all around me.

You can do the exact same thing, dear parent. You were literally born to EMPOWER your little one to leadership; the way you already lead so many others. Open your heart to this process, to yourself, and *you got this*!

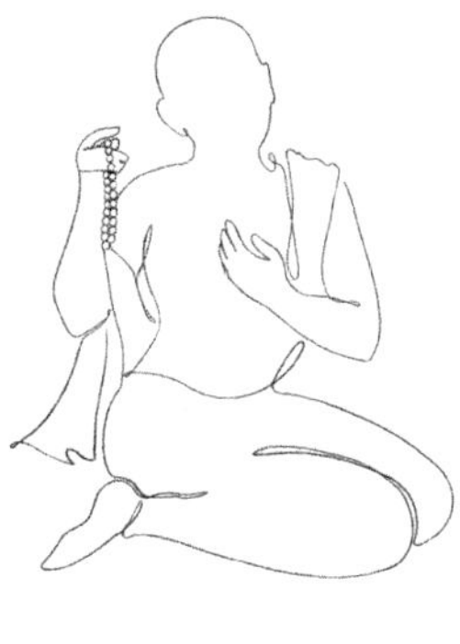

* * *

Mantra Affirmations: I Begin

* * *

This first set of mantras begins our journey. As stated earlier, mantra means a shift in mindset. You can do these meditations either alone or with your child. Ideally, fifteen to thirty minutes of alone time before your child wakes up. Realistically however, you probably don't get much time alone, so do this when you're in the shower, when you're driving to work, at lunch, after bedtime. Just sneak fifteen minutes into your day. Sometimes, parents do these when they're reading a bedtime story to their children, or quietly in their hearts as they're waiting for their child to fall asleep.

When you sit in your meditation space, imagine the climb ahead of you. Feel the excitement and nervousness in your hearts. Feel my presence by your side. Remember that we are divinely guided. We offer respects to our own mentors, touch the ground with reverence, and with gratitude we begin this difficult climb. The challenges ahead will be minimized by this first mantra.

First recite the Sanskrit mantra 10 times. Imagine your child in front of you, and offer their heart to the mantra. Remember, a mantra is a mindset shift. With a mood of prayer and service, recite the English affirmations three times each. When you say the last line, place as much belief in it as possible, in order to reframe your mindset.

idam guru gaurangaya idam na mama
Let me find the courage to climb to every level.
Let me commit to the hard work required.
Let me bring my child to the Garden of Harmony, Mayapur.
I am ready. I am eager. I begin.

PART II

DISCOVER

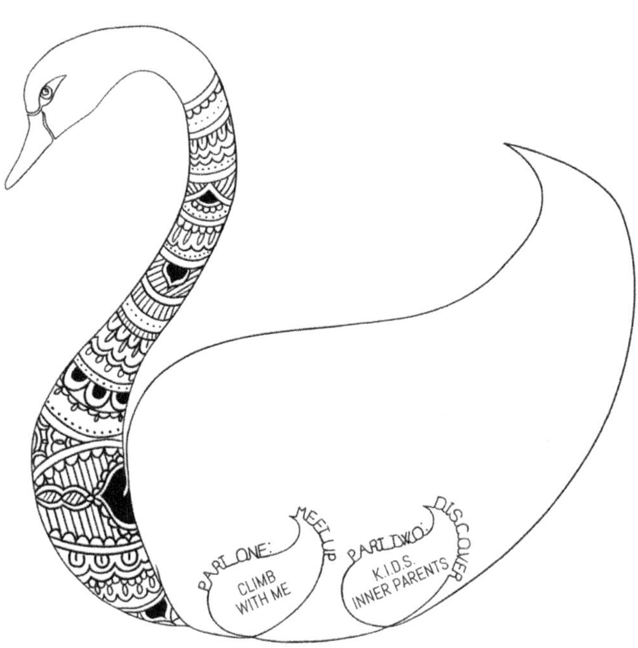

4

WHY DOES MY CHILD FEEL SO BROKEN?

"The seed already is what God designed it to be. The gardener is not trying to make the seed be what the gardener wants it to be. The gardener wants to create an environment where the seed can become what it wants to be. The gardener can provide nourishment and support but cannot force it to be something it is not. There is a real arrogance in that."

— WILL SMITH

LET IT ALL OUT

Envisioning the Garden of Harmony is all fine and dandy, but reality is that you're here because things are broken in your child's social environment and most of your days are filled with I Quit moments.

Have you ever had a really long day at work, and just wanted to share it with someone? You talk to your partner, or a friend but can't really get it all out. You worry you'll bore them, or you feel guilty about complaining.

Here's your chance. I'm right here and I will hear you. Let it all out. I know you've been holding in it. Imagine me sitting right next to you, eyes locked with yours (in a non-creepy way), open and available. I know you're stressed and I really want to make it better. I'm not going to judge you or interrupt you. I've literally got twenty-five years of hearing and feeling the worst of parenting scenarios. So, here's your chance.

TELL ME ABOUT YOU

Today, you can just write it all out. Better yet, press the microphone button on Facebook messenger, Google Keep notes, or any recorder on your phone and start talking. What you say will help us identify your top challenges. This is what I want to know.

1. What is your child's name and how old are they?
2. What are they struggling with and where are they when they face these struggles?
3. Do they fight with their friends or do their friends fight with them?
4. How do they react (e.g., crying, reluctant to discuss) and what words do they say when they talk to you about it?
5. How do you respond?
6. How often do these issues occur?
7. Does anyone else know about these? Your partner, their siblings, parents at school, teachers at school, family members? How did they find out?
8. Has your child been able to fix their issues temporarily or come up with solutions?
9. What worries you the most about your child's struggles?
10. What qualities is your child showing during these interactions?
11. How does all of this make you feel?

As you share the answers, get everything you need off your chest. It's okay to not answer all of them. Here's an example.

"I'M NOT GOING TO BE YOUR FRIEND ANYMORE"

"My daughter is Nickie and she's five. She struggles with making friends and staying happy. She's usually fighting with the other kids on the playground. I think the fighting is two-sided; whenever the kids start interacting, it turns into a fight. Usually both girls involved don't get their way and don't want to listen to the other one. After literally like fifteen minutes of being on the playground, I'll hear, 'I'm not going to be your friend anymore. I just don't like playing with you.'

"Usually, it's my daughter saying that. When I hear that, I realize, *okay this isn't working.* I don't generally want to get too involved because I think it'll just make it worse, so instead I just tell them, 'Okay, we're going to stay for ten more minutes.' Or I let it go and just watch until one of them is in tears and tells me they want to go home. It happens every time we're in a park or a playground or our backyard and my daughter is with other friends.

"Other parents know about it because their kids also tell them that they don't like playing with my daughter, and I've had a few emails from the teachers at school, which is so humiliating. I'm trying to teach my daughter what words to say to be kind, but it feels like she has to make an extraneous endeavor to do that. She hasn't been able to come up with solutions other than to just not like people and stay away from them, which I guess works too but then she doesn't have any friends.

"She only tells me all about it when she's upset, so usually she's explaining it to me with tears in her eyes. Sometimes at nighttime, she'll say it matter-of-factly, 'today such and such told me she hates me, and she wasn't going to be my friend. I said the same thing too. I don't like her at all.' It worries me like something crazy because I don't understand why she can't just get along, and I don't want to keep putting her in the situation where she's getting her heart broken by another kid who doesn't understand her.

"I think she's too young at this point to have boundaries and I don't want her primary memories of interactions to be fighting with someone ese. It makes me feel sad, depressed, and worried. I have a loss of appetite and am hesitant to send her back out in the world. I feel like I'm a really bad parent because I can't figure this out for my child. I don't really know why this is happening. My child is showing dominance, aggression, loneliness, pain, feelings of not being good enough, feeling of unworthiness, clinginess, and meanness during these interactions. What really bothers me is when I'm not there, I'm not able to help her and I have no idea how the other kids and teachers respond to her when she is upset. I have no idea if they're giving her the tools to help sort through her feelings. And I am frustrated that she can't just figure this out. How hard can it be? I feel sad for her, and it makes me feel angry as well."

After you write everything down or talk it out like Nickie's mom did, think about the qualities you see in your child that you've mentioned and write them down.

In the example given, these were the qualities Nickie's mom listed:

- Unworthy
- Clingy
- Mean
- Aggressive
- Lonely
- Sad

ALSO NOTE down what you're feeling. In the example given, Nickie's mom wrote:

- Worried
- Lack of appetite
- Hesitant
- Depressed

- Sad
- Angry

Thank you for sharing all this. I'm sure it wasn't easy. Do you know why this is so upsetting? Because you are a leader. You have an intense desire for your child to be completely the opposite to what you see. You're just not okay with the circumstance the way it is, and you want a change.

So, let's start with a total shift in mindset, shall we? Help me to see where it is you want to be. We step into Level 1, the first "E" in EMPOWERMENT.

* * *

Level 1: Envision Your Dream Child

* * *

We're going to step into the opposite now of what you shared. Take a deep breath. Think: If your child could be completely perfect in your eyes, and exactly the way you want, what would you see? Stephen Covey shares in his leadership book, *The 7 Habits of Highly Effective People,* how important it is to begin with the end in mind. As we make this climb toward the Garden of Harmony, who do you see when you arrive? Close your eyes. Actually, close them.

What is your child doing? Who with? Where are they playing? Imagine a beautiful life for your child with beautiful experiences that you expect right now. If there were absolutely no issues, no problems, no challenges, if everything was exactly the way you wished it to be, what does it look like? What qualities do they embody?

Write down (or record) all that you see. As you share, think of their top ten qualities. Which qualities would you like them to embody the most? Actually, your child was created through an act of love. They have manifested because of your heart's call. This process will help you recognize that your child already has these qualities you see within them. I will help you nurture the qualities you see.

QUALITIES

What top ten qualities do you see? Here's a list of leadership qualities you can choose from, but don't let it limit you. Narrow it down to your top ten.

- Kind
- Compassionate
- Endearing
- Patient
- Brave
- Resilient
- Attentive to details
- Full of integrity
- Innovative
- Honest
- Self-confident
- Visionary
- Strong communicator
- Delegator
- Decision maker
- Problem solver
- Inquisitive
- Self-motivated
- Humble
- Self-disciplined
- Passionate
- Resilient
- Accountable
- Supportive
- Tech-savvy

- Empathetic
- Learning agility
- Empowering

Really think about which of these are very important to you. Start off by choosing twenty, then distill it down to ten.

Draw a simple drawing of your child. It can be a silhouette as shown here, or an actual drawing. It doesn't have to be perfect. Using different colors, place your top ten words around the body of your child.

EXAMPLE

Nickie's mom envisioned her with swings, as she saw that most of Nickie's negative interactions were near the swings. She drew a picture of her daughter taking turns swinging. She wrote ten leadership qualities around her daughter's body. She envisioned her dream child. This process helped her reinforce that identity in her heart.

SEEING THE WORLD THROUGH THE EYES OF A CHILD

When I was a little girl, I remember being surprised by how adults saw me. One dewy morning in Detroit I sat with a few friends on a ledge with flowers. Older friends (they were ten or eleven and we were four or five) at with us as well. My friend's mom pulled out her polaroid camera to take a picture of us. After she clicked the button, a small white square came out of the camera, and the image started appearing. She waved it around a bit and showed it to us.

I remember being shocked. *Was I that small?* The "big girls" were like a foot taller than me! I was clearly much younger than them. But *that much younger?*

We studied together in a one-room schoolhouse, with multi-level classrooms. We went to temple together, played together, and I could recite all the Sanskrit prayers in the morning even better than some adults! They would question me: "Wow, how are you able to read the words off the board?" I thought that they struggled with it too – not realizing that indeed I was just a four-year-old girl. Looking at this picture was almost like an identity crisis for me – *how could I be so small?*

That image lingered in my mind for quite some time. I'd stand up on the edge of the bathroom tub, which faced the mirror so I could size myself up in my reflection. It started sinking in, *you're just a little girl.*

My thoughts were not little. My desires were not little. My interests and goals – none of it was little. But my body was little.

I've seen children experience the same epiphany. Four-year-old Susan just told her teacher last week that she was older than all of the children in the Lower Elementary class. She's not purposefully trying to be defiant. She just doesn't see the world the way adults do.

Eight-year-old Kristina, struggles with letter and number reversals but can diligently and persistently work for more than an hour on her work. Although 41 is always 14 and 385 is very mixed up, she works right alongside others doing the best she can. Although her Us and Ns and Hs are taking more than two years to decode, when asked what her favorite subject is, she responds confidently, "Reading." She doesn't see herself as any less than anyone else. It's only the adults who label.

I was watching a baby girl and her older brother. The older brother was walking fast, and the baby girl was crawling alongside him, just as fast. She wasn't comparing herself to her brother, "oh I can't move fast enough; only my brother can." She felt her own movements and was fully immersed in them. She felt the sense of getting to the destination just as much as he did, even though she was crawling and not walking! She did not feel any less than him.

A CHILD'S WORLD

Children live in a world where they're big enough and smart enough. They want the same opportunities as everyone else and to be accepted for exactly who they are. It's the adults in their lives who belittle them unknowingly, place them in boxes of ages and grades, and limit their capabilities. From the moment a child is born, they are equipped with incredible capabilities; the amount of intelligence and muscle work that is displayed in the first year alone is incredible. Sadly, even though they're extremely capable, adults frequently doubt them.

Imagine constantly feeling inadequate and inconsequential! Imagine feeling like you're a nuisance if your parents are talking to their friends and shushing you every time you speak. Imagine your frustration at not being tall enough to go on the roller coaster ride, or smart enough to give your perspective. Imagine a world where everyone is taller, bigger, and better and these big giants are in control of your every move.

THREE CORE NEEDS

How can you turn that around and understand your child's needs? How can you empower them to develop those leadership qualities you envisioned? First, we will explore three sets of core needs. Leadership qualities, or even happy interactions, can't manifest when these needs are unmet.

The first set of core needs are connection and belonging (*sambandha*): "I know myself. I know you."

The second set of core needs are free will and agency (*abhidheya*): "I can do it."

The third set of core needs are achievement and completion (*prayojana*): "I did it."

These needs were established in bhakti texts more than 5,000 years ago. Contemporary modern psychological philosophies have discovered similar needs. The upper three tiers of Maslow's hierarchy of needs holds belonging, freedom, esteem, and self-actualization. Edward Deci and Richard Ryan, from the self-determination theory of psychology, identified similar needs and categorized them as autonomy, competence, and relatedness. There are many words used to encompass these three needs. The most powerful ones I have found originate in the bhakti texts.

This entire EMPOWERMENT process depends your ability as a parent to empower these three core needs. At every level, in every chapter, you will learn how to bring your child to the height of their core needs being met. Once their needs are met, they step into higher levels of purpose, empathy and leadership. Here's an overview of what to expect and a comparison of the needs introduced in psychological philosophies.

	Leadership Parenting	**Child's Feeling**	**Bhakti Texts**	**Maslow's Hierarchy**	**Self Determination**	**Erik Erikson's Stages**
Ch. 6-7	Connection & Belonging	*"I know myself. I trust you."*	*sambandha*	Belonging	Relatedness	Trust vs Mistrust
Ch. 8	Free Will & Agency	*"I can do it."*	*abhidheya*	Freedom	Autonomy	Autonomy vs Shame/Doubt
Ch. 9-10	Achievement & Completion	*"I did it!"*	*prayojana*	Esteem	Competence	Industry vs Inferiority
Ch. 11	All Three Needs Chapter 11	*"I know what I'm meant for."*	*dharma samadhi*	Self-Actualization	Motivation	Identity vs Confusion
Ch. 12	Others' Core Needs	*"I can understand what they need."*	*vadanya*			Intimacy vs Isolation
Ch. 13	Win-Win	*"We can help each other."*	*sanga*			Generativity vs Stagnation
Ch. 14	Win-Win-Win Leadership	*"We can serve everyone together."*	*sankirtan*			

CORE NEEDS 1: CONNECTION AND BELONGING

The first set of core needs a child shows is the need for connection and belonging (*sambandha*).

Humans, and especially children, need a very secure foundation of connection. From ancient bhakti texts, we understand that the very existence of the soul is based on connection. The Supreme Soul had a need for relationship and so manifested into all the individual souls, in order to experience love.

The first few years of a child's life are important for fulfilling this need. Children need to trust that there is a real live human who will be meeting their needs, no matter what. Every time you have responded to your child's needs in a peaceful, non-reactive manner, you are enforcing this sense of connection.

Connection is what links a child's heart to our heart. Yoga actually means to link or connect. Connection is the foundation of all the other needs. As in Maslow's hierarchy, if a primary need is unfulfilled, it is difficult for a child to step into fulfilling the later ones. The most important need a child will have is the need for connection. Much of social dysfunctions are based around disturbances in connection. Further on, I will teach you how to reenforce that connection.

What Does It Look Like?

The connection need manifests in many ways. When children communicate, and want to spend time with others, this need is manifesting. When their friends leave and they get upset, it's manifesting. Children with a high need for connection are people-oriented. They love talking to their friends, making gifts for others, touching base with you frequently, sitting on your lap and cuddling more.

When Connection Need Is Met

A child whose need for connection is met can connect with another with security. They walk up to others to play with confidence. When their friends disagree with them, they don't feel rejected. When things don't go their way, they don't take it personally. They feel confident that it was just a one-off, but they're okay. They smile a lot; they make others smile. They attract others to be around them. They are confident that if Mom or Dad aren't there, they will be okay.

When Connection Need Isn't Met

Sometimes the need for connection manifests stronger at different times like when there's a new baby, or when there's been an illness or hospitalization, or after Mom or Dad have gone on a trip. It also manifests at different ages like when school has just started, or when they're beginning separation anxiety at eight to fourteen months.

They get clingy in their relationships, acting out with their friends. They get attention by hitting, saying nasty things as a joke, poking, or making fun of other kids. They complain a lot about their friends, and they need help for simple conversations. When they approach their friends to play, they start off with a negative attitude, "why can't you such and such." They don't feel confident. If a friend disagrees with them, they take it personally. They have difficulty sharing. They don't feel good enough and if a friend disagrees, they feel they aren't worthy or important. They'll say things like, "They don't like me. They don't want to be friends with me."

Other programs label this need for connection "attention-seeking," or a "highly clingy" child. But it's not a need for attention as much as just a need to connect. This is a soul-deep need and crucial for every human being.

Red Flags

Young children who are left alone for long periods of time have severe unmet connection needs. Children who must get their own meals, get themselves ready for school, stay in their own rooms, or watch TV or gadgets for long periods of time are experiencing neglect. They struggle the most in social environments. Children who suffer that form of neglect can become bullies, because they "force" others to give them the attention they seek. They can also become victim to bullies, as they do not have healthy interactions where communication and connection has been modeled. They don't have skills to stand up for themselves and feel their worth.

Connection Summary

When your child's connection and belonging needs are met, they will feel:

- I have someone I can connect to, who will hear and understand what I'm trying to say.
- I belong to a social group, my family, and a group of peers in my classroom or community.
- I can trust those I am connected with to look out for my welfare.
- My needs for intimacy, comfort, and love are met in healthy ways.

CORE NEEDS 2: FREE WILL AND AGENCY

The second set of needs a child exhibits is the need for free will and agency (*abhidheya*). Free will is another intrinsic quality of the soul. Many philosophies debate this intrinsic need of a soul, free will or determinism, and if there is such a need for free will, where does fate and destiny come in? Those conversations are beyond the scope of this section, but I will say that bhakti texts very comfortably clarify that. Since the soul is made in love, to connect with the supreme source, and love can't be forced, the second quality given is free will. The soul gets to choose how and who they wish to love, and that love can't be forced.

What Does It Look Like?

Free will is the basis of desire and autonomy. When a child desires something, they exert their free will to attain that desire. Agency is the ability to make choices to get that desire fulfilled. This free will need is a need to matter, a need to make choices, and should be attended to as frequently as possible. It empowers children to be successful in establishing independent, healthy habits.

This need can manifest in opposite ways for children. One baby may prefer sleeping in total quiet; another may fall asleep easier in a room full of people. It manifests when they must do things their way. When my older one was three, he had this phrase, "*Daju Kare*." (His nickname is Vraju – daju, and *kare* means, "going to do it.") He always said that. He had to be the one to tie his shoes, put on his jacket, pour his milk. I loved it and I allowed it! Soon, he was toasting bread, layering cream cheese, and making breakfast. He mixed the pancake batter, flipped them, and did so much more. All as a three-year-old.

Some children may also manifest a higher need for free will than others. They want things their way and need to make their own decisions. Also, it can manifest more powerfully at different ages. Generally, toddlers and early adolescents have incredibly strong needs for free will and agency.

When Free Will Need Is Met

A child who has their free-will need met is content, knows they have choices, and knows what to do with the choices. They act responsibly even if an adult isn't around. For example, a five-year-old will confidently walk into a room full of activities, choose one, and sit down. They don't need to be forced to do basic activities. They know which activities they enjoy. They're also content in working and doing chores. They can accept when a choice isn't available because their free will is replenished, so a desire that doesn't get fulfilled doesn't make or break them. They are content, peaceful, and settled. They are okay with boundaries, as they have had plenty, and the boundaries have helped them increase meeting their free-will need.

When Free Will Need Isn't Met

When free will isn't met, it becomes stronger and begins manifesting in other ways. The child is labeled defiant, out of control, and power-hungry. They have difficulty sharing, empathizing, or getting along with others.

They get reactive quickly. For example, if they don't get the toy they want, they break it. They may be obedient and submissive when with authoritarian parents, but as soon as they have a lot of freedom, they don't know what to do with it. They may physically run around chaotically. They have difficulty in environments without structure or boundaries. They argue a lot more. They hit if they don't get their way. They have difficulty self-regulating, and they struggle with boundaries and consequences. They don't like rules, asking for help, or asking for permission.

Other programs call this a need for power or a need for control. It's unfair to label children that way. It gives this impression that children are egomaniacs who are power-hungry, control freaks. But that couldn't be farther from the truth. This need is an intrinsic need for a child to manifest key skills of independence, decision-making, completing tasks, and finding their purpose.

Red Flags

Young children who are raised in an authoritarian environment with overly strict rules of behavior will act out. Children forced into submission for long periods of time will struggle with healthy decision-making. Children who don't have healthy boundaries, and who haven't been taught how to make choices, and which choices can be made will struggle in structured environments like classrooms and other people's homes. For example, a little boy had such a high need for free will that when he saw the Montessori classroom, he didn't know what to choose and how to place it back. He was haphazardly grabbing things, kicking over other's work and more. On the playground, he got into so many altercations. But when given the choice to "sit down for two minutes or sit down for five minutes," he literally would yell very happily, "I'll sit for two minutes!" He was unaccustomed to healthy boundaries and healthy choices, and this manifested in an extreme way.

Free Will Summary

When your child has their free-will and agency needs met, they will think:

- I inherently know how to reach my full potential.
- I don't want to be forced to do things I don't want to do.
- I want choices in my life.
- I want to be trusted to make decisions.
- I want to be respected for the decisions I make.

In later chapters, I will show you how to empower that free will while still maintaining healthy boundaries.

CORE NEEDS 3: ACHIEVEMENT AND COMPLETION

With the achievement and completion needs (*prayojana*), the child has a need for reaching a goal and for completion (I did it!). They're trying for a specific outcome or result. Bhakti texts teach that the world is perfect and complete, as is the creator who designed it all. Anything that looks incomplete actually has perfection hidden within it, and individual souls are but a small manifestation of the complete whole of the universe. Souls are on a path to achievement and full completion, and every endeavor they make is a part of this path. This sense of completion can be had at any stage of the path, and once the goal is reached, that is not the end. It's a mystical cycle that is amazing to experience, but that's for me to share with you in another book.

How It Manifests

For children, this need for achievement/completion manifests in so many ways. From the moment a baby starts moving their arms around at two weeks, to rocking back and forth on all fours at eight months, to grabbing at the table dining cloth at fourteen months, and onward, they are pregnant with a sense of achievement. The baby who's moving their arms around wildly is trying to grab something – they got it! Soon they're moving, from point A to point B. Watch a baby and it's like their literal being is driven to move. Once they get there, a sense of completion, ahhh, and soon they're raring to go again.

I was teaching my four-year-old how to ride a bike and his younger brother, only two years old at the time, had to learn as well. Suddenly I'm teaching two kids at once to ride a bike! The "baby" was just adamant – he *had* to learn! Our whole week of spring break was spent outside, with him *tantrumming* and pushing and forcing himself to learn this difficult task. He had a very strong need for achievement. The achievement need manifests as a strong feeling of "I did it!" "I'm competent!" "I can achieve and complete."

When the Need for Achievement Is Met

A child whose need for achievement is met has an internal sense of confidence in tasks. They know that they can do it. When someone asks for a volunteer, they're usually the ones with their hand up. They're confident to help others. They're good finishers.

They like the feeling of completion, of the activity coming full circle. They love games that have higher and higher levels. They like to stick with something until it's done, and they don't like to leave tasks until they are done. They are interested in completing that puzzle, cooking that meal, building that drone or robot or Lego creation. Children with this need met are confident, ambitious, and happy.

When the Need for Achievement Isn't Met

Children who haven't had their need for achievement met aren't very confident, nor able to finish things. They don't raise their hands often; they leave things out, they're not good at starting new things, or finishing old things. They may get distracted very easily. In the classroom setting, we see that they are unable to complete work and activities, though they may be good at choosing.

These children may also be hesitant to start activities because of fear of failure. They may be perfectionists so they take longer, checking too many details. On the one hand, they could drive you crazy by never finishing because of perfectionism, because they're too goal oriented, or on the flip side, they may just drop it because they don't care for the outcome.

Red Flags

A red flag in achievement is when a child becomes extremely self-conscious about completing things. Parents criticize them for doing a poor job or redo their entire task because the outcome wasn't perfect.

I have a high need for achievement, and this showed inappropriately with my child once. I actually redid his entire science fair experiment board, taking every piece off and re-gluing it. He also had an unusually high achievement need. He shared years later that these types of interactions made him feel not good enough.

The opposite can also happen. A red flag is a child who is completely unmotivated for anything. They have no desire to achieve anything, complete anything, and spend their days watching T.V. or playing on screens. They don't know what to do with themselves and they just act out when they're bored.

Achievement Summary

A child whose achievement needs are met feels:

- I have an intrinsic goal I wish to reach by my actions.
- I want to be trusted in my goals.
- I have a reason I'm doing what I'm doing.
- I achieve and complete things.
- I am good enough.

Understanding these three core needs in children is extremely eye-opening. Observe your child. How are these needs manifesting? Which red flags do you see in your child? Which need is not being met appropriately? Journal it. In the rest of the book, we will identify exactly how to fix it.

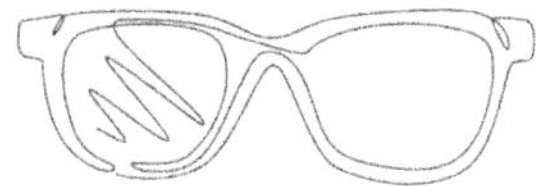

GOLD-TINTED GLASSES

Through your observations, you will realize that your child is so much more intelligent than you ever thought before. They have just as much intrinsic intelligence as a fully grown adult; they have to! Like newly-built AI machines, they are constantly evolving, growing, and learning new things.

Now that you've learned your child's core needs, you'll view them from a completely different lens. We will call them gold-tinted glasses.

Usually, kids are viewed with glasses with a little bit of crap on them. They're not good enough. They're not strong enough. They're prone to make mistakes. "OMG, I can't believe you just dropped the milk again!"

We're going to make a strong switcheroo of those beliefs in our head. We're going to the store to pick up the sleekest gold-tinted glasses. They may be more than we can afford, but these beautiful gold glasses will change your family's life.

Picture yourself picking them out. Imagine how good it will feel to see your child in a completely different light. Now you have them on? Good. Read further. What you learn may blow your mind. You may decide you don't even believe it. When I told these same bhakti truths to a room full of sannyasi priests in the world headquarters of the ISKCON society in India, I had five sannyasi monks questioning me, they couldn't believe it as well. Although I was up at the podium shaking a little in my boots to be asked tough questions by prominent religious leaders in the bhakti society, I ever so humbly was able to confirm, "hey, these aren't my words; these truths come straight from our bhakti literatures."

You can choose to take off these glasses any time you want and get back to your regular ol' life of parenting your kids the way you've been for all these years.

NOT AN ORDINARY CHILD

The undeniable truth and complete fact is that your child is not an ordinary child.

Let that sink in for a few minutes. (I know some of you have secretly already known this.) That you are a spiritual-minded intellectual who will read a leadership parenting book shows that your child is special enough to warrant that preparation.

When a king comes to a city, all his ministers prepare for his visit ahead of time. They find out what foods he can eat, and what stores are nearby that carry such foods. They stock the dressing rooms with clothes he will wear, bring his work, set up his schedule, and more. Sometimes weeks of preparation can go into a two- or three-day stay.

It is described in bhakti texts that when the Supreme Lord Krishna arrived 5,000 years ago, gods and goddesses from the heavens took birth in different ministers' homes to prepare the kingdom for his divine birth. The constellations, the planets, the weather, the earth's bounty of vegetables, minerals, fruits, flowers all aligned perfectly to create a pleasant environment for Krishna's new life on Earth. Any time a great personality is born, there is special preparation.

SPECIAL ROOM

Before my first baby was born, at seven months pregnant, I was perched on the top of a ladder painstakingly ripping off old wallpaper. I loved

Home Depot and learned what a miter saw was so I could install a new chair rail in the baby room. Did you also prepare a special room for your child?

All this preparation shows us that we know our child is no ordinary child. We have prepared our external circumstances (the baby crib, the baby registry, the ceremonies) and now it's time to prepare their social spaces.

K.I.D.S.

Bhakti texts explain how rare the human form of life is. Just the fact that your child has taken a human birth means they're ready for things that animals can't even conceive of – inquiry, growth, and compassionate love.

Actually, your child is so special that they are even spoken of in the Bhagavad Gita, the primary bhakti text spoken 5,000 years ago. It is a dialogue between the foremost of Gods, Krishna, and his friend, the warrior Arjuna on a battlefield. They are fighting evil, and thousands are slain. Arjuna shares deep concerns about the spiritually minded individual who dies: "What happens after death? Is that individual like a riven cloud, lost materially and spiritually?" With deep compassion, Arjuna feels the pain of those warriors who are laying down their lives for the sake of establishing goodness in the world.

Krishna responds mystically. "Don't worry," he says. "They're covered." These rare souls who have already started a journey of leading others through service – these transcendentalists – they take birth in the homes of aristocratic, spiritually-minded individuals. Krishna alludes to the process of reincarnation, a very foundational belief of bhakti. We are eternal spirit souls. Our journeys don't end at the time of death. The universe arranges for us to continue whatever internal progress has been made. While material circumstances do change, the internal growth of a soul continues in another life. This is called the law of karma and reincarnation.

Your child has very purposefully been matched with you and entered your home through destiny. You are the perfect person for your child. You are a high-minded, spiritual being, choosing leadership in your life. You are your child's destiny, and you are the spiritually powerful being that Krishna speaks of for your child.

With this perspective, and these gold-tinted glasses, you will redefine what your child exemplifies. Here's a cute acronym to help you do this:

- K – Kings and Queens: My child is royalty, a king or a queen.
- I – Intellectual: My child is an intellectual, highly-intelligent being.
- D – Demigod: My child is a demigod/ demigoddess.
- S – Sages: My child is a sage.

Yes, dear one. That snot-nosed little booger of a four-year-old who won't stop saying no to you is an aristocrat and a sage. Maybe now it makes more sense as to why their fights are demigod-sized!

As K.I.D.S., your child already has everything needed within them to solve the problems they face around them. All that is needed is an expert guide (you) and a healthy, safe environment to help bring those qualities out.

This also means that they are born leaders. They *inherently* know how to serve; how to work with others; how to inhabit all those powerful leadership qualities you had envisioned in your dream child.

LAW OF EXPECTATIONS

But wait a minute, I started this chapter with hearing from you all about the difficulties your child is having, so I understand that just putting on gold tinted glasses isn't necessarily going to work. But that having been said, it is a really powerful practice. That is why it's the very first step, to just envision. Of course, as you continue reading this book, I'll give you many more practical examples.

Bruce Wilkinson, author of *The Seven Laws of the Learner*, shares a powerful story of expectations.

He was a rookie professor, teaching his first set of classes in college. He was assigned sections one, two, and three of the course. A seasoned colleague of his expressed surprise that this brand new professor would be teaching section two. Apparently, section two was the class where all the honors kids from high schools around the state were placed.

On the first day of school, Bruce was ready to teach. He felt like his first class – section one – went well, "a good give-and-take session with a solid group of young men and women." However, when section two came in, he couldn't believe the difference in energy. "From the ring of the bell, class just flew by as we learned at almost warp speed. It was like stepping on a surfboard and riding the crest of the wave the entire hour." During the semester, he felt a vast difference between the students in section two and the students in his other two classes. "Everything seemed different – their questions, their eye contact, their facial expressions, even the way they sat in their chairs. It was incredible. My colleague was right: these students pulled the best right out of you." The other students in the other sections were good, but nowhere near the caliber of section two.

Halfway through the semester, the academic dean asked him how he enjoyed teaching college. Bruce waxed on and on, singing the praise of the section two class and all the students in it. He expressed his delight and gratitude for being chosen to teach the honors students even though it was his first year. He shared the amazing differences between them and the rest of the classes.

The dean was quiet, and after Bruce finished, shocked him by saying, "I need to tell you something that may surprise you – but there's no honors class this year. We canceled it. We decided it would be better to spread the top students through all the classes."

Bruce was dizzy with disbelief. He excused himself and ran to confirm this with the registrar. It was true. There was no honors class.

Bruce regrouped himself and looked up the grades of the different classes. The difference between the section two students and all the others was staggering. He compared the pile of work completed by the section two students, with the other two classes. Section two had more pages than the other two sections combined! He "went through the papers, one by one, page by page, and the difference was dramatic. The section two students outshone their peers again and again."

Bruce realized, and shares with his readers, that this was the most dramatic learning experience of his life. What he believed about his students made an incredible difference in how they learned and acted.

That professor did not know that there was no difference between the supposedly high-achieving students of section two in comparison to all the other classes. What was different in his approach? How were their responses, their energy, their mood, their grades, their papers – how was it all so drastically different from the other classes?

Imagine how he leaned forward when he talked. Imagine that he must have spoken faster, knowing the students could keep up. He might have given more material, explained things with bigger words, pushed the kids more, expected in every one of his spoken and unspoken actions that he wanted more from them, and he would *not settle for less*.

If you see someone climbing Mount Everest, you won't worry about whether or not they could walk up a small hill.

I went on a 5K run with a few friends. One of them was a marathon runner. Another hadn't done any exercise for a while. When the marathon runner paused to tie shoelaces, no one blinked an eye. When the non-active friend paused, we all worried: "Hey, are you feeling okay. Let us know if you need a break."

Do you see the difference? Because we knew what the marathon runner was capable of, we responded differently. Do the same with your child.

My parents envisioned my sister and me with gold-tinted glasses. My mom told me that our home Deities were installed because, and I quote, "You were the reason we became spiritually focused. God came to our home because of you". Umm what? When she told me that, I was a just a little kid – nothing special, definitely not that spiritually qualified, but she empowered me.

"You are special to me. You have arrived for a purpose. I'm so grateful you are here. Our lives have been enriched by you being here."

Let your children feel this from you.

Now just because they are K.I.D.S doesn't mean they no longer need to conform to societal expectations and have set limits and boundaries. Quite the contrary. Because they are in a family of leadership, the expectations of conduct are way higher for them. Chapter 8 will guide you through establishing those boundaries.

We began this chapter with the list of everything you're feeling overwhelmed with. We end with you envisioning your dream child, through high expectations and gold-tinted glasses. Remember, all those soul qualities we spoke of in the dream child are already inherently existing in your child. That knowledge itself can help your responses.

Don't worry, I will work with you on the details. But now, it's your turn to become their willing guide. In the next chapter, we talk about you.

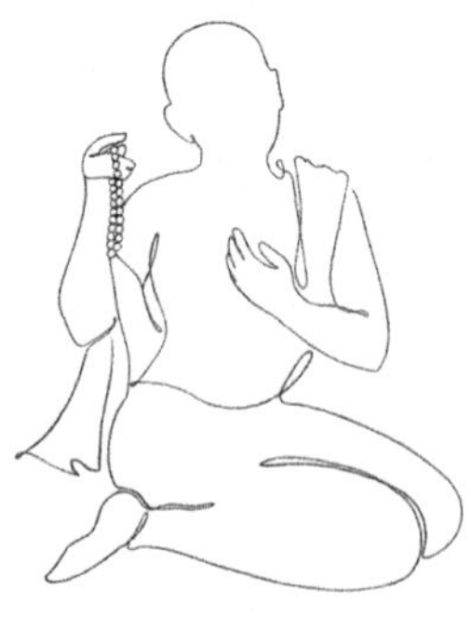

* * *

Mantra Affirmations Level 1: I Envision

* * *

As we work on solidifying your child's identity, we remember that bhakti texts share that the intrinsic identity of a soul is "eternal, full of bliss and knowledge." That means *your child intrinsically already has everything within to be happy, show their intelligence, and have patience and grit*. Crazy, isn't it?

This identity is discovered through mantra meditation. Mantras use sound to shift one's consciousness and mood. You can experience sound shifts easily – put on a sad tune that reminds you of an ex and suddenly your whole body can feel demotivated. Listen to classical Bach or Beethoven versus rock and roll, and you feel completely different shifts in your energy. Sound is very powerful for unlocking what's deep within the heart. The first sound introduced by bhakti texts is *om*. *Om* is considered the sound of the universe, the primeval sound.

By reciting this word, you and your child will reach your higher selves. The Sanskrit mantra words *"Bhur bhuvah svah"* denote the different levels of the universe, and past, present and future. By reciting the mantra below, you are channeling the ability to uncover their identity in any sphere and any time space.

Om bhur bhuvah svah
Let me see my child as an intelligent, capable, powerful spiritual being.
Let me change my mindset and internal expectations.
Let me trust that their divine qualities will emerge.
I envision. I trust. I accept.

5

WHY HAVE I BEEN CHOSEN?

"Leadership is this intense journey into yourself."

—JEFFREY IMMELT

At this point, it's natural if you're having doubts about this child of yours who is supposed to be this amazing demigod and royalty. It's natural when you feel those I Quit moments to throw down the gold-tinted glasses and question your parenting abilities.

"Why me?" is a question that comes up a lot. "Why am I having to go through this stress? How am I supposed to know how to navigate this?"

During those I Quit moments, when you feel alone, lost, and helpless, you feel disconnected from your child and from yourself. First, we will identify and accept your parent personality type. Later, we will journey deeper to meet your source, your Inner Parents.

YOUR PARENT PERSONALITY TYPE

Once I attended a birthday party where there was little to no structure for the children. There were a variety of activities set up, but no adult giving clear directions and no schedule. The kids got their snacks when they wanted, ate it wherever they chose, and played with whomever and whatever they wanted. Because it was a bit of a free-for-all, I was uncomfortable. I recognized that it was just not my personality to be okay with so little structure.

Later, I overheard two moms talking. "What a cool party! Isn't it nice to let the kids choose what they want to do?"

"Yeah, kids are so controlled these days. This gives them a chance to discover the activities and their friendships on their own."

It was eye-opening. While I was judging the party for no structure, here were two moms feeling liberated for their children. It wasn't that my way of throwing a party was wrong; nor was there anything wrong with the unstructured, open event. It was just natural as we are all unique individuals, I had different needs than they did.

Let's take a few minutes to figure out what is important to you. What is your personality?

There are many detailed personality tests such as the Myers-Briggs Type Indicator and DISC personality test. For the sake of this lesson, we're going to do a simple set of questions to get you started. However, as is the case with all personality assessments, the results are not set in stone. You will lean toward one type or another at different ages and stages, and different circumstances.

PARENT PERSONALITY QUESTIONNAIRE

Question 1

It's an hour before the school bus arrives. Your child just told you he forgot about his test during first period. He needs your help.

1. This is upsetting and you let him know. You practice tough love and don't help him. If he fails, he will learn an important, powerful lesson to not leave things until the last minute.
2. You are upset and you let him know. Even though it's last minute and inconvenient, you sit next to him and ask him the study questions to help him.
3. You listen to his freakouts. You empathize with his predicament and let him figure it out. He'll come to you if he needs help.

Question 2

Your three-year old has already rejected two shirts this morning. She doesn't know what she wants to wear and is in tears. You're running out the door and running out of time.

1. You tell her if she doesn't put the next one on, you're going to give her a time-out or take away her favorite toy. She needs to learn consequences and stop playing games with your time.
2. You bring her to another room, start feeding her breakfast with no shirt on. Once she's fed and distracted, you ask her which one and put it on her.
3. That's okay. You understand that she can't easily decide and pull out a few more shirts for her to choose from or reject. Or why doesn't she wear all three?

Question 3

You're in the middle of making dinner. Your eighteen-month-old is sitting in a highchair with a bowl of dry cheerios. Every time you give her a bowl, she dumps the bowl upside down on the floor, with a big giggle on her face.

1. While she's really cute, you know you need to teach her

proper eating habits. After a few reminders, you take the bowl away, remove her from the highchair, ask her to pick up all the pieces, and tell her mealtime is over.

2. You look for an alternative. Removing her from the highchair, you sit with her on the floor, and help her eat the cheerios. You explain why and what you're doing.
3. It's okay. She's young and you love seeing her laugh. You laugh alongside her, pick up the cheerios off the floor, pull up a chair, get more and eat them with her together. You don't mind cleaning up, if need be. Let her have fun.

QUESTION 4

You're picking up your child after school. Your daughter's friend's mom lets you know the girls have made arrangements and your daughter will be going to her house right now and she'll be back in time for dinner.

1. What! How can she dump that on you? You say, "umm not today. We already had plans." Even though you didn't, it's not okay for your daughter to make plans with other families without talking to you first. You tell her friend's mom, no.
2. You pull your daughter aside and talk to her. You expect that she'll come home first, finish her work, and then decide whether it makes sense to go to her friends. You communicate this to her friend's parent.
3. Yes! You feel great that your daughter made some of her own decisions and will be out of the house for a little bit longer so you can get that much needed work out in your day.

Question 5

You're on the phone with your friend and your child keeps interrupting you. Again, and yet again.

1. You put the phone on mute, ask her to please stop, walk out of the room and slam the door, not purposefully. But she gets the point. It's rude to interrupt.
2. You ask your daughter if it's an emergency. If it's not, you ask her to wait ten minutes until the phone call is done and then she'll have your undivided attention. If she's young, you find something else for her to do, or take her outside in the backyard to play.
3. You tell your friend to wait a minute, put her on hold and listen to your daughter explain what the issue is, which takes some time. By the time you get back to your friend on the phone, you hear a dial tone. You call her back and apologize.

Question 6

Your fifteen-year-old comes home after curfew. It's a school night.

1. You've called a few times. No answer. You wait up for him on the living room couch. When he's finally home, you tell him he's lost privileges for the next few weeks.
2. When he finally gets home, you ask him if he's okay. The next day, when you're calmer, you have a conversation about the curfew, why he was late, and if the curfew time needs to be changed or if it can be followed.
3. You go to bed. He's old enough to figure out where he wants to go and to manage his own time. You trust him and his decisions.

Question 7

Your boy's friends from school are suddenly coming over for a homework project. Your boy's room is a mess.

1. You rush upstairs to clean it all.
2. You make your son clean it before his friends can come in
3. You leave the mess, does it really matter? Let them have fun.

Question 8

Your idea of a good time with your kids is:

1. Reading a story together with a moral instructive lesson.
2. Hanging out with them and watching them do something they're excited about.
3. Watching a Disney movie with nachos and popcorn.

Question 9

Your son doesn't complete the dishes today, tomorrow, or the day after.

1. You threaten to take away his phone and get in an argument. After his phone is in your hands, he finishes them.
2. You have a discussion, giving him the benefit of the doubt and figure out why he's putting them off. You re-work the chores arrangement so he can commit to it.
3. It's okay. He's busy. You end up doing them yourself.

There are three primary parent types: trainers, facilitators, and witnesses. Remember, it's not a thorough evaluation, but just a basic quiz to see which style you lean more toward. Count how many you chose out of the nine options.

- Mostly As lean toward being Trainers.
- Mostly Bs lean toward being Facilitators.
- Mostly Cs lean toward being Witnesses.

TRAINER

You are a trainer! It's important to you that your child make the right decisions. You like to be in control of your environment. You know best for your children and expect them to stick to your established rules. You're ready to set them up for success and will instruct them accordingly. Your relationship with your child is a bit reverential type. Trainers generally will continue an argument until their children accept. You will expect more from your child and help them reach out of their comfort zone. You have a high need for achievement, and focus on completion, the product and the end goal

When it goes right: Trainers set their children up for success. Their children give them a feeling of accomplishment, and they like to showcase their children to others. Children admire trainer parents. When they're young, children of trainers feel safe with strong boundaries.

What to be aware of: Trainers will get into ego battles with their kids, tantrums when they're young and arguments when they're older. Their kids will have a need for distance in their early adult lives, in order to find their free will. Because trainers are perfectionists, they can feel disappointed when their children don't measure up. Children of trainers may feel they're not good enough.

FACILITATOR

You are a facilitator!

Facilitators have a high need for free will and agency and love to support their child with the space to discover on their own. It is important for facilitators to neither smother their children with too much control or attention, nor to be completely permissive. Facilitators enjoy active conversations where all sides are discussed and don't shy away from an argument. They are good listeners, but also know how to guide conversations to healthy conclusions. They like to treat their children with lots of respect and let their children guide activities and decisions in the house.

When it goes right: children of facilitators are innovators, deep thinkers, and have a sense of purpose. They like to invent and create and have had many opportunities to develop their thinking skills. They feel confident to make their own decisions because they have had just the right amount of guidance.

What to be aware of: children of facilitators may have difficulty respecting authority or other's opinions when they're young. They may also have difficulty accepting if they've made the wrong choice. They can get inflated egos and have difficulty seeing others' perspectives. They don't do so well in highly structured environments and need to make their own way.

WITNESS

You are a witness! Witnesses have a high need for connection. You love to be a part of your child's happy experiences and love to watch your children make their own choices. You are a pleaser, a smile-maker. You like to go along with the flow and not make waves. You don't like confrontation and prefer to let things play out. You trust that your children will learn from their mistakes. Harmony and peace are more important to witnesses than being right.

When it goes right: witnesses create a loving, peaceful environment in the home. Their children usually feel comfortable, loved and happy. They feel free to make their own decisions and not constricted. They have a lot of independence.

What to be aware of: because they are conflict-avoiders, witnesses can be too permissive and have difficulty enforcing consequences and boundaries. Their children may wish for more structure and feel lost as they grow up. They may take time to figure out who and what they want to do.

ACCEPT YOURSELF

All three parenting types have pros and cons. Identify what you can be proud of and what you can work on. As you learn more, you'll be able to see how your parenting type responds and reacts to the strategies in this book. You can accept yourself and know that you are perfectly matched for your child. Identify which core needs your child has, and what your parent personality type is. How are you matched up with your child perfectly according to their core needs? When you observe your child's core needs in conjunction with your parent personality type, you can be more aware of your responses. What do they need more of? What can you help them with?

PARENTING INSECURITIES

Figuring out who we are as parents also means addressing your insecurities in that role. Remember the misconceptions we debunked in Chapter 2? We parents have so many insecurities. One of the greatest parenting challenges is to parent among those who seem to do it expertly. When you get unsolicited advice from others it can make you question yourself. That is why the public display of your child's negative social interactions disturbs you so much. You will feel that parents and teachers are all aware of your ineptitude.

I understand these insecurities. For example, I love to sing and have been singing since I was five. Many have complimented me on my voice and invited me to sing at their events. My voice isn't where I would like it to be as I tend to be pitchy. But after I practice, I think I sound amazing. My sister, on the other hand, is a Grammy-nominated singer. She has over two million followers on social media and is world-renowned, performing concerts internationally. When we do live broadcasts together, and she asks me to sing with her, suddenly I completely shut down. Insecurities cloud everything, my throat closes up, and even a basic tune eludes me.

That's the power of insecurities. Having your child's social inabilities played out in front of the "experts" (teachers, other parents full of 'wisdom'), magnifies your insecurities and can make you feel like a failure. It makes this whole experience all that more intense for you.

Then when your child pours out their feelings about what's happening at school, they look to you to help them. If you don't know how to respond, you feel helpless, and it can make you feel like a fraud.

Identifying your parenting personality can help quell the insecurities. When you observe how you're responding to your child according to their needs, you will begin knowing what to do. All of the lessons in this book are to help you overcome those insecurities.

YOU ARE ALREADY A GURU

Remember when I was sitting in the hospital wondering if I had been a good mom? I questioned whether I had prepared my child for navigating difficult life circumstances. Remember how those magical Sanskrit words floated into my thoughts?

One of the mantras that came to me was a powerful one from the oldest bhakti text, "Srimad Bhagavatam." *Gurur na sa syat sva jano na syat; pita na sa syat na janani na sa syat; na mocayed yah samupetya mrtyuh.*

The simple translation is, "A guru is a father is a mother is someone who has the power to liberate their children from the fears of this mortal world."

You as a mother, as a father, are as revered as a guru, are as anointed as the top spiritual leaders of society and have been directly given this responsibility because of how qualified you are to free your child from their fears. Believe in yourself. This has been given to you by the Supreme Source itself.

Those words put moms and dads in the same category as gurus, spiritual monks who have sacrificed their lives to serve humanity. You know the ones who wear saffron robes and markings on their faces and have renounced all material things, dedicating their lives in service to God and his people. Think: Jesus Christ, Mohammed, Mother Teresa, the Dalai Lama, etc.

What a surprise that us mere mortals – regular old moms and dads – are being given the same position as gurus. Such is the sanctity of parenthood.

This sanctity of the parent-child relationship is one of the most important tenets of leadership parenting. You have been divinely empowered and personally called to serve your child. Out of many thousands of births this child could have had, he has been perfectly placed in your home.

Bhakti texts teach that souls move from one body to another, experiencing desires, and working through their good and bad karma. When they finally take birth as a human, they enter a specific family, guided by their desires and needs. I like to visualize a divine being peering through all the homes across the earth planet, looking at all the potential moms and dads, looking at the list of psychological and spiritual support this baby needs, and bam, seeing you and gifting them to you.

It doesn't really matter what your personality is. You are already perfect in the eyes of the supreme and in the eyes of your child. Shake off those insecurities and stand with conviction. You are enough. You are chosen. This child needs you, and only you.

As you take a deep breath, and fill your chest with confidence, we will now reach the next level, the "M" in EMPOWERMENT.

* * *

Level 2: Meet the Inner Parents

* * *

We will step past your insecurities and step into greater empowerment. At this level, we will meet two powerfully divine beings seated in your heart. They are the Inner Parents.

The Inner Parents are always with you. They are your Source, my Source and the Source of every living being in this world. Call them the universe, the divine, nature, God, or whatever name you wish. They are your protectors and caretakers.

I remember watching *Bambi* as a child. When he was born, he was a cute, wet pile of long limbs. Only moments later, he started stirring. He lifted one leg, then another. He teetered and tottered and fell. But up he went again, trying to balance his legs. Soon, he was on all four legs. "Kinda wobbly, isn't he," Thumper commented. Finally, he took one step, two, five, and within a few short hours – only hours! – he was frolicking and playing with his friends. *Who is guiding his steps? Who is teaching him how to walk?* Even as a little girl, I knew the answer to that and was amazed. *Inner Parents are guiding his steps.*

What about a spider? How does it know how to spin a web? In *Charlotte's Web*, Charlotte creates her nest, a massive puff of white web hanging off the corner of the barn doorway. But then, Charlotte dies! Although the pig Wilbur is heartbroken, he has this little hope. "I'm going to take care of the little ball of white web yarn like they're my own babies." One day, the white ball opens up, and explodes into little puffs of tiny spiders flying away. "Where are they going?" Wilbur wonders.

Who's telling them what to do and where to go? I wondered, too. Their momma isn't, and nor is Wilbur, who's just scratching his little pig head in wonder. *Inner Parents will care for them.*

I remember when my first-born was placed on my stomach right after birth. He looked in my eyes and I looked straight into his. There were few words between us, but he knew that he could drink my milk and trust me. How did he know that I was his mom? How did he know to trust me? *Inner Parents guided him.*

Scientists give all kinds of fancy terms to what the Inner Parents do: instinct, biology, hormones, parent's intuition.

Each and every one of us has Inner Parents. They are conscious supreme beings, full of personality, and deep, loving compassion. They are both male and female, mother and father, and have also experienced being a daughter and a son. All leadership qualities arise from them and they will be able to empower you to fulfill your child's core needs. They are simultaneously your core essence, and your eternal parents who will nurture you. They know who your child will impact and how.

Your Inner Parents are not constricted by time. They know what has happened to you in your past, what growth you will accomplish with your child today, and what the future holds. Through you, they are preparing the environment for your child's total success. All experiences are known to your Inner Parents. They will guide you when you are torn and lost.

Just as you are so eager to solve your child's problems, because you can't imagine them suffering, similarly the Inner Parents' only purpose for existence is to relieve your suffering and solve your problems. They will maintain, nourish, and give you what you desire.

Have you ever felt that parent's intuition? Like you just knew something was wrong with your child? That was the Inner Parent's nudge.

Judy Blume, author of children's books, wrote a lovely book that I read in my childhood called, *Are you there, God? It's me, Margaret.* As Margaret navigates social issues, she reaches out to God in her mind, as if He's her bestie. Though it was whimsical, it struck a deep chord with me. I would do the same. *"Are you there, God? It's me, Gopi."*

When we reach out to the Inner Parents, we need to trust that they hear us and will answer. The problem is that we don't believe they will respond. Years of distrust in our own abilities, of second-guessing ourselves, has broken our connection with Inner Parents. We can reconnect through self-reflection and meditation.

Any time you feel I Quit moments arising, take a step back, close your eyes, and listen. *I'm having a hard time with this. How do I handle it? What would you like me to do?*

When you're centered, the message will come loud and clear. It may come directly as a thought in your mind and heart. Or it may come indirectly through someone else's words, an email, a social media quote, or a variety of "signs." When you see it, know that this answer is for you and stop doubting.

Finally, I need you to hear me, you are never alone. You are not meant to raise this leader alone. You work hard in your environments. You are a gift, and you serve others. You will always be supported by the Inner Parents. They are here to help you. And I will, too.

In the next chapter, you will learn how to connect with your child by hearing them. For now, take a break and do the meditation below.

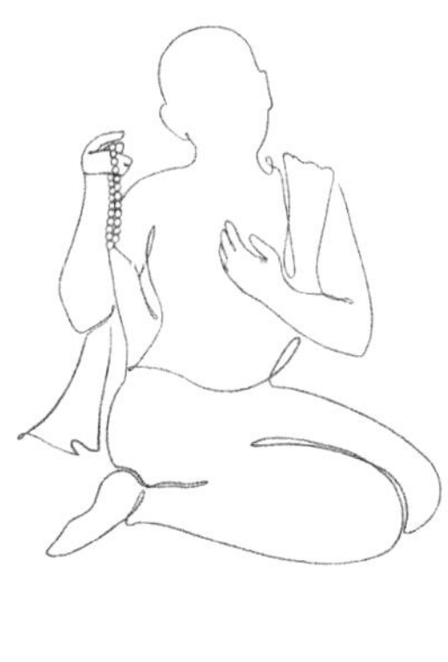

* * *

Mantra Affirmations Level 2: I Am Worthy

* * *

THIS MANTRA directly connects you to the Inner Parents. It was taught to five-year-old Prince Dhruva, when he was rejected by his stepmother. (Read full story in Chapter 13.)

Sit with your back erect, in the lotus pose of yoga. Close your eyes and open up your heart. Recite the Sanskrit mantra ten times. Ask the questions you don't know the answers to and be open to hear the answers throughout the day. Recite the English three times each.

This mantra means, I offer my respects and call to (*namo*) the Supreme Persons (*bhagavate*) who reside within me (*vasudevaya*) eternally (*om*). As it was spoken to a child, today you become a child in front of your Inner Parents. You can also recite this mantra with your child for compounded blessings.

Om namo bhagavate vasudevaya
Let me accept my responsibility as guru.
Let me trust that my parent personality is perfect for the child given to me.
Let me hear my Inner Parents every day.

I am worthy. I am enough. I am meant for this.
I am nurtured. I am empowered. I am never alone.

PART III

CONNECT

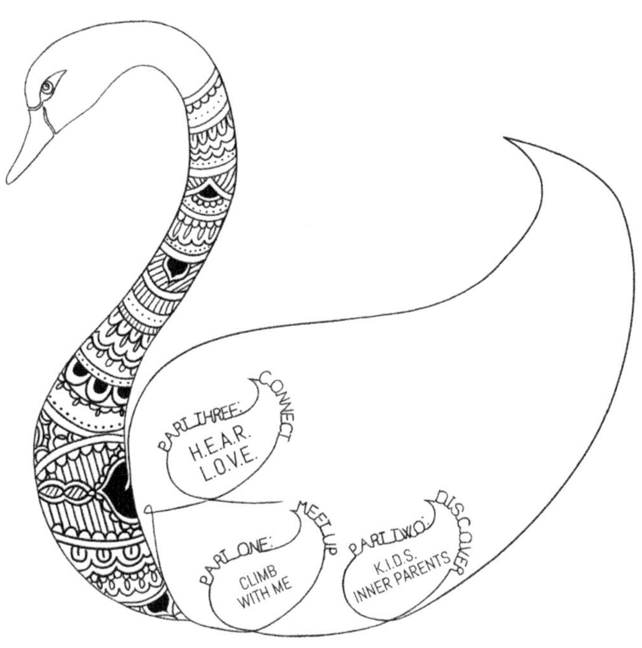

6

HOW CAN THEY CONNECT WITH OTHERS?

"Learning to stand in somebody else's shoes, to see through their eyes, that's how peace begins. And it's up to you to make that happen. Empathy is a quality of character that can change the world."

— BARACK OBAMA

ON THE PLAYGROUND

A group of littles, preschoolers and kindergarteners, are sitting with their dark blue uniforms and pretty pigtails in the grass and mulch. One has bright, yellow-blond curls, another a red ribbon winding through her braids. They're so cute; their teeny voices having just fashioned their vocabulary words, still with the Ls sounding like Ys and the words not precise. But how lovely and confident they speak to each other. They are making a garden and discussing how, by digging with that stick, they're going to dig deep enough to put plants in there. One of them stands up to break off a few little leaves from the nearby shrub to "plant in the garden."

Another young girl, the same age, named Angela walks over. She's looking for friends to play with and has gone from group to group trying to figure out who to spend time with today. I've had my eye on her. Her mom is a client who's worried about her daughter's social issues, so I'm here with my ears and eyes open to observe.

Angela wants to be a part of their "garden-making club". She grabs a stick and starts digging really close to the other girls. "What are you all doing? I want to play with you too. Can I help?"

In her exuberance, she doesn't notice that she has started digging into the other girls' hole, and it's getting a bit messed up. The sweet little conversation between the four girls suddenly changes in tone.

"Well, we're already working hard on this." "Well, we're doing this ourselves." Immediately the older girl sets a few boundaries, closing to one more person joining the group. I'm surprised at how quickly the mood has changed, from little cutie pies working together to stone cold "leave me alone."

Angela retorts back, "how come you never want to play with me? Why don't you ever want to be my friend?!" Her voice rises, becomes shrill, and I can see she is on the verge of tears.

I come a little closer, hesitant to step in and wanting to let it play out, but at the same time realizing she needs tools to know how to involve herself and they need tools to learn how to accept another playmate in. Somehow the conversation seems to have become a habit: Angela asking to play with others, not knowing how, and the others saying, "well we've already started," and Angela immediately jumping into accusatory tones.

Indeed, as I observe some more, this is what has happened to Angela at every group she has tried to become a part of. Something is broken, and she can't seem to connect with others.

This scene has played out more than a thousand times on the playground in the last eighteen years I've been at this school. Young and old, during break, they navigate how to hang out with each other.

Where do they belong? Which group? How do they connect? How do they feel worthy? How do they find a friend? Who can they count on to be their friends? Even with a playground full of kids their age, many children feel alone.

TODAY, just as I see her meltdown coming up, I bring Angela to the side and give her a few words to use to start working with the other girls. It works. She encourages the other ones; she communicates more gently. She doesn't mess up their existing plots and she starts digging and talking and playing with them. Again, the conversation turns to cute nothings about flowers and daisies and butterflies and unicorns and how beautiful their gardens will be. So, I leave.

Sure enough, just a few minutes later I hear agitation again. Angela has started telling everyone else what to do. "You need to make sure you put those flowers in there, on that side, and not on that one. I told you we need to water these otherwise the flowers will wilt. What kind of garden are you making anyways? Why are you not listening to me?" She has become bossy, and no one wants to follow her instructions. She starts taking it personally. She runs over to me, now fully crying. "No one wants to be my friend. I hate it here. I want to go home. No one loves me!" Tears are pouring down her cheeks.

I remember these ups and downs. I remember wanting to play with my "friends" but not knowing how to. I remember my friends rejecting me as too bossy. Are these the types of conversations we had?

Again, I listen, and again I give her the words and work with her and the other girls to sort through it. I know that I will need to do this a few times until they get comfortable. This is why we teach empathy courses in the morning spiritual classes.

However, not all parents have the luxury of knowing how to work with their children. Not all can sit at the playground during snack time and lunch time and watch their children interact with each other, see what's not working, and help them speak to each other expressing their needs and understanding each other.

I'm sure you've heard many of these types of conversations with your child, and this is one of the reasons you're reading this book. There are many things at play here. The most important thing is the little child doesn't know how to connect with others.

BROKEN CONNECTION

Remember we spoke of three needs – connection, free will, and achievement? In these scenarios, the internal need of connection is broken.

Here are some signs of broken connection:

- When you see your child trying to engage with a group of children and they're not accepted into the group
- When your child doesn't get invited to playdates
- When your child is invited to playdates but there are fights immediately afterward
- When friends get up to leave, or the game is over, as soon as your child joins.

When these scenarios happen all the time, it can break your heart. You'll wonder, *why can't my child connect with their friends?*

NOT GOOD ENOUGH

The underlying issue is an intrinsic feeling of insecurity. Children who feel uncomfortable in group environments where they go from "no one wants me around" to "I'm going to be the boss," are navigating internal security dysfunction. Whether it's genetic, a product of their nature, only-child syndrome, or just their personality, these little ones just need some extra support in boosting their self-worth.

For example, Angela doesn't feel worthy; it is why she moves from group to group, not knowing how to fit into someone else's world. It is why after only one sentence she starts complaining loudly, "Why don't you want to be my friend?"

No one said anything about friendship – they were just trying to figure out where Angela's garden would be made – but Angela has taken it as an indication that she's not worthy.

Another child, John, has also decided that. He is also trying to fit into a group, but the only way he knows to is by poking at the kids, teasing them, smacking them on the butt, calling them silly names, annoying them so they will give him attention. He has also stepped into a negative interaction to make friends, because he too doesn't internally feel worthy. He doesn't know how to garner the attention and love in positive ways.

Mike is the same. After a few minutes he's hitting, punching, grabbing the ball, and running away. This scenario happens countless times. An interesting pattern I notice is that these children are not insecure children per se. At home, in the classroom, or in other environments, they're good at what they do. They're confident in their spheres. They can read and write and speak well and present themselves to others. They can teach other children important things when asked to. They do tend to be bossy, but they are figuring out their worth in collaborative spaces, and *that* makes them a little insecure.

HOW THE GODS CONNECT

Let's hear how the demigods connect. It is described in bhakti texts that when there was chaos or turmoil in the world, the demigods would journey to the Ocean of Milk to connect with Lord Vishnu. Seated on the banks, they would meditate on him, communicating their needs through their hearts. His response would be transmitted powerfully through the heart. He understood their feelings, and they understood his responses. The only words spoken were mantras. The connection was a heart-to-heart one. They were deep in the knowing that at any point, they need only communicate through their hearts, where the solutions would also manifest. With this security, they were empowered to manage the variety of responsibilities that demigods needed to.

I will teach you to establish a heart-to-heart connection with your child through empathic communication. We are stepping into Level 3, the "P" in EMPOWERMENT.

* * *

Level 3: Preserve Their Hearts

* * *

The very first step in the connection process is to hear. The way we connect with our child's hearts is literally as simple as that. We hear them: the words they speak, the feelings they have, the thoughts they share, all this needs to be fortified first. If you show your child every single day that the feelings in their hearts are valid, meaningful, and worthy of attention, they will become more secure in their ability to engage with others.

After allowing them to talk to us and by listening to their feelings, their underlying needs come out. We will empower them by preserving their hearts.

When we hear our children's feelings, we are telling them, "I see you, I accept you. My heart accepts your heart."

You know the movie *Avatar* where the large blue animals connect with the other animals through their tails? After they fuse their tails together, they look at each other deep in the eyes and say, "I see you."

Through properly hearing our child, again and again, that's what you will do. You will be telling them, deeply, internally, "you are worthy."

Now, you may think you have already heard your child and you spend time listening to their crying and whining forever. We're going to bolster this process by hearing them in such a way that they can learn to solve their own problems, and we're going to give them specific words to help them do that. But the first step is just to hear them. Hearing doesn't mean listening and giving advice to them. There are many different types of empathy programs out there. Here, I lay out a simple one.

Here is the process.

EMPATHY B.L.O.C.K.S.

Imagine their words to be a gentle (or rushing) stream of water coming from their heart to yours. Their need for connection is flowing very strongly toward you when they come to you with thoughts and feelings.

In this flow, there are rocks that stop the flow of connection. These are known as empathy B.L.O.C.K.S. These communicate to the child that they don't need to be feeling what they're feeling and that they can't trust their hearts. Here they are.

B – Boredom

Boredom is pretty self-explanatory. When a child shares their feelings, you're disinterested. You don't look at them; you continue doing the dishes, watching T.V., reading, playing on your phone, texting, or whatever else.

At the end of my day, I would pick my boy up from school and as I was waiting in the car, I would check my phone. Because we were at the same school, my workday ended when he was signed out. After a long day of being around kids and in back-to-back meetings, I could finally look at my phone texts. So the first thing he would see after school was me on my phone. Although certainly for the rest of the evening I wasn't on the phone, he repeatedly said, "Mommy, you're always on your phone!"

After he said that too many times, I realized why he had that impression. He needed my undivided attention when he climbed in the car after a long day at school. Instead, he got B from me: boredom. This signaled that he was uninteresting, and not worthy of my attention.

L – Lecturing

Another block arises when we lecture a child in response to their feelings. If they mention getting a bad grade on their homework, we launch into, "This is because you didn't study hard enough."

Or, if they complain that they're still hungry and we see their lunch isn't finished, we might say, "You're supposed to eat three hearty meals a day! Do you know how much I pack for you? If you don't eat at the right time, you'll get weak, and you won't have the strength to play. Do you know how many starving kids there are in Africa that would die for that lunch that I've packed for you? Why didn't you eat!?"

Perhaps a child yawns and is tired. "How many times have I told you to go to bed early? Early to bed, early to rise, makes one healthy, wealthy, and wise. If you sleep early, you'll be able to rest your body and you'll have energy for the rest of the day!"

We lecture kids constantly; the more feelings they have, the more we need to lecture their feelings out of them. After all, isn't it important for us to impart all that wisdom we have? How else will they learn? Lecturing assumes that our children are unintelligent, and that their feelings are useless, sentimental, unimportant things that need to be snuffed out of them. Lecturing is a very big empathy block and needs to be minimized.

O – One-Upping

One-upping is when we compare our experiences as more difficult in response to our child sharing their feelings. Here is an example: "You know how many miles I had to walk to get to school?" Every parent says this. I've noticed even I have said this. "You have it so easy! You can't imagine what I had to go through when I was a child. I had way more homework than you. My work was so much more complicated than you deal with. This is so simple. Why are you complaining?

"You guys live in luxury. I had only one pencil I was allowed to use, and I never got all these fancy pens, pencils, and shoes. And still you're complaining?"

One-upping minimizes what's in our children's hearts; it tells them their experiences are not valuable.

C – Contradicting

Our child might say, "I'm not cold."

We respond with, "You have to be cold. It's sixty degrees out there! Put on your jacket!"

Perhaps they say, "I'm not tired."

"It's already 8:00 p.m., you must be tired! You've had such a long day; you've been playing all day and working hard. You must be tired. Go to bed!"

"I'm so upset my friend did such and such."

We counter with, "Oh, it isn't so bad. Stop being dramatic; just chill. It will be fine."

(I'm not saying that we shouldn't get our children to put their jackets on and go to bed at a certain time, just that the feelings they're expressing need not be blocked and contradicted. More on how to get your child to put their jacket on and do things you ask in Chapter 8.)

K – Kiss It

You know how when kids approach us with small *ouchies* and many times we just kiss it to make it better, without figuring out the cause? We do this with our children's feelings too, and while it's better than the other blocks, we aren't helping them find solutions to their feelings.

"Kiss it" is when we offer a pat solution, without really hearing them. We're taking the responsibility off them and onto us. Sometimes this is warranted, but not always. Most of the time, with "kiss it," we're just looking for a way to shut down the problem as quickly as possible, stuff down their feelings on it and move on. "That sucks. You should just stop hanging out with them," or, "I'm sorry to hear that. Let's find another jacket for you to wear." Perhaps we say, "Here, take my phone, you'll feel better." "Don't worry, we're leaving soon anyways." "That's not working. Let's just never come back here."

S – Sympathy

Sympathy gets confused for empathy many times, but it is not empathy. Sympathy is when we feel the same our children feel and get sad, angry, or frustrated with them. Instead of being a neutral facilitator who can allow the child to process their own feelings; we make it about us. This is natural for parents, as we're biologically tied to our children's emotions. When our children are sad, tired, or hungry, it can literally mess with our own feelings.

However, it is important for us to separate our own feelings from theirs so they can separate *their* feelings from *ours*. They will need to stand on their own two feet when they're not around us. The goal of empathy is for them to recognize what they feel, work through, and find solutions. It's not about us.

"Oh, you poor dear. That makes me so sad to hear!"

"That sucks so bad! I'm so angry!"

Any therapist can tell you that giving sympathy to a client who's struggling with an issue or some pain is not going to help them. Those who are processing difficult feelings may actually get angry if you give them too much sympathy, like, "wait a minute. I'm not to be pitied."

I know this from repeated illness in my family. I didn't want people to look at me with those sympathetic eyes. Any time someone gave me a reflection instead of making it about how they're also hurting, showing they really heard me, that soothed me. Sympathetic expressions just made me mad.

All of the above B.L.O.C.K.S., while helpful in certain circumstances, do not help our children to recognize their feelings and work to a solution. They inhibit the flow of feelings. Your child needs you to just hear and reflect so they can feel fully understood.

THE H.E.A.R PROCESS

Instead of using the empathy B.L.O.C.K.S. with your child, use the H.E.A.R. Process. This process involves being 100 percent attentive to them.

Because days are busy, and it is not always possible to be completely attentive to your children, set times in your schedule when you can H.E.A.R. We don't want to create spoiled, attention-seeking children who think the world revolves around them. At the same time, with H.E.A.R., you'll see their feelings settle on their own and they won't need as much attention as before. Practice H.E.A.R. when you have time and when their feelings are strong. After practice, it will become automatic. Important moments are when your child wakes in the morning, mealtimes after everyone is seated, or when you pick them up from school. This practice will remove any insecurities they may face when they're not around you. Consistent empathic H.E.A.R-ing strengthens our children's core connection need and produces powerful results.

H – Hearing

More than 75 percent of communication is nonverbal. When your child speaks to you, literally turn your body toward your child. Lean forward, make eye contact, and use facial expressions that show them you are fully engaged in what they are saying, like it is the most important thing you will hear at that time.

Children can understand if they're valued or not, and they can tell if they're just a bother. By the H step, we're energizing their feelings by just being fully present when there are intense feelings to work through. H means fully hearing with full body language and attention, including your posture, eye contact, and physical body moving toward them. A simple gesture or sound to make it seem like you're listening is a great addition, such as, "Hmm," "Ooh," "Wow," or "Okay."

Back when I would visit my grandparents in India, whenever my grandfather would speak, my dad would respond, "hmmm." After every other sentence, my dad would have a soft, "mmm." Recently, I heard a podcast by Jay Shetty, social media influencer. The renowned Radhanath Swami was speaking, and Jay kept responding, "mmm." He hadn't done that on any of his other podcasts. It was intriguing!

I mentioned this to my dad. He said a cultural practice that has become involuntary is when a mentor, or guru, or elder speaks, because every word they say is so valuable, the listener will respond with a quiet "mmm." I noticed as my dad was speaking that I did the same to him. It was a bit funny.

Give your child the value of a guru, a mentor, a great personality. Turn your body toward them. Make eye contact and respond.

E – Emotion

Your child may share a bunch, pouring words out in frustration. Look for the emotion they're feeling and name it. Can you sort through it all? For example:

- "Sounds like you're feeling sad…"
- "Sounds like you're feeling angry…"
- "Sounds like you're really frustrated right now…"
- "That was so important to you and you're feeling disappointed…"

To help name their emotion, here's a variety of options:

- Depressed
- Fearful
- Angry
- Miserable
- Agitated
- Unsettled
- Anxious/ worried
- Annoyed
- Sad
- Uneasy
- Tense
- Nervous
- Dismayed
- Disturbed
- Challenged
- Stressed

When you identify the emotion, it's okay if you don't get it right. In fact, your child may correct you, "No, I'm not mad, it's just that I'm…."

This is important, and means your child is learning to sort through and name it themselves. This is self-reflection, vital to the H.E.A.R. process. Now they can learn to own their feelings, and release blame. The empowerment process is working.

A – Action

After you've identified the emotion, listen for what action (actual physical behavior) caused that emotion. When you connect the emotion your child feels to a physical behavior, you ground the child and move them from emotional space to a rational space. You will need to ground yourself as well to avoid getting too worked up over it. If it's an intense situation, pause on speaking, step out of the emotion and look for the physical action that caused it. Do this without any blame, judgment, or evaluation.

Any action can be spoken of with or without judgment. Think of the following examples. Some have negative or positive connotations, and some have no connotations.

- The dirty towel was left in the bucket.
- The lazy boy left the dirty towel in the bucket.
- He grabbed the toy out of the child's hands.
- He took the toy away from the child.

In the above examples, the word "lazy" and "grab" turn the sentences into judgments. Judgmental language increases the dependance on someone else for our feelings. The goal of H.E.A.R. is to help the child own their feelings and discover a solution.

Finding an action without judgmental language when your child is pouring out intense feelings is difficult. It is natural to become defensive for our child. It takes time and patience.

- Instead of saying, "you're feeling angry because Jamie snatched the toy away from you," try: "You're feeling angry because your toy was given to another child without anyone asking you."

- Instead of, "you're feeling sad because the other girls made a garden without caring about what you wanted to do," say:

"You're feeling sad because you wanted to make the garden with the other girls. It was important for you to do it with them."

- Instead of, "You felt sad that they were being mean to you," try saying, "You felt sad that they didn't invite you to join them. You wanted to be invited with words. You wanted them to ask you to stay and play with them."

Do you see the difference between these statements?
Some more examples of action words being used are below:

- "You saw your toy being given to someone else."
- "The art piece you worked on was torn apart and scribbled on."
- "Your Lego creation was demolished."
- "The sink still has a ton of pots in it."
- "The socks were strewn on the floor."
- "The wet towel laying on the bed made it wet."
- "The homework wasn't completed."
- "My brother was hit and started crying."

Notice in identifying the action, there is no blame, judgment, or evaluation of good or bad within the sentences. It is purely stating the action, which is a fact.

Here are examples of the differences between facts (only stating the action) and judgment.

- Fact: The dirty mop was left in the bucket of dirty water, instead of hung to dry.
- Judgment: He was lazy and left the dirty mop in the bucket.
- Fact: Your grades were lower than you had hoped.
- Judgment: Your grades were low because you didn't study enough.

R – Respond Reflectively

In this step, combine all the above and respond, repeating back using your own words to name the other person's emotions with the accompanying actions (facts). For example, "When you saw your low grade, you felt disappointed," "You're scared that I might crash the car," "You're worried about college," or "Your friends are important to you so you're nervous to tell them the truth."

You will start noticing most of the time (unless there are some serious bullying issues happening), empowering your child to understand and own their feelings through this H.E.A.R. process will solve the issue! With your help, your child will understand what is important in their relationships, seek out those that fulfill their needs and stay away from those that don't.

PROBLEM SOLVING ON THE PLAYGROUND – A TRUE STORY

Robert: "Mother Gopi Gita! Mother Gopi Gita!"

MGG: "Yes? What's wrong?"

Robert: (very dramatically) "Chris keeps throwing the ball at me and it really hurts, and I tried telling him, but he just won't stop. It's hurting my head and my arms and look; I even have a bruise!" (Holds out his arm with nothing on it.)

(I resist the urge to jump up. I resist the urge to run and get Chris and raise my voice at him and give him a time-out.)

MGG: "Oh my. Sounds like you're really upset! You even have a bruise on your arm. Let me see it." (Leaning toward him, giving care, showing concern. I notice no bruise.)

Robert: "Well, it doesn't really hurt that much. It's just that I keep telling him to stop throwing it at me!"

MGG: "Hmm. It sounds like you're frustrated because he doesn't seem to hear what you're trying to ask him."

Robert: "He won't even listen to me! Anyways, it was *my* ball first! I had it before him!"

(The story changes as he sees that Chris isn't getting in trouble.)

MGG: "Oh, I see! You're feeling upset because you were playing with the ball before Chris had it. Now you want it back?"

Robert: "Yeah! And he's not letting me play with it! All the other kids keep grabbing it away. Even when the ball comes my way and they're not even letting me grab it first!"

(I look to where Robert was playing with all the children and realize they're in middle of a game. Robert is frustrated that the other kids are faster than him. This has nothing to do with Chris.)

MGG: "Looks like you wish you could grab that ball first! Seems like you want to be faster."

Robert: "Maybe I can ask Lindsey to join my side. She's really fast. Maybe she can get the ball for me." (As he's speaking, he runs off back toward the game, ready to solve his own problem.)

This example happens countless times in homes, on the playground, and in classrooms. An adult inexperienced in empathy would have jumped up to correct Chris for bothering Robert. But a little bit of the H.E.A.R. process uncovers the real issue.

Children's emotions can be equated to a grand big iceberg, which you only see the tip of. The H.E.A.R. process allows for the superficial to be released, so that deeper feelings can arise. Avoid reacting to the first words. Resist the empathy B.L.O.C.K.S. Practice H.E.A.R. and watch them solve it on their own. It can be kind of magical.

SETTING BOUNDARIES

When you're practiced in H.E.A.R., your child will value their feelings. They'll develop deeper confidence. They'll be able to self-regulate, accept themselves for their emotions, see the behaviors tied to them, and decide to stay away from those behaviors, or the people who cause them. This is the beginning of setting boundaries. Through self-awareness, they fortify their identity. Their need to run to you will lessen. H.E.A.R. helps create a balance in their social dynamics.

After you become adept at H.E.A.R., you will hear your child practicing empathy on others. That is your goal.

SOCIAL EMPOWERMENT

A self-aware child can be internally connected no matter the circumstance. They're not insecure or scared of emotion, because they've practiced owning, naming and resolving that feeling. They become aware of what areas bring out the uncomfortable feelings, and which environments to avoid. They can communicate their needs without blaming others and aren't dependent on others for their emotional happiness. If an environment makes them sad, they can communicate it, and resolve it with their friend.

SEEK FIRST TO UNDERSTAND THEN BE UNDERSTOOD

Stephen Covey shares his fourth habit, "Seek first to understand, then be understood" – such an important one. If we stop giving children our own idea of what they need to be doing each moment, and if we just try to understand them, to H.E.A.R. them, it will give them not only the internal acceptance of themselves, but also give them the tools to doing this for others.

Imagine little Angela's conversation happening with H.E.A.R. Instead of taking it personally that her friends don't want to play with her, she would understand their needs. "Oh, so you're feeling disturbed because you wanted to play alone right now?"

Angela would have recognized that she was digging in her friends' garden, instead of making her own. She would have moved over, without automatically assuming that it was because she wasn't liked. This paradigm shift can happen when you give value to your child by avoiding empathy B.L.O.C.K.S. and practicing H.E.A.R. regularly. You will see the difference quickly.

RESULTS

By mirroring and reflecting, you're doing a great service to your children:

- You're giving them confidence of worth and being heard.
- You're setting them up to identify their feelings.
- You're giving them the tools to communicate these feelings.
- You're empowering them to solve their own problems.
- And you're giving them the very important message that they alone are responsible for their happiness (fulfilling their needs) and another being's actions or lack of actions shouldn't mess with their happiness.

GARDEN OF HARMONY

In the Garden of Harmony, elegant Saint Gaura gracefully meets with every single child and hears their hearts. As they are playing, building, creating, collaborating, and helping each other, he listens. He fortifies their activities just by hearing what they are up to, what their dreams are, how it's coming along, what plans need to be changed, what things may not be working out, what plans need to be changed, and what they've learned about each other. He just hears their hearts, first and foremost.

GAURA AND THE DISMISSIVE PHILOSOPHER

Saint Gaura had the arduous task of establishing the path of bhakti, the path of loving service, during a time in India when many philosophers propounded the opposite – impersonalism. Impersonalists propose that the ultimate spiritual perfection is devoid of loving relationships; the bhakti philosophy teaches the exact opposite. As Gaura preached the importance of spiritual love (bhakti), he was met with fierce opposition.

A renowned scholar in Orissa, Sarva, rejected his path of love. "How can love be the ultimate destination – that understanding is for the less intelligent, sentimental folk! That young Gaura must learn from me." Because Gaura was younger than Sarva by many decades, he dutifully followed, out of humility and respect for an elder. For seven, long days, Saint Gaura sat across from Sarva, and heard his lecturing on dry Vedic philosophy, devoid of spiritual emotion.

Saint Gaura's goal was to change hearts; the way he did it was by hearing. He patiently listened for hours upon hours. He taught us that the beginning of establishing a loving connection (bhakti yoga) was by hearing. It wasn't just the external words that Gaura heard, which were surely upside-down conclusions of ancient scriptural texts. Gaura heard deeper: what is it that has brought Sarva to these conclusions of the Divine? What past life experiences must he have endured? Just by seeing this majestic golden Gaura giving him such solid attention, grumpy old Sarva felt worthy, accepted, honored. That feeling of connection opened him up to hearing what Gaura would have to say.

Of course, Gaura did respond after the seven days of listening. But before any of those responses, Gaura had put in the time, and listened. We will learn the nuances of the words Gaura used to empower and yet course correct as well in the next chapter, as we gain insight in how to use words.

By this encounter, Gaura taught us that loving connection starts through hearing. Through hearing, one can change the hardest of hearts. Empower your child by your empathic presence. They will be so much more ready to hear your instructions.

TOWARD LEADERSHIP

If you truly want your children to navigate guiding others in leadership, they need to learn how to hear. They will learn this from you. You are being called to put aside your boredom, lecturing, one-upping, contradicting, and forced solutions; just H.E.A.R.

Hearing takes humility and trust. Accept that your child, as a spiritual being, has the answers intrinsically. By you reflecting their words and accepting their feelings, they will solve the dilemma themselves.

Once your child has the experience of you hearing them empathically, they will naturally do this with others. They will change others' hearts the way Saint Gaura was able to.

For those who practice mantra meditation, every day we get the opportunity to speak to the Inner Parents. We offer our joys, sorrows, and daily needs with our mantras. For two hours each day, bhakti followers share their hearts through these mantras, while the Inner Parents just hear. Here is the mantra you can recite. Any time you want to step into leadership in any conversation, you only need to hear. It automatically places you as the caring valuing elder.

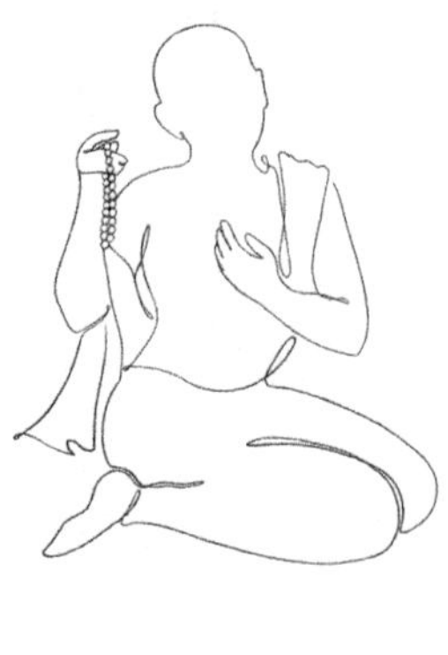

* * *

Mantra Affirmations Level 3: I Hear

* * *

THE FIRST PROCESS established by Saint Gaura for the bhakti path is hearing. Hearing mantra sounds connects one to the Inner Parents immediately. There is an invisible tube from the ear to the heart – a subtle one, invisible to the eyes – that brings emotion from what you hear. That is how music plays such a big factor in uplifting or degrading one's mood.

As you continue your mantra practice, ask Inner Parents to connect you directly to your child's heart. Because they reside in all hearts, the time you spend with them through mantra meditation will rejuvenate your child as well. You will begin to understand what your child needs and how to fulfill those needs.

At Level 3, I introduce you to one of the more powerful mantra words in bhakti texts – *krishna*. Krishna is the Supreme Personality of Godhead. Krishna is so personal that He has a form, a complexion, likes and dislikes, and is full of charming sweetness. His soul essence is to be deeply connected to each living being, the way a magnet is drawn to iron, immediately bound together. Krish means "magnetic, to be pulled toward, to attract." Krishna is "the source of magnetic attraction."

By reciting the word *krishna*, you and your child increase your deep connection with each other, and with the Inner Parents. Your child becomes more able to connect with others on a spiritual platform. This internal sense of connection draws others to your child in a pleasing way.

krishna krishna krishna krishna
krishna krishna krishna he
Let me truly hear my child's needs.
Let me reflect their feelings when they are chaotic.
Let their emotions settle, find sanctuary, and find answers.
I am peaceful. I am listening. I am connected internally.

7

HOW CAN THEY BE UNDERSTOOD?

"Handle them carefully, for words have more power than atom bombs."

— PEARL STRACHAN HURD

BEING DRAGGED BY A HORSE

I loved the feel of the soft hair on my skin, a living, breathing animal under me, so much bigger than I imagined. I was riding a pony in the hills of Maharashtra, India, a tourist spot called Mahabaleshwar. We went horseback riding every day, and though we were on guided ponies behind our parents, at only nine-years-old, I felt powerful. I was amazed by how I could get this large animal to do what I wanted.

Suddenly, my sister requested her guide to gallop, so her horse took off in front of me. My guide had gone to get a bottle of water and was no longer beside me. Seeing my sister's horse running ahead, my horse started galloping too. Full of fear, I lost control and my little body tossed up and down in the saddle. My left leg came out of the stirrup, it swung over and I fell to the ground. Unfortunately, my right foot was still stuck in its stirrup, so I was dragged for quite a distance, my head hitting the rough terrain and rocks. I screamed but the horse would not stop. I remember hearing my parents' screams. It was traumatic.

I was taken to the local doctor up in the mountains. My hair and face were covered in blood from my skull being gashed on the rocks; I still have a big bump today. I didn't get to do all the family activities for the next few days, as I needed to heal. After a few months, this trauma became just a memory to share with others.

I had heard that quote, "if you fall off a horse, you need to get back up again," so I tried another time two decades later. In Dallas, I climbed on a beautiful white horse at the community ranch, feeling a little fearful because of my childhood experience. I kicked my legs in, asking the horse to gallop but in the middle of its running, it suddenly stopped. I was literally thrown far off the horse, to the other side of the pasture gate. I lost consciousness, and when I came to I was crying and totally shook up.

So many friends were there riding comfortably, *but what did horses have against me!? Why have I been unable to control these horses so they don't hurt me!?* I wondered. Full of emotion and tears, I decided, *that's it, No more horseback riding. You've tried twice and you just shouldn't anymore!*

THIRD TIME'S THE CHARM?

However, I'm not one to be easily defeated. Another decade later, a beautiful summer in 2019, we journeyed to southern California, where my husband's family lived in idyllic Pacific Palisades. Our kids were grown, and we decided to go up the Malibu Hills on horseback at Will Rogers State Park. There would be only one guide for all five of us. Both my boys were grown teenagers, and they said they would help me with my fear.

We met the guide, a soft-spoken young man named Jim Curtis. "I really need to make sure I can control this animal," I told myself pensively, choosing the largest, most beautiful black horse there was. I was determined.

Horses are grand, and you can tangibly feel their power. Their big eyes, their soft, long hair and tails. They have an eerie calm. They reminded me of children. Their beauty and calm draw you in, yet at any moment, something could go wrong leaving you uncertain how to manage it.

We climbed up and started a scenic ride through a meandering trail up Southern California's beautiful hills. The views were breathtaking, the weather was perfect, the breeze was light – it was a perfect day for horseback riding. I asked our guide to give me tips and tell me his story. "So, how do you control them?"

CONNECT NOT CONTROL

Jim immediately corrected me. "It is not about controlling them. It's about connecting with them."

Knowing that all creatures have powerful, dynamic souls in them and that animals communicate just as clearly as humans, I was intrigued by what he said. I have spoken to quite a few horse guides, trying to understand their methods (really, just to make sure I wouldn't get thrown off the horse!), but this was the first time a guide was intuitively confident of his relationship with his horses.

"I make sure I'm very present when I'm with my horse. I want to be responsive to its cues. This takes observation. This is why I don't want you to take pictures. I feel gratitude to the horse for allowing us to ride on him and use him for our pleasure. If you're present, it will be some of the best moments you're going to have."

What a difference in the way he viewed the horse versus what I had been thinking for decades.

He showed that he was so aware of his horses that he could tell when they might become reactive. He was aware that they may shake this way or that because of what was around them.

It was just like being a parent, that observation, that closeness a mother and baby have in knowing when the child will get upset, what their different cries mean, and what the child may need.

As I heard his words, I was reassured and realized how foolish I had been. My goal had always been to domineer over these animals, not to respect their identities, desires, and thought processes. I had egotistically assumed that I, as an all-knowing human – would just be able to control them.

WHEN THEY BECOME REACTIVE, BE RESPONSIVE

Jim continued, "Horses do get upset. When they get spooked, they will lift up their front legs and throw you off. They can get spooked by the smallest of things: a wasp flying around, a far-away airplane or helicopter that's too low." We were across from some massive mansions, and I imagined them with their helicopter pads nearby.

"If we jump into a reactive space when they're reactive, we'll never win. They're much more powerful than us. We need to become responsive to their reaction. If we're observant, we'll know it's about to come. When your horse rears up on you, don't react – or it'll spook even more. Instead, jump into a responsive space. Take a deep breath, work on your fears, stay calm, and it will calm down.

This made much sense to me, and I hoped for an opportunity to try it. Could I see that my horse is upset or spooked or in need of something and connect with it first? Could I respond with a calm voice if my horse reared up? I began to see every opportunity with a horse to work on connecting and responding to their reactivity.

So, it is with children. I thought. Instead of understanding our children, we react when they react. They need you be in charge and stay in charge, not through control but through connection.

As Jim Curtis continued speaking and as I responded, my horse's ears would point toward him and then back to me. I could feel that he knew what we were talking about. I hoped the horse saw that I was no longer interested in controlling but connecting. I began speaking softer and relaxing my body into the horse's. Yes, I was the horse's guide, but through connection and not control.

LUNATIC SELVES

What's interesting is that when our children react, oh boy, that's when our lunatic selves come out. We can be the most dignified, peaceful humans in the world to everyone we come in contact with and somehow, in front of our children, we turn into raving banshees. Little things can set us off.

In the previous chapter, I shared ways with you to stop and listen to your child's responses. In this chapter, you will learn what words to use and what not to use in response. When your child is navigating their own reactive horses (friendships in the world), they need a solid place at home to learn all the tools of reacting and responding. You are that place.

SAD ENCOUNTERS

Most adults don't see the impact of their words. They can't see that the things they say can be insidiously hurtful.

I was in an alley in New York City and a young child climbed into the front seat of a taxi his family had been waiting for. Suddenly, the dad yanked him out of the front seat and dropped him in the back, yelling. The whole time I stood there, the dad was yelling. The rest of the family remained quiet, as if this was the norm.

If you observe kids and their parents the way I have been, and you open your ears to how children are spoken to, it's deeply saddening.

Parents yell about their kids right in front of their kids, about how useless they are, how difficult they can be, how they don't do their chores or brush their teeth, or about how long it takes to get out the door in the morning. Parents complain loudly for all to hear about the horrible qualities of their child with their child right there, listening. How must it feel to be that little girl or boy? It's downright humiliating.

I have also had these moments and felt deep guilt afterward. Because of the illogical irrationality that children bring, we adults fall into patterns of yelling or screaming, feeling so damn frustrated. Because we somehow feel that because we love them so much, they will be okay with us at our worst.

EMOTIONAL CHILDREN

A child's amygdala – the emotional center of the brain – is not yet fully developed. They take reversals more intensely. When they're upset, we react the way our parents reacted with us. The habit of negative language gets reinforced through the generations.

Here is a list of reactions you may have. Become aware of this list. Observe your tone, your body posture, your words. The reactions make up the acronym R.E.J.E.C.T. Every time you speak to your child with these moods, you reject their sense of self-worth and teach them what social interaction is supposed to look like. You break a core need of connection. They internalize that experience, and it shows in their friendships.

R.E.J.E.C.T.

R – Rebuke

Rebuking is giving harsh, sharp criticisms. It's the worst form of rejection. "How could you ever think they would like that? How could you be so dumb? You're insensitive! You eat like a pig. No wonder you have no friends."

E – Embarrass

Around others, you make them feel small and useless. This can take the form of pointing out a fault of your child's in front of others and talking bad about them in front of their friends, family members, or teachers.

J - Jab At

This occurs when you nitpick your kids. Everything about them is wrong. A parent might say, "Fix your hair, your shirt, or your shoes." Parents might also complain about their child, "your friends are..." "your handwriting is a mess..." "your nails are dirty...." To jab at is when you berate your kids about the negative.

E – Exaggerate

To exaggerate is self-explanatory. This is when you are so affected by something your child does that you spiral and make a mountain out of a molehill. It becomes the only thing you can think about and the basis for all your conversations. For example, "did you know he couldn't even figure out how to go to the bathroom by himself? Did you know he peed in the bed every day this week? How can you be so forgetful? I'm telling your dad! I'm telling your grandma! You spilled the milk all over the entire kitchen floor! You can't get along with anyone ever! I can never leave you alone! You're always fighting with your brother!"

C – Collapse

Collapsing may come across like this: "this is too much for me, I can't deal with this, go talk to your dad/ mom, here take your iPad," or

"I have no idea what you expect from me, don't you know what a stressful day I've had? I don't have energy for this! Yet again! The same drama! Can't you stop? I can't handle this." Collapse is when you turn into the child and need more attention on your difficult day rather than helping your child with their needs.

T – Threaten

An example of threatening is, "if you act like that, no one will want to be your friend ever again," "no one will invite you to their house," "I'll never have a friend of yours over," "I'll never take you out," "I'm going to lose all my hair," "Your stress is making me old," "I'll take your iPad away," or "I'll take you home and never bring you back here."

OBSERVE YOUR HABITS

Some of you read this and think, *OMG, I never do that*. Some sneak into your language when you're unaware. Or you may gasp and realize you do a few of these way too many times. It is important to observe yourself. How often do you speak these types of sentences? Which ones do you use more than others?

Take a few days to listen to your language. Write down different scenarios and look at which ones you use more frequently than not.

THEIR INNER VOICE MONOLOGUE

When our words R.E.J.E.C.T. our children, we take away their confidence. We create an inner monologue where they don't feel they are good enough.

Do you have an inner commentary? When you look in the mirror, do you think negative thoughts, like, *I look horrible, I look old, I look tired.*? When you get in a fight, do you think, *man, they suck; they're horrendous; why in the world would I even talk to them? I need to shut them out of my life.*

All those thoughts are negative habits. Make sure your kids learn good habits of proper self-talk. There is an Indian saying my dad used to remind me of, *"Jab mu kholo tum, mithi baani bolo tum,"* meaning, "When you open your mouth, speak sweetly."

It doesn't mean you can never yell. Anyone who knows me knows I'm a yeller. I have to go outside to scream or shout in my journal. The difference is as a parent, I shouldn't yell at the children and reject them.

What you tell your kids day in and day out is more powerful than you know. Seemingly harmless jokes make up their dangerous beliefs about themselves.

I had a client who heard her entire childhood how much of a slob she was. When she got older, she became that. Her home was never clean – she had just given up on the idea that she could be neat. After some work with me, she realized that she would even get angry when she had to do the dishes or cleaning, because internally she felt it to be a waste of time. She was a slob, and it wouldn't change. She noticed she used the same language with her children.

On the flip side, another client's dad always told her she was the brain, the smartest in the family. She could have literally moved a pencil from the desk to her notebook and her dad made her feel like she was the smartest thing since sliced bread. She always felt that internal sense of confidence about her intelligence.

That's what you need to tell your children, every moment, even when they mess up – especially when they mess up! It is not necessary for us to remind them of their shortcomings.

How will our children be comfortable to succeed and work with others if they feel rejected? They will be scared to be themselves. They will hear others' words as R.E.J.E.C.T. and they will be insecure.

Another bhakti term is *vaco vegam;* basically that's shut your mouth. Any time you see the R.E.J.E.C.T. thoughts starting, put a lid on it and keep them in the head space. Don't verbalize them.

If you find a need to yell a lot, it's time to jump to Level 7 Rest as a Spiritual Practice in Chapter 10, take a break, do some self-reflection and come back to center.

What do we say instead?

Now you will practice the words that are used by everyone in the Garden of Harmony. Words are used to nurture relationships and love. Those words need to become the monologue of your child.

Now, we move into the fourth level, the "O" in EMPOWERMENT.

* * *

Level 4: Offer Your L.O.V.E. Boost

* * *

A L.O.V.E boost means using words in a way to bring out their leadership qualities. Remember your dream child we envisioned in Level 1 when you wrote out all those qualities? During this exercise, you will energize their qualities with your words. Even if your child is irresponsible, you will look for when your child is responsible and energize it. By doing this, we're going to shift the way they look at themselves.

L – Limit Your Words

"L" means limit your words. It isn't necessary to get your point across with long lectures. As a matter of fact, the more you go on and on, the more the child feels they are only worthy of your disdain. They take that with them into social spheres and become okay with being mistreated or mistreating others. Say what you need with one sentence.

It may be impossible for you to completely stop R.E.J.E.C.T. communication, especially if you were raised in a household where you were R.E.J.E.C.T.-ed frequently. So just observe yourself and limit the words. Develop awareness of how you speak.

Those who have been raised in collectivistic cultures can attest to relationships where words aren't so necessary. Through body language, eye contact, and connection, you can communicate to your child how you feel about them.

My father was an incredible L.O.V.E. booster. He saw leadership qualities in me. As a child, I don't remember him actually praising me out loud, but I know he noticed me. He didn't have to use any words. His glance, his nod, his eyes and body language told me everything and inspired me to do more. His simple, "yes, ask Gopi, she'll be able to do it," was more than I needed to know that he knew I was qualified and that he had faith in me. Because of the sheer light in his eyes when he saw me, what was important to him became important to me. I could feel his utter acceptance of me.

O – Observe the Opposite

We tend to comment on the negative in our children. We need to switch the dynamic. When they are peacefully playing, completing their chores, spending time on their homework, and just being "good," do we really notice it? The only time we use our words is when things are wrong. Where energy flows, that grows. Every time negative energy is placed on an action or behavior, that action gets reinforced, and grows. You will look at the opposite – look at the positive. Observe the opposite of what annoys you, even if it is just a small thing.

I've noticed an interesting phenomenon. Most kids on the playground who complain about other kids secretly want to play with the one they're complaining about. They don't even know it themselves! "He hit me." "She took the ball away from me." "She didn't give me the swing when I asked." When I practiced H.E.A.R., the real story came out. "I wanted to play with them." They start with the negative because they know how to get an adult's attention. Can you blame them? The only time they get attention is when something negative arises.

So, observe the opposite every day. Flip the negative sentences in your head, pause before you say them, and just observe.

V – Verbally Record It

What is going on in the situation? Like a video camera, record the action verbally. What is happening here? Do this frequently. Don't ignore the positive things you see. You'll notice their leadership qualities emerging with different actions.

For example, "I noticed that you picked up the grocery bags from the car and brought them inside without me asking." "I see that all the pots are lined up with no suds in them, and you spent forty minutes doing them." "I can see that you're ready to throw that block because you're feeling angry at your little sister, but you held it in the air and didn't actually throw it." "I can see that even though your brother hit you and it made you really mad, you didn't hit him back."

E – Energize with a Quality

Here is the time to bring out all those qualities that you see in your dream child from the first exercise.

"I noticed that you picked up the grocery bags from the car and brought them inside without me asking. That shows responsibility."

"I can see that you're ready to throw that block at the tower because you're feeling angry that it's messed up, but you held it in the air and didn't actually throw it. That showed me a lot of self-control – probably even more than I would have had!"

"I can see that even though your brother hit you and it made you really mad, you didn't hit him back. I can tell you really love him, even when you're mad."

These qualities that you wrote down in your dream child activity have actions that come with them. What does a responsible, compassionate, humble, focused, efficient child look like? Start looking for those actions in your child – even the smallest one and energize them. Internalize this type of language, dear reader, literally inhale it. When you connect a quality to an action, your child solidifies their own identity. They create powerful images of themselves – as K.I.D.S. – royalty, sages, and more.

Your child is being propelled into the future by your words. The more L.O.V.E. boosts you can give during the day – for both positive and negative interactions – the more confident your child will be when they go out in the big, scary world of friendships. Make it part of the very fabric of your being to avoid being critical and to do the exact opposite. You will see the difference it makes in less than fifteen days.

My seventeen-year-old son has just finished spending almost an hour cleaning the dishes. Elated, I see his completed work in the kitchen, only to find gross stuff in the sink strainer. I call out his name. I'm just about ready to yell out, "why can't you also take out the crud in the strainer!" Mind you, I've been practicing, teaching, and working with this L.O.V.E boost for decades! And yet, I still find my bad habits of R.E.J.E.C.T. in my heart. I resist, wait, and observe the opposite.

Hearing me yell his name, he comes downstairs. Instead of what my mind was telling me to say, what do I say? I verbalize the action and energize with a quality. "I see you spent forty-five minutes cleaning up all these pots and they're so neatly organized and drying on the counter. You're so efficient. Thank you."

Yes, it did take him a whole day to get to the dishes. Yes, there is still crud in the strainer. Yes, the dishes are dripping a little off the towel, and one of the counters nearby isn't clean, but do I really need to focus on the negative when he's put in so much effort? Guess what. Next time he does the dishes, he's going to remember that I said he was clean and efficient, and he's going to make more effort. Believe me, start when they're five and you'll get kids who take care of it all!

ON THE PLAYGROUND

An ABA therapist working with one of our students on the playground was observing our students with us. One of my favorite meditations is playground time – seeing the change in interactions as each year passes by. Though one boy has been told repeatedly not to throw the playground mulch, he continues to do so. We have spent a whole year telling him not to. It is frustrating to say the same thing repeatedly. Today, a playground teacher calls out his name sharply, and motions for him to stop.

The therapist has had a intense morning, with her student *tantruming* while she stood her ground. I notice she has great patience and ask her about it. She shares her techniques with us.

"See how they're all playing, and the only time we call their name is when they do something wrong? This is how all kids are treated. They get attention only when something is negative. Very young children, and neurodivergent children, can't easily distinguish between negative and positive attention – attention is attention." She reiterates the principle I teach so many clients – don't spend more time interacting negatively with your child. Make sure your positive words far outweigh the negative. How nice it was to be reminded of this.

I wonder how to change the dynamic of the young, energetic boy who continues throwing mulch in the mud, away from the playground area, though we have all expressed our displeasure at it, given him reasons for a long while now. I ponder: *How will I offer the L.O.V.E. boost to him?*

First, I practice O – Observe the Opposite. I see that he is enjoying throwing the mulch in the mud. He's kinesthetic, loves movement, has a high need to use his gross and fine motor skills. Have you ever felt rose petals or rice grains between your fingers? It's quite a fun experience. He is thoroughly enjoying the way the mulch feels in his hand, and he's filling in the muddy, liquidy area with all that mulch. He has a need for completion – to make it so the small muddy area isn't wet and thick anymore, and his free-will need is strong – he wants to do this the way he wants to do it, and no teacher yelling his name is going to stop it. How can I turn this around? As I walk up to him, I continue observing.

Now I start V – Verbally Recording the Action. I comment on how he must love throwing, how he likes the feeling of spraying it – which is true – it is quite fun. "It must be so fun to feel the mulch through your fingers. Are you trying to fill in that muddy area so it can dry up? What if we turn around and use the mulch through our fingers to fill in that area near the swing? That way the expensive mulch doesn't get wasted in the wrong area." This is different than the usual response! His eyes widen. He was technically doing something wrong, but I looked at what was right in the situation and commented on that.

As I pick up the mulch and finger it with him, I start showering it toward the area under the swing. It worked! He turns his body around and starts throwing it there as well, creating a pile. "Look how resourceful you are. Thank you for refilling the swing area." I practice E – Energize with a Quality.

Guess what. He never threw the mulch in the mud again. His needs were met. I've connected. I've hijacked his negative behavior, and I've showered him with a L.O.V.E boost.

Dear reader, you will do this today, tomorrow, and every single day after. Reject those R.E.J.E.C.T. words from your vocabulary and use the L.O.V.E boost. Limit the words you're using. Observe the opposite action by visualizing it and verbally record it to your child. Add a powerful quality next to it, and there you are. Watch as your child demonstrates dream child qualities and enjoys spending time with you. Do this as many times as you can.

Have you read the story of Pollyanna? It was my all-time favorite book as a child. An orphan girl comes to live with her grumpy aunt and sprinkles the town with energizing positivity. There are grumpy neighbors who she bakes cookies for, a grumpy doctor, and even a grumpy old man living up the hill in what the kids called a Haunted House with real actual skeletons in his closet. By the end of the book, she has turned around everyone's grumpiness just by noticing and commenting on their cheerful, kind qualities. With her good heart, she was able to turn all of those grumpy people into happy, loving friends who became charitable to the orphans in the town.

RAISING PRAISE JUNKIES

As you're practicing this, it is crucial that you are not just using a fake, loaded phrase of praise. Unnecessarily praising your child for every little thing they do isn't helpful. The positive comment *must* be tied to an action and a quality, otherwise it increases their ego and arrogance, not their humility that is needed in leadership. These phrases, without an action or quality, sound like this: "Wow! You're great! You're amazing! You're so smart!"

Our children don't need empty words that are not backed by actions. Remember, I shared in the Introduction that a primary definition of leadership was service with humility? Service is action and service requires humility. Love is also an action word. Sitting around, not actually picking up one's body to work or to perform action, is not worthy of being noticed.

Here also I'm not asking you to praise your child, I'm asking you to notice your child.

Here's what the difference is.

Parent's	L.O.V.E. Boost for the Heart	False Praise for the False Ego
Body Language	Facing forward, not hesitant, full eye contact, not embarrased	Exuberant, a little nervous, trying, not confident
Tone of Voice	Calm, confident, trustworthy, strong, kind	excited, overexuberant, fake, singsong, higher pitched
Words	Speaking actual behaviors, movements, and specific leadership qualities	"You're great! You're amazing! You're a star! The best! Wow! " (superficial words without details)
Hidden Message	*"Mom/dad notice me. I can see that I'm the quality they're saying. I want to do this action again. I know who I am and what I'm meant for."*	*I'm not really all that. Why are they making such a big deal. I have to be perfect now. I don't know what I did exactly. I love the praise.*

SPARE THE ROD AND SPOIL THE CHILD?!

Also, right at about this time in my coaching sessions, when I ask parents to stop using R.E.J.E.C.T. sentences, and I introduce the L.O.V.E. acronym, I get this question: "What about discipline?!" The tone of voice that accompanies the question is usually one of angst, blame, and criticism toward me and my methods.

When parents say "discipline," it's said in an accusatory way, full of intensity. Being Asian and raised in a tiger-momma-kinda environment, I can literally hear their thoughts; I have had those same thoughts when I read similar philosophies years back. *What kind of namby-pamby, airy-*

fairy philosophy is this where we are to never correct our child or rebuke them or tell them where they're off? Are we just raising spoiled weak kids? This thought process is full of frustration. If you don't know any other way to raise a child, it is natural that you will get a little uncomfortable with all this positivity.

The good news is that I have been exactly that parent, the one who wanted to control and who *has* controlled my older one for a large part of his childhood. Remember all that we said about not associating leadership with being bossy, but with being collaborative; remember all that we have said about children and their needs – their very real human needs – about them being treated as if they weren't good enough. And be ready, dear reader, to do the hard work. There is no quick fix, no smacking them into submission. You can do that, but then get ready for them to run away from you as quickly as possible as soon as they're out of your home. After that, they will not know what the hell they want to do with their life, or who they are and will struggle when they are in any leadership position, or even sadder, with their own children.

What it all boils down to is that we think that the only way to engage our children is through words of criticism (rejection). We need to completely rethink the way we ask our children to complete tasks or engage in activities. The words you use for them to do that are extremely powerful!

Did you know that discipline doesn't mean force, anger, guilt or shame? The word "discipline" is from the Latin word *disciplina,* meaning "instruction and training"? It is derived from the root word *discere,* "to learn." We're going to learn how to guide our child in the right type of discipline in the next chapter.

HOW THE SAINTS ACT

Saints have an amazing ability to bring out the most powerful dynamic qualities in others because they are so pure that they only see purity in others and energize it. My grandfather and guru Swami Prabhupada noticed the smallest things and energized them. Once his disciple gave him a small gift. Mind you, this is a world-renowned guru who traveled the world and got luxurious personal gifts and very large cash donations for his temples, and projects. One day, his disciple Deva handed him a little envelope with a twenty-dollar bill. She described how he lifted the bill, fluttered it in the air, and was beaming, his chest filled with love. She said he waved it around in the air as if she had given him a million dollars. He made her feel as special as a million dollars. He amplified her love.

Won't it be nice when you make your child feel this way? Imagine, once they feel so energized, they will be able to energize others naturally and authentically. It will come from deep within their soul, as they have been so supported by you. Can you imagine a world where every small act of a child's was as if they felt like they were giving you a million dollars? That is what is meant by treat your kids like K.I.D.S. – Kings and Queens, Intellectuals, Demigods and Sages.

SAINT GAURA AND THE PROUD PANDIT

When Saint Gaura was only sixteen years old, he opened his own school of students. He taught the lost art of *nyaya* – logic and grammar. His lofty task was to change the hearts of other stuffy logicians and dry renunciates who clung to hardened thoughts of impersonalism. They "happiness is temporary" and "love is useless" type of philosophies. How would he do this?

He began energizing them. He started with the proud scholar Kashmiri. While Saint Gaura was teaching his students on the banks of the Ganga one day, proud Kashmiri arrived. He was a *"digvijay pandit"* or a scholar that had won competitions across India. He even had a signed victory document *(juya – patrika)* with signatures from scholars across India to prove his dominion in debate. He had heard of Gaura's intellect at such a young age, and desiring to add Gaura's name to the list of who he had conquered, arrived there with the sole purpose of defeating Gaura.

So much pride filled his heart; indeed, he was an excellent linguist. In front of Gaura and his students, he composed 100 verses of complex poetry glorifying the sacred river Ganga, right on the spot. He proclaimed that his understanding of language was much better than Gaura's, insulting young Gaura in front of all his students.

No one had been able to correct Kashmiri up until then. Gaura peacefully and respectfully admired his poetry. Gaura had memorized all 100 verses that Kashmiri recited as quick as the wind. Though surely Gaura could see the pompous nature of this proud scholar, he used sweet words in praise. "There is no greater poet than you in this world!" Then, Gaura gently asked about a specific verse, "Kind sir, can you explain to us the faults and embellishments of this specific verse?"

To which Kashmiri replied, "You're merely a child. How can you know anything about literary embellishments? My verses have no faults."

To which Gaura responded, "I pray you not become angry by my words. Indeed, your poetry is magical. However, upon scrutinizing it, one can see five faults and five literary ornaments." Saint Gaura proceeded to break down the Sanskrit grammar and found redundancy, contradiction, and a few more issues with the poetry.

Kashmiri stuttered, tried to respond, and learned his lesson. He was shocked! He had never been corrected and his pride was completely crushed. He couldn't rationalize the faults in his poetry and was embarrassed and humiliated that this young teenager found them. Still, Gaura gently responded. He glorified the embellishments, trying to lift up

Kashmiri's heart. Because the poetic champion had been defeated, all of Gaura's students started to laugh – but Gaura stopped them.

"It may be my mistake. I'm just a child and new to these literary devices. Please go home and don't worry yourself about all that I've said. We can meet again tomorrow after you have rested. You've had a long journey here, and we have been benefited by your presence. I look forward to learning from you tomorrow."

Surely Gaura did not need to learn from this scholar; Gaura had divine intelligence within him and indeed was the source of such intelligence. Surely Gaura did not need to "cater" to Kashmiri's overwhelming pride. But he did. Though Kashmiri had lost and been corrected, he was able to gather himself, and smile peacefully. Though he left the unable able to prove that he was the reigning champion of linguistics, he felt happy within. Indeed, when Saint Gaura corrected anyone, it was so dignified that the person felt happy in their hearts. Though Kashmiri had arrived with the aim of totally humiliating Gaura in front of all his students, Gaura corrected him with grace and dignity. Kashmiri's pride was gone; and he became humble. Gaura energized the opposite qualities within everyone he came in contact with.

As mentioned in the previous chapter, it was Saint Gaura's arduous task to change the hearts of all these older scholars and bring in the pristine tradition of divine love. How expertly he did it. He used love in every interaction, establishing the practical path of bhakti for us to learn from.

A WORLD OF UNDERSTANDING

Can you see how important it is to energize our children with our loving words? Imagine how they would be so comfortable and confident in their identities that they would energize everyone around them They would be able to save those who are bullies and those who are sad and suffering.

Dear mothers and fathers of the world, can we not do this with our own flesh and blood? Can we please preserve their dignity when speaking to them and when correcting them? I don't want to see children being R.E.J.E.C.T.-ed anymore. It isn't fair to them.

If a mere dog, through Pavlovian behavior modification, can be taught how to salivate when a bell rings, surely with our direct words and nonverbal thoughts and feelings, we can empower and blossom our little children into what they were meant to be: kind, generous beings.

You have that choice. Make it a habit, do it every day, and practice it. It will become natural to you.

In the next chapter, I teach you how to energize their work. I speak more on that difficult concept of discipline, and I teach you how to get your child to do what you wish for them to do while becoming more confident doing so. However, do not turn the page until you can implement these important principles: the L.O.V.E. boost, and the R.E.J.E.C.T. words.

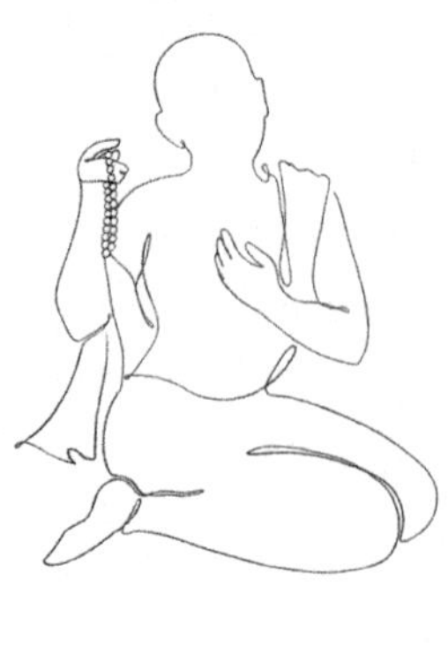

* * *

Mantra Affirmations Level 4: I Speak Love

* * *

As we settle back into our meditative space, we ask the compassionate Inner Parents to help us implement all this. For some of us, we may need to change a whole childhood of R.E.J.E.C.T. words and negative inner monologue. This will not be easy. It takes divine guidance and will.

Krishna, the God of connection, appeared on this planet over 5,000 years ago. He connected in deep, loving relationships with every living being: his friends, parents, and even the animals. There is a wonderful folk song with a mantra embedded in it that tells of each interaction they had. When they wished to speak to him, even if they were frustrated, they chanted the following mantra, and the frustration in their hearts, arising out of love, turned into acceptance. As you recite this mantra, you internally connect with Krishna, who will give you the power to change your words from R.E.J.E.C.T. to a L.O.V.E. boost. As you recite it, you can offer your interactions to the mantra, even if they are full of frustrations of the past day's events. Like the previous mantras, reciting this ten times daily is very beneficial.

he krishna he yadava, he sakheti, govinda damodara madhaveti
Let me control my tongue and reject harshness.
Let me speak sweet uplifting words.
Let me energize their beautiful qualities.
Let me create an empowering inner monologue for my child.
I am centered. I preserve dignity. I speak love.

PART IV

PRACTICE

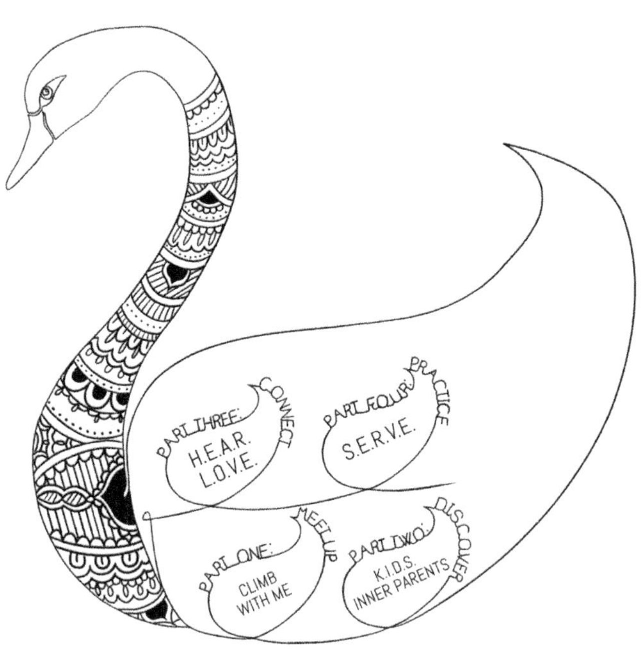

8

HOW CAN THEY ACCEPT BOUNDARIES?

"To serve is beautiful, but only if it is done with joy and a whole heart and a free mind."

— PEARL S. BUCK

When your child feels internally connected because you fixed your communication with them (as was covered by Level 3 and Level 4), they will be ready to meet the next set of needs: free-will and agency. They won't be able to meet their higher needs until connection is established.

No matter how well you communicate with your child and your child communicates with their friends, there will always be social challenges – that is the way of this world. To ensure that your child will not be intensely affected by those challenges – friends getting upset at them, fighting, hurt feelings, even bullying – it is vital that your child engage in meaningful activities which will empower their free will and agency. Having free will means I, as a spiritual entity, have choices. I do not need to place myself in difficulty and can find my own happiness. When your child knows they can make choices, they won't be tied to the choices of their friends, forcing themselves to do what others want for them. Having a sense of agency means, I am useful and worthy, and I can find activities where I feel that worthiness and usefulness. When your child knows this, they'll be able to manage those few times when they're feeling left out or unneeded in a social environment. They will be okay to hear *nos* because in their hearts, they'll have a lot of *yesses*.

You will now learn how to fortify those second-tier needs of free will and agency.

Little Simon has been lashing out, hitting and kicking others. He angrily pouts because I've asked him to sit down for a few minutes to reset. I ask, "Why are you hurting others? What's wrong?" I know that if a young child starts hurting others, it's not because they're purposefully trying to cause others' pain. There's something upside down inside. He gradually shares what he's feeling. He really wanted to play with a friend, but that friend didn't do what he asked. "He doesn't like me! He's not my friend!" Simon says.

Inevitably, the tears start pouring. "I hate all of them! None of them are my friends! I want to go *home*!" He wails, his little body shaking with pain. Emotional pain, scientific studies show, hurts as much as physical pain; the same nerves in the brain "light up" when affected.

I pull his little body into my lap and comfort him. I drop into empathy mode – this is not a time for me to be correcting him for kicking others. I allow him to accept his pain, "Sounds like you're feeling really rejected right now. Sounds like you were really looking forward to playing with that friend and you're really hurting." He settles in, taking his time to respond to me between whimpers.

"I'm just so mad! He's so mean to me!"

I say, "You're really angry! What happened?" (I'm practicing H.E.A.R. from Level 3 and looking for the action that accompanied the feeling.)

He was making a hill by digging mulch with a few friends. His friend "wouldn't let him use the yellow shovel." As the story unfolds, I see that Simon didn't want to use any other shovel and wanted to take the yellow shovel from his friend, who was already using it. When the other boy said no, Simon felt rejected, uncomfortable with the boundaries being placed on him during playtime. He wasn't okay with hearing a no.

All that is required of me is to practice H.E.A.R. The consequence of him sitting out has already been given. I don't give him any other solution. Now calm, he runs off to give it another try. I watch him continue playing and watch him throughout the week. Here is another level of social conflict: children who are unfamiliar with finding options when they hear a "no." They come off as bossy, selfish, and overly controlling.

When your kid acts like this, you're probably yelling at them, "The world doesn't revolve around you! Why aren't you sharing! You can't always have what you want!" That's a hint their needs of free will and agency are unmet.

You may notice that your child gets along with docile kids: a younger child who's okay to follow their advice or one who follows them around. They may also have many older friends who think they're cute enough to do what they want. An unhealthy power differential may follow this child's relationships into adulthood.

To fix this dynamic, we enter the next level, the "W" in EMPOWERMENT.

* * *

Level 5: Worship Their Work and Tasks

* * *

I NEED you to know this level will be much harder than the previous levels. Basically, you need to undo all the previous years' habits you've established with your kid. You'll need to reexamine the way you engage your child in work and tasks, enforce rules and consequences, and whether or not you keep your boundaries strong. Expect that you will be repeatedly pulled back to "status quo" of previous habits. There will be plenty of times where you won't want to continue. If you sign up to work with me directly, I'll hold you to it and provide a safe space for you to do so.

This is also one of the questions parents ask me the most about: "How do I get my kids to do what I want them to do and be okay if they can't do what they want?"

Without completing the two previous levels, where you learn how to establish a loving connection, this process will be accompanied by fear, shame, and guilt. Make sure you apply those processes first.

There are three results you can expect at the end of this level.

1. Your child is confident about their choices in work and tasks.
2. Your child knows what they really love doing.
3. Your child accepts your boundaries and consequences.

IMPORTANCE OF MOVEMENT

"You will be remembered by what you do. The things we do are the most important things of all. They outlast our mortality. The things we do are like monuments people build to honor heroes after they die. Like pyramids that Egyptians built to honor the pharaohs." That's spoken by August in the book *Wonder*. Taught in elementary schools across the country, it's about a young boy with such a severe facial disfiguration that his mom has homeschooled him until fifth grade. Because he loves his work so much, he has enough confidence to tolerate all the bullying he has to deal with when he finally enters school.

The more you're able to empower your child in their tasks, the more they will be able to withstand and navigate social environments, just like Auggie in *Wonder*.

Your child has spent the last five years in major movement, reinforcing their gross and fine motor skills – how to pick up a small item, stir, pour, lift things, jump, leap, dance, do cartwheels, and more. With each physical movement they have made, they discover what their bodies can do, and what they really love doing. Amazingly, this discovery in movement lays the foundation for discovering their life's purpose – covered in Chapter 11.

For now, you're going to find out which tasks bring your child joy, what work you can hold them accountable to, and what they start getting really good at.

BHAKTI SERVICE

Bhakti texts teach us a Zen state of movement; indeed *Bhakti yoga* directly means "devotional service." Service is the combination of physical movements, engaged senses, and loving connection to the Inner Parents, the universe, and the community. This service empowers the needs of free will and agency. Your child will get deeper satisfaction in completing tasks if they see it as service, not a job or chore.

If you go to the Kalachandji's temple in Dallas, you'll find the inner sanctum or *pujari* room. This powerful little space, with incredible spiritual energy, is where all the worship paraphernalia and holy items are kept. Here hundreds of priests work alongside each other in perfect harmony. There are a thousand little tasks completed all day, from 3:45 a.m. to 9:30 p.m. Each task has detailed instructions. The worship articles are seen as expansions of the divine and treated with high value. Nothing touches the floor, is banged, or dropped. Each item is placed delicately in its respectful position – on the shelf, in the drawer, on a tray. Articles frequently used are hand-held bells, water cups, small spoons, lamps, and mini trays. When they're washed or polished, the water needs to be just right (not too hot, not too cold) and not scrubbed too vigorously. Every task, and all the items required for that task to be completed is an intentional, love-filled interaction with the body and environment and a mood of service. It's an incredible experience to participate in.

Bhakti texts teach us that the home is an extension of the temple. We give honor to all items that enter it and have a mood of respect toward work that needs to be done. With this mood, worship the work and play of your child. Do not see it as a waste of time.

HELPING YOU OUT

I know your days are really busy. Most days you feel overworked and overtired managing everyone's needs and the thousands of items on your to-do list. From work, to home, to community, to self-growth and rest, honestly, who has the time for it all.

The beauty of worshipping your child's work is seeing that *you don't have to do it all yourself*. Your child is perfectly capable to take on some of your responsibilities, without the nag and drama! I know this because I've been able to depend on my boys every day. I had to get out the door by 7:30 a.m. with two little kids each morning. There was no way I could finish getting them ready, breakfast, packing lunches, getting all my stuff together, doing some meditation, and morning exercise without their help. Working on the process in this level will be a win-win for both of you.

THE TO-DO LIST

Let's get started with some observations. Make a list of your child's daily tasks, either with you or alone. Divide them into morning, noon, and evening. Find at least ten tasks for each category, but don't limit yourself to ten (you might have many more). You can use this basic list below as an example but personalize it to make sense for your child.

Morning	Afternoon	Evening
Wake up	Come home from school	Eat dinner
Get Ready: brush teeth, take a shower, put clothes on	Eat snack	Brush teeth
Eat breakfast: Sit in chair, eat without spilling too much, put bowl away	Play in the backyard	Put away the dishes sometimes
Pack up backpack	Ride their scooter, bike and hoverboard	Play inside with toys
Play with Legos and cars	Do homework	Play with friends or sibling
Drive to school	Watch T.V.	Read a book with mom or dad
School drop off	Play screen games	Bedtime

ONCE YOU HAVE WRITTEN out your child's daily tasks, think about how they're working out. Which tasks are a struggle? Where are the meltdowns or frustrations? I've placed a letter X near those tasks that were full of drama.

Morning	Afternoon	Evening
Wake up	Come home from school	Eat dinner XXX
Get Ready: brush teeth, take a shower, put clothes on	Eat snack XXX	Brush teeth XXX
Eat breakfast: Sit in chair, eat without spilling too much, put bowl away	Play in the backyard	Put away the dishes sometimes XXX
Pack up backpack XXX	Ride their scooter, bike and hoverboard	Play inside with toys
Play with Legos and cars	Do homework	Play with friends or sibling
Drive to school XXX	Watch T.V.	Read a book with mom or dad
School drop off	Play screen games XXX	Bedtime XXX

As you can see, some of these tasks are for the household, and some are play. We're working on both.

FOCUS ON ONE AT A TIME

The problem with tasks is how many mini tasks go alongside any single activity. "Eating dinner" is no longer just about eating dinner. "Make sure they're not eating too much sugar, give them vegetables, oh, and not cooked, raw are the best. Or, serve them crushed up in tomato sauce so they don't know it. They need all the different colors of veggies. Are your veggies organic or sprayed with pesticides? Don't give them cancer from those sprays! If you're washing the veggies, use that healthy spray. When you cook them, steam them – don't boil them." On and on, for every task.

It gets so overwhelming even for us adults, what to speak of for the kids! Is there ever a correct way to do anything?

Do me a favor. You are fricking busy. You have a zillion things to accomplish in your day. It's quite okay if things don't get done perfectly. Remember, you don't need to do it all. Just pick one of the tasks that are important to you. Focus on that.

Don't worry if your mom gives you a lecture about the utility drawer that hasn't been organized, or your child's clothes aren't folded perfectly in their drawer, or if the toys aren't all organized. Oh well.

Maybe those things are important to you but not that your child eats salad. Decide what's a high priority for you and stick with that. Cross all the other items off the list for now. We'll move to the next one once this one's down.

THE S.E.R.V.E. PROCESS

Here's how you will worship your child's work and get them fully absorbed. It takes two days of doing this with your child to see results. Seven days for long-lasting change. One month and you're good to go for a few years.

- S – Show it step-by-step
- E – Energize the task with enthusiasm
- R – Reinforce with reason
- V – Vary the task with choices
- E – End the negativity: boundaries and consequences

S – Show It Step-by-Step

If you've been at work all day, getting stuff done with high powered adults, hitting objectives and what not, it's hard to transition into a little world of four- or five-year-olds. It's like entering another world. As you enter their world again when you get home, *slow yourself down.* Just as you needed to slow your breaths down when you were trying to put them to bed as babies, pause right now and think the way they think.

Children need activities to be broken down to mini steps. How you walk, how you move, where the item is taken from, where it goes back, every single detail needs to be modeled. You should even model the wrong way to do it, so they're aware of exact expectations. They love the fine details – five- to seven-year-olds are working on their fine motor skills – and they'll pick it up quickly.

Have you walked into a Montessori Early Childhood classroom? It's an enchanting, magical, mini world. You'll see two dozen children peacefully working: rolling out mats, picking up simple work off the shelf, placing it on the mat, completing the work, doing it with friends, putting it back on the shelf, rolling the mat back up respectfully and putting it away. *How do they do that?!*

I learned the magic of it while completing my Montessori certification. I was so surprised that *every single movement of every single activity in these classrooms* is slowed down by the teacher and modeled step-by-step.

The teacher shows the exact way to roll a mat, and then asks the child to do it himself. During that lesson, nothing is more important than that child's ability to understand this process. Many times, no words are even needed; the focus is on the physical motions. It's so beautiful, like a Zen experience for children. For every activity, whether it be cutting a banana (yes, knives are used by four-year-olds!), spooning beans, polishing silverware, tracing numbers and letters, or even difficult multiplication activities, the child is shown the *exact* way to do it. Details like where their fingers go, how long it can take, and where to sit on the mat with the work are covered. Then the teacher gives the opportunity for every child to show the rest of the group how it's done.

To fully immerse your child in any task, you need to be the one doing it *with* them. Showing them how to do it means *you do it first*.

Around Christmas time, I noticed that my boys would lose interest in new toys only three days after unwrapping them. I decided to build the new Lego set with them. I'd build rocket ships, fly it around, make engine sounds and step into their worlds of fantasy with them. This reenergized their interest in playing with Legos. For another month, they would be absorbed again. Any time I wanted their engagement in a task or play, I did it with them. Just thirty minutes spent with them on a task was enough to boost their interest for weeks.

To be fully absorbed in a task and feel the full effects of their free will, your child needs to be engaged in the task in a positive collaborative space doing it happily and lovingly with you.

E – Energize with Enthusiasm

My Montessori professor showed us how to roll out a mat with a big smile on her face. "Look children, what I'm going to show you now! I'm going to show you how to *roll out a mat*!" With a sing-song voice full of bright, cheery sunshine, she brought pizzazz to a basic and boring task. Entering a quite state, she used her fingers to roll it out, massaged the palm of her hands on the flat part of it to press it to the ground, ran her fingers along the edges to un-crease any curls, and man, it was like she was making love to the mat. That energy transfer was infectious.

So that's how they do it! I thought. That's how a room full of two-dozen preschoolers will stop jumping off the walls and channel their energy into their work. With your enthusiasm, you can channel all the energy of your child into completing the task you want them to do.

This means you better like the task you've chosen. If you absolutely dread taking out the trash, do me a favor, don't put it on your child's list early on. For any task you're introducing, be aware of negativity that may seep into your comments, "I know it stinks, ugh." "Its super disgusting, let's just get it over with." Or even, "I know it's hard to do but it's good for you."

Maybe you associated the task with negativity from your childhood, but it doesn't make sense to get that idea in your child. Change the cycle for your child. Remember, children love to serve and will any chance they get. I have experienced years of seeing my class littles literally bounce up when I ask for a volunteer to take out the trash.

I don't like cleaning dishes at all. It was an uphill battle getting my boys to do them. When my mother-in-law was doing the dishes once, she commented, "Isn't it so nice? It's like your hands are getting a soft bath in sudsy water." Wow. What a perspective. Now when I do dishes, I pretend like I'm getting a manicure (sans the nail work). I clean them with my kids, and we've turned around the negativity. It's a sweet bonding experience.

When my younger one was four, he was given the task of cleaning the toilet because he was still peeing all over the floor. I wanted him to clean up the pee so he would be more motivated to pee directly into the toilet. It wasn't a punishment, but just a "hey, honey, would you take care of that toilet. There's a lot of pee on the floor. Here's how you do it." To my surprise, I checked on him twenty minutes later, and he was singing while cleaning the toilet! He was literally in the zone, suds all over, fully absorbed. It was so cute, I had to grab my camera and record it. What was totally disgusting to me was just a fun task for him.

Remember, young children love to serve. They are eager to complete work, and don't have an intrinsic negativity associated with household tasks, or their play. Let's not mess it up for them.

R – Reinforce It with a Reason

Always give a reason for every task introduced. Especially if their interest has waned. Ask, "Why do we do this? What's the meaning behind it? How does it help the family?" Don't expect your child to do things that have no meaning to them. As highly intelligent sages and intellectuals, they will not do things "because I told you so". Even Krishna confirms this in the Bhagavad Gita – your highly intelligent spiritual children will shy away from ritual without purpose.

Ask them why their enthusiasm may have waned. "Is this really annoying for you? Why don't you like it?" You may find out that the peppermint in their toothpaste is really gross, or that their fine motor skills aren't developed enough to know how to get the toothpaste out of the almost empty tube. You may find out that they don't know how to turn on the hot water to do the dishes and they don't want to do the dishes in cold water. You may find out that the garbage bags to get for taking out the trash are under a whole bunch of other boxes and it's too much of a trip for them to take it out. They may not even know why they're hesitant to do that task, but doing it with them, walking the steps with them, enjoying their company, hearing their reasons will help you get to the bottom of it and reenergize this state of Zen associated with this service.

V – Vary the Task with Choices

Another important way to engage your child in the tasks is to give choices. Allow your child to make decisions for themselves, for you and for the family. Become an expert in identifying guided choices.

Unfortunately, the world children live in today offers very few choices. At school, every thirty or forty-five minutes, kids are being told what to do and how to do it. Like robots, who sit solely at desks, all the children, no matter their interests or personalities learn the same things and take standardized tests to prove they learned something. It crushes their need for free will and agency.

Since alternative, choice-based schools aren't practical for everyone, let's ensure that when we're with them, we fill this crucial need. You will give them lots of choices. Trust your intelligent child to reason, make decisions, and be trusted to do so.

Some parenting philosophies promote total choice making, with very little structure; some call for rigidity and guidance. Bhakti, the classic system of parenting that is beyond the constraints of the latest fads in child development, is a balance of all these philosophies. It asks for parents to look at the specific needs of the child and the expectations they put on the child. Choose options that meet their needs and your expectations, and make sure the choices are acceptable to you, according to the leadership qualities you envisioned in Level 1. (For example, don't offer a choice that's selfish if you want them to develop selflessness.)

You will see the activities they enjoy through the choices they make. You'll be able to increase those options and begin their discovery of purpose. Here's a list you can start with.

Choices in Meals

Bhakti texts teach us that service begins with taste. The mood with which a child eats matters, as each morsel infuses the cells with positive, nourishing energy. Anything food-related should have conscious intention. These meals are offered to the Inner Parents through different prayers of grace and gratitude. For this reason, bhakti meals are vegetarian – full of compassion for animals and kindness. Preparing, offering, eating, and sharing meals is a whole spiritual practice.

But, you say, "Our mealtimes are nutty!" "I don't want to eat that!" followed by, "You have to! You can't just have Cheerios and ice cream for breakfast!" As a new parent, I was so surprised at how hard it was to get my kids to eat what I made! Because it can be an exhausting chore, this is the best place to shift the energy with choices. Use your creativity. Give them options they enjoy. Pastas with a robust veggie tomato sauce. Pizza breads with veggies and cheese on top. Curried veggies with chapatis or naans. Tacos and enchiladas with veggies and beans. Bread, potatoes, and corn. Veggies hidden inside items also works. Every culture has their favorite healthy foods, so figure out a few staple options. There are so many resources online for helping your child eat healthy, so I'll leave it at that.

If you get them in the kitchen helping you for meal prep, you will see them broadening their meal choices. My boys were lucky to learn gardening every week at school. They discovered so much and loved helping me cook. Five-year-old kids love helping in the kitchen. They probably already have a small cooking set, with those Velcro veggies they can cut and "prepare." Get them started as early as possible. Involve them in the grocery shopping as well. "We're going to make a menu. Then we'll go to the store on the weekend and buy the key ingredients."

If they are completely dead set against eating something, don't force them! My older one hated eating salad (lettuce, tomatoes, carrots); anything that required deep chewing. I didn't understand it. Years later, when we saw an impression of his teeth at the orthodontist, we learned his molars didn't line up! He was literally unable to chew highly textured food like lettuce. *He wasn't just being defiant.* I felt rotten for forcing him to eat stuff he couldn't chew, and he was too young to explain to me why he couldn't eat those items. Remember, trust your child's internal likes and dislikes. And give them choices in what they do like. I can help you navigate your specific child's needs if you sign up to work with me.

Something to remember: Make sure you're good with the choices you're offering. Make them guided, not completely open-ended. They're still too young to choose long-term benefit over short-term benefit and if it was up to them, they might choose to eat mac and cheese every day.

Choice in Household Tasks

Giving a choice in tasks can look like, "Would you like to do the dishes, or take out the trash, or sweep the floor, or clean the dining room table? You pick which ones you want to do and I'll pick which ones I want to do." Make a schedule with them and put it on the fridge. Keep it simple, and make sure you've followed the previous steps to show them how to do each one.

Choice in Clothing

As above, your child can be involved in all the decisions around getting ready. Which color clothes do you like? Shoes? Uniforms? Where will your clothes be stored? When will laundry happen? How will you both fold? Which accessories will they wear?

Take them with you to the store. Involve them in every aspect of the getting dressed process and it'll go smoother.

Choices in Schedule

When you come home from school, ask, "Would you like to eat first and then do homework, do homework first, or play first?" "What should be our schedule this year?" "How do you want to make sure everything gets done?" "Do you need my help on anything?" "Do you want to help with dinner on Monday, Wednesday, and Friday?" "Do you want your friends over on any days?" "Which extracurricular activities would you like to be a part of?"

When summer break started, we would make a list of all the things we wanted to do and the vacations we wanted to go on. This was a fun tradition we had, and we'd start knocking those off the list.

List of Activity Choices

Here's a list of a ton of activities your kids could be guided to do. Play activities are just as important to your child's free-will needs as household tasks and should be given the same respect and attention.

- **In the kitchen:** cutting veggies (show them carefully how to, and have them practice with you), boiling veggies, toasting, pouring, rinsing, stirring, (teach them the importance of staying careful with the heat, and going slow), wiping, cleaning, transferring leftovers, cleaning dishes, emptying dishwater, sweeping and mopping the floor, organizing the containers with lids, or pots with lids, polishing silverware

- **Building and creating:** Legos, Tinkertoys, marble towers, train tracks, Lincoln Logs, Brain Flakes, Magna-Tiles, Jenga, pickup sticks, blocks of any sort, large and small floor puzzles

- **Household tasks:** sweeping, mopping, stacking containers, matching container lids with containers, refilling the grains (rice, beans, etc.) with a funnel, cleaning dining table with Windex spray, wiping windows, folding clothes (YouTube has fun ways to do that), loading and transferring laundry, emptying trash, watering garden or potted plants, cleaning the patio with a hose, dusting, arranging books/shelves, and more. You can get mini-sized dusters, brooms, and dustpans, if you'd like.

- **Art:** painting with watercolors, oil paints, acrylic paint; children can learn to lay out the newspaper, put the canvas or paper on it, get the cup of water, do their painting and then clean it all up and put it away. Remember to start with the S and teach them how to step-by-step. They can also make cards, draw pictures on the cards, write notes for Daddy, for grandma, for friends at school; buy them a variety of glitter pens, stickers, and markers and have a little station for that. How fun their little treasures will be.

- **Make-believe:** dolls, action figures, old clothes, community hero outfits, Halloween outfits, fun scripts, and dialogue.

> Make-believe is such a fun way to engage kids. "We're going to make Kryptonite and play Superman; do you want to make it with me?" Even just hiding and playing, saying different voices, putting different types of outfits on, and becoming another person with cool scenarios. I so loved doing this with my boys and all my students year after year. Five- and six-year-olds love this.

Did you know that every single one of those activities up above helps them in their academics at school? Make-believe helps with language, arts and creative writing. Working in the kitchen helps them with math, and so does art! Look out for another book on this topic!

E – End the Negativity: Boundaries and Consequences

There will be plenty of times where your child just doesn't do what needs to be done. You need to make a commitment to stay in a positive state, no matter how difficult it gets. Or drop the task.

As I write this, my seventeen-year-old has his clothes gathering in front of the dryer. I put on a cheeky grin, grab him by his hand, lead him to the pile of clothes, and say, "Let's do it together." Though he groans outwardly, he starts smiling as well, like "um, I'm not a little kid" smile. But I make him sit down with me and we fold the clothes together. I pull out an interesting video of special shirt folds. He continues groaning "Mom…" but I won't let him go until it is done the way it needs to be done. All the while, I'm cheeky and fun, and even if he was annoyed, I keep my positivity strong enough for both of us.

I could have yelled. (I wanted to.) I could have lectured. (I have before.) He could have yelled back. But after years of being in this home, he knew when mommy means business, and I didn't have to be negative.

Whenever you get angry, frustrated, and negative about a task, your child's interest in that will wane. Instead of getting angry that a task isn't getting done correctly, recognize it needs to go through the process of S.E.R.V.E. again. Reenergize it.

I know this is easier said than done. You've had a long day. Having to walk them through brushing their teeth right is the last thing you want to do. That's fine, then drop it. Remember, they're only a little kid. They are undoubtedly going to forget. Yelling about it isn't going to help anyone.

If you frequently find yourself yelling about incomplete tasks, jump to Level 8 and get yourself a break.

EXAMPLES

Here are some examples of S.E.R.V.E. used with five- or six-year-olds who do tasks. Let's imagine a child who isn't brushing their teeth in the morning.

S – Show It Step-by-Step

Grab your toothbrush. Let your child choose theirs (pink, orange, or blue?). Stand in front of the mirror together and brush your teeth together. Make sure you share all the details, where the toothbrush sits, where the toothpaste sits, where both don't sit, how to roll it up at the ends when it's getting finished, and how to put the lid on without all the yucky toothpaste coming off of it.

E – Energize with Enthusiasm

There are a ton of fun YouTube videos that show kids how to brush their teeth with dancing cavities and bad guys. You can sing a song, show the bubbles in your mouth, and show them how to spit it out. There are so many ways to make things interesting for children and to incorporate enthusiasm.

R – Reinforce with Reason

"Why do we need to brush teeth? There are many good reasons." Tell a funny story at bedtime about a guy who never brushed his teeth and what happened to him. After your child is done eating, ask them if it feels different when they run their tongue across their teeth. Make brushing teeth relevant and have meaning to them.

V – Vary It with Choices

"What color toothbrush would you like?" "Where should we keep it?" "What flavor toothpaste?" "Before bedtime reading or after?"

E – End the Negativity

If they skip any steps, or just don't brush their teeth, don't yell or let it go. I know it can be so annoying. Let your feelings settle, then go back to the Show It Step by Step and model it again when you're ready. Do it with them, energize it, give choices and keep it positive.

FIRE OF MOTIVATION

When a child chooses, they show their *will* to engage in the task. This *free will* ignites their fire of motivation. They'll show interest with increased veracity than if you forced them to do the same thing.

Once this free will is ignited, when they have issues with friends, maybe they'll be annoyed, but it won't break them. *Okay, I'll try something else.*

Remember, when those disturbances do arise, practice H.E.A.R. and L.O.V.E and avoid the empathy B.L.O.C.K.S. Add S.E.R.V.E and you will see fewer social freakouts.

C.A.N.T.

Inevitably, children refuse to do what they need to do properly. At first, you will hear their refusals more often than complying happily. Here's how they get out of doing their tasks.

C – Crying

The most common way a child get out of doing a task expected of them is to cry. If you say no to something, or ask them to do it correctly, and your child starts shrieking and crying (and they are not tired or hungry), that is a *big red flag*. Don't give in to their crying. Are they fed? Have they slept? Fulfill their physiological needs. Drop into the H.E.A.R. "I hear you're feeling really upset about this. I know you really wanted to…. Yeah, it's so sad, huh. I wish I could give you that/ do that with you/ let go of this boundary. It's okay to feel sad about it. You'll get through this. I believe in you." But don't you give in. If you're planning on giving in to their crying, don't expect that task or say that no in the first place. By giving in to your child's crying repeatedly, you're doing the worst disservice to them. I'm going to say it straight: *you're raising a spoiled brat*.

Find out what about it is disturbing them. Reason with them. Give them choices that they may be okay with. But hold them to it. Holding them to the decisions made collaboratively is being a safe space for them. Most likely, you'll see that their crying had nothing to do with the interaction or expectation you have, and that they're just needing to let out emotion from a prior event that day. But hold them to the task you've all decided on.

A – Arguing

"Well, my friend doesn't have to do this." "They all have an iPad, why don't I?" "They got to watch that movee all night, why not me!" "You're so unfair!" Arguing can be a wonderful display of your child's reasoning skills, and if done in a respectful tone, you can discuss it if you want. Sometimes after they present their sides, you may even change your mind. But if your decision is firm, don't let their arguing change your mind too often. If it's an absolute no, don't waver and don't let them argue. "I respect you too much to argue," was a great one-liner I would say to my boys. If they continued arguing, I would literally walk away. It would start making me mad, so I would remove myself from the location. If they're arguing, and you start getting mad, guess what – they will continue arguing, because they know you're either going to lose it, or give in. Stay firm. "I love you, and I respect you too much to argue." Stay patient and let them know. *Okay, this one is non-negotiable.*

N – Nagging

Kids like to nag, begging and asking for the same thing *again and again.* Your child will learn quickly if by asking you'll give in, so identify which items are important to stay firm on and then decide if you're okay to give in if your child figures out ways to beg you.

My kids figured out the best time to ask me to play video games. After my long day at work when I was chilling on the computer or taking a nap, they would ask. I would say no. They'd come back twenty minutes later. I'd say no again. *I always gave in on the third ask.* They wore me down and I would give in! It became a joke (like they would literally crack up about it at the dining table). I realized and wisened up. I decided instead of saying no, to just schedule it in their day with a time limit.

If it's a no, it should be a no. If you find that you're changing your mind on it because they really want it (or don't want to do that task), change the no to a choice-filled yes.

T – Tantruming

Sometimes your child can get so mad when you firmly hold them to their standards that they'll start calling you names, threatening, and totally falling apart. "I hate you!" "You're the worst mom in the world!" "I'm going to tell dad on you." "I'm going to tell all my teachers." "I never want to be in this house again!" "All my friends are going to leave me." "I hate this!" They may throw, shout, and pummel their bodies to the ground. Man, we've all been there and it's difficult to take.

Guess what. This is also normal, natural behavior for a child whose free-will and agency need is all messed up. They don't have confidence in their ability to make choices, to know what is good for them. They're still too dependent on you for their happiness and this is the breakdown of that. Working through that tantrum and staying firm and loving through that process is how they will strengthen this need.

It's healthy for your child to learn that the world isn't always going to move according to their wishes. What you can do here is jump into the H.E.A.R. process, hold them, give them a safe space to feel their feelings have been heard, but in that process *do not waver on your decision just because they're tantruming.*

If you do give in, you're letting them know you're weak. You're handing them a calendar and writing a date for a future tantrum. Don't do it.

What you can do instead is wait until they calm down and discuss it. Maybe there was a really important point they needed you to understand. Let them be heard. It is possible that once you hear their reason, you'll come to a new understanding and that's okay. You're connecting with them, and not an inflexible, demanding robot parent. But never change your mind *simply* because of their tantrum.

BOUNDARIES

By sticking with the expectations and decisions you've both made, you're giving your child the safety of boundaries. Imagine riding your bike down a road with a fork in the road and seven other paths to take. How will you know which path is yours? You'll look at the roads in detail – one may have snakes on it, one may have thorns on the road, one may have sweet-smelling flowers, one may have a lion in the distance. By seeing the lion and the snakes and the thorns, you'll realize, *okay, that's not for me*. That boundary – that option that's not viable – will help you focus more on your own destination.

So it is with our children. By knowing what they ought not to do, they have so much more energy to focus on what they *can* do and what they *should* do. They will not be able to discover their purpose, or what they're good at, and what they enjoy doing without the boundaries you enforce.

They will also struggle immensely with friendships if they have limited boundaries in their home. They will get the sense that the world revolves around them (and it doesn't) and being in a social environment will be a rude awakening. By being lax in your boundaries, and constantly giving in to their demands, you're raising what is called in layman's term, a spoiled brat. I'm sorry to say hard things, but no one wants to be around a child who doesn't respect others' boundaries and needs. Since you've come to me, I will hold you to high standards. You must increase your boundaries so your child can exist peacefully in the world when things don't go their way. The majority of social dysfunctions I see in my clients' children are caused by the fact that their children do not have a healthy sense of boundaries and are unable to accept a no.

Here are some example statements of holding boundaries at home. Memorize them.

- "The toothbrush goes in this container – not over there. Show me you remember where it goes."

- "The bowl on the dining table needs to be placed in the sink when it's done. Show me that you know how to place it in the sink and that you can reach the sink. I can do it with you today."

- "When we're upset, we don't hit someone else. We use our words instead. Do you need to scream? That's okay. Let's do it together. I FEEL ANGRY! But don't hit." "Here, say this, and I'll help you resolve it. Repeat after me…." "Thank you, does that feel better?"

- "When it's 30 degrees outside, you need to wear your jacket no matter what. I know you don't feel cold, that's because you're so engaged in your play! But your body feels cold and it's my job to make sure you stay warm no matter what, so you don't fall sick. Here's your jacket. Show me you know how to put it on even when you don't want to."

- "If you don't feel like you can do that correctly, that's okay we can practice it together five times until you do. No worries – I've got all the time in the world and I'm not going anywhere until this is practiced and you can show me that you understand how important it is."

- "Just as I'm speaking to you respectfully, I do expect that you speak to me with respect. Can you say that again? I know you might be really tired/ annoyed/ stressed and let me hear about that. But do talk to me with respect."

- "Look, I would so love to do that art with you again, but the problem is last time all the water in the cup spilled all over

> our new carpet and it made me so sad, and the carpet got dirty. Until I can see that you're able to clean up for yourself, we'll keep the art away, okay? As soon as you show me that you can clean up a few days in a row in other areas, we'll pull it back out. I know you can! It will take a few days of practice – then I can't wait to pull it out again!"

Navigating boundaries without negativity will be the most important gift you can give to your child. Most children who struggle in social atmospheres struggle because they are not used to someone else saying no; they're used to getting their way, and they have difficulty seeing that others have important needs, too. Your child *needs* you to say no to things that are unhealthy or selfish and your child needs to know that it is okay for the "no" to come. Your child is dependent on you to show them that a no isn't the end of the world, and comes with a few yesses, but that you believe in them and trust them enough to be able to stand firm.

By holding firm to decisions you've made regardless of the C.A.N.T.s, the crying, arguing, nagging and tantrums, you're literally empowering their leadership skills. They're learning resilience, determination, responsibility, accountability, dependability, grit, and more. Most importantly they're learning self-respect. They're empowering their self-efficacy. They're seeing they can do stuff *even when they don't want to.* They're learning what they're made of. They're learning that the world will not always bend to their will. But that no matter what the world gives them, they can use their free will and agency in finding alternatives. They're learning to be in control of their own happiness, *no matter the circumstance.*

CREATIVE BOUNDARIES

Here's a few ways to hold firm to boundaries while staying positive.

Hiding a No as Two Yesses

"You absolutely can't eat ice cream before dinner, but you can have ice cream after dinner, or right before you brush your teeth."

"We do need to leave now, sorry, but you can come back here next week or tomorrow afternoon, which would you like to do?"

"Sorry, you can't wear the unicorn outfit to the church event, because it's important to dress according to our environment. I know it totally sucks; sometimes I wish I could wear my PJs to work too, and I'm sure the police officer gets really tired of having to wear their thick heavy uniform to work every day. Wouldn't that be crazy! But guess what – you can wear it as soon as you come home or tomorrow when you have your play date for your friend! Do you want to do that?"

"I know you were really engrossed in that puzzle, and it's not done, but it's dinner time. So, tell me which one you want to do – after dinner, we can do it together. Or we can put it all away right now. Which would you prefer?"

The two yesses need to be intriguing, exciting things. Additionally, they need to be options you are okay with. Get their mind off the no and get to think of other ways to fulfill that desire. You'll start seeing them figure out other options for the nos in their life. This is a powerful skill.

"Oh, I know! I can't do that, but maybe I can try this instead." That right there is a statement from a child with a healthy free will and agency and is our goal.

When to Then

Another cool technique is to give them what they want when something else is completed.

"When you put all your toys away, then we'll go have dinner together as a family."

"As soon as we leave here from your friend's house, we'll get to see Daddy and hear about his day!"

"When dinner is done, we get to read that book that you love."

"You can play games on the phone for fifteen minutes as soon as we're done making dinner."

I try to avoid using phone games as a "reward" and use it as a last resort because there are so many more creative things you could be discovering that your child is doing.

THE THREE CS

Clarity

For any task, expectation or boundary, make sure you've followed the S in S.E.R.V.E. and they know exactly how they should do it before you jump in and say it's wrong, or not the right way. This is why practicing S.E.R.V.E. again is the best way to address when things aren't going right.

Consistency

If you've worked on a task a specific way, and need to enforce it, do it the same way every time. Arbitrarily changing rules makes it difficult for your child to trust you. Allowing them to get out of it through C.A.N.T. ruins their confidence in themselves. They start equating a loving relationship with someone who will give in a lot. When others don't give in, they'll doubt their self-worth. Be consistent on decisions you've made. Hold them to the decisions and choices they've made.

Consequences

When you're following the S.E.R.V.E., that's when you talk about the consequences of completing the task incorrectly. "Oh, if we don't wash our bowl right after, it means we're probably not going to have a bowl to have to eat out of next time, or it means Mommy has to wash them and Mommy is tired." Let them see that consequences arise naturally.

Consequences aren't punishments and should never be viewed as such. "Uh-oh! Someone's gonna get in trouble!" Take that out of your vernacular.

Life already has natural consequences built in it. The law of karma (a bhakti concept) is that every action has an equal and opposite reaction or consequence.

Here's a simple list so you get the idea. Punishment isn't needed. Keep the tone positive. You can even turn it into a joke, and I do that all the time.

- You break it, you fix it. Or you don't use one of my things again.
- You spill it, you clean it up.
- You don't put it away, you don't use it again next time.
- You hurt a child on the playground, you sit for a few minutes.
- You tantrum when it's time to leave, we don't go there next time.
- You don't do the task we all decided on, no matter, next time you can do mine and yours. (I'll do it with you.)

But always, with all of these natural consequences, the mood needs to be with compassionate love. There should be no R.E.J.E.C.T. language, only L.O.V.E. to help hijack the mood and energize it. When they're upset, there should be only H.E.A.R. Don't say, "well what do you expect. I told you so." All that negativity doesn't help them. They will undoubtedly fail and forget and spill and make mistakes. Show them kind compassion by sticking with boundaries and consequences, without you becoming a mean angry parent.

I love to get silly when I show consequences. "Ooo, I'm so excited. This means you'll need to sit *right next to me* and eat your lunch because you're just throwing it at your friends! Maybe I'll even *feed* you."

"Oh man, that sucks. These toys weren't cleaned up and now they need to be put away for a whole week! It means I can't play with them either!"

"Hmm, seems like you forgot to take the trash out and now it's overflowing and I couldn't wipe the counters. Yay! You can wipe the counters for me too, I'm so happy!"

It's hilarious actually, and it confuses my students and my children every time.

If you sign up to work with me, I have a whole list of funny, silly ways to enforce consequences that have worked for so many parents. I can trouble shoot yours with you.

LET IT GO

Ultimately, if you've used the S.E.R.V.E. meticulously and still your child isn't doing it right (after ninety days of trying), do me a favor and let it go. Make sure this isn't a decision being made because they're nagging or crying. But let's save your valuable time, shall we? Look at the list of other tasks and focus on another one. If one out of ten tasks you've identified as priority items aren't working out so well, that's quite okay. You will find others that your child enjoys engaging with you in.

MY EXPERIENCES

Because I'm a go-getter much like you are, and because leadership calls for getting things done, I absolutely loved the level of Worship Their Work. I loved showing my children tasks, engaging them in choices, and watching them dance through their days with me. They helped me cook, clean, and so much more. We avoided things that weren't important to me and found house cleaners and organizers to help with those. By the time my sons were ten and twelve, they were cooking once a week, and had a steady list of household tasks that I never needed to nag them on. They still complete those peacefully and we do it together.

Because the older one loved puzzles, reading, and computers, we bought him circuit boards, physics kits, science toys, and tons of books at age five and six so he could thrive. By twelve, he created a whole data system for the school, a way to gauge attendance, and he helped my husband in his hobby of running the sound for massive festivals with 5,000 to 7,000 people. Now as an adult, he does all that on his own and more.

My younger one loved to use his hands and loved building with Legos, marble towers, blocks. Then he moved to origami, stacking cards and cups, making fidget spinners, and taking apart fans and computers. When he was thirteen, he built a drone, flew it, and won first place in a university championship. Now, at seventeen he has a makerspace Etsy store where he sells artsy chess pieces that he makes on the 3D printer he built. This all started when he was five, because I engaged him in S.E.R.V.E. tasks. He still chops all my veggies and slices and dices the lettuce and tomatoes like a master. I depend on both of them quite a bit.

Even in my classroom, my students show me every day how they love being useful. For eighteen years, I've had children organize the cabinets, move books off shelves, wipe, dust, clean. When I need to carry too much from the car to the class, they'll run over and help me, without being asked.

Dear parents, kids love being useful and feeling worthy. Engaging their nature empowers their free will and agency and provides a powerful foundation for them to discover their purpose.

SAINT GAURA AND THE PILE OF DIRT

SERVICE IS at the heart of the *bhakti* lifestyle. Though leading a major movement, Saint Gaura showed by example. Every year, the Jagannath temple in Puri, Orissa held a massive festival where major chariots are pulled through the streets. During this period, Saint Gaura personally asked to clean the temple full of dust. He personally engaged his followers, taught everyone to clean with detail, got down on his hands and knees and did it with them. This "cleaning festival" he inaugurated is called Gundica Marjanam.

Other leaders and saints were shocked. This was not a task the leaders engaged in. With the caste system, they had the luxury of just ordering others around. Why would they lower themselves when there were more important things to do?

But not Saint Gaura. He taught that every task is a service. It increases humility in one's heart and he showed this by his example. By cleaning the temple and the home, one's heart is cleaned, and leadership qualities can shine more brightly. His thousands of followers learned from him. When they saw his commitment to cleaning the temple, they joined as well. Soon, the cleaning service went much quicker! History tells us that at the end of the day, when everyone gathered to see what was completed, they saw Saint Gaura's pile of dirt was bigger than all theirs put together. He was so absorbed in this service, and completed his work so thoroughly, that the results were miraculous.

Dear parents, empower your child to service tasks and teach them how to use their bodies in full absorption. Now that you know about the second set of needs, we're moving on to the last set of core needs: achievement and completion.

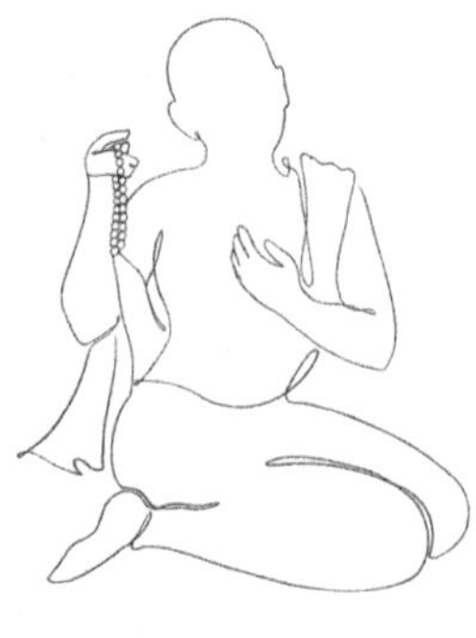

* * *

Mantra Affirmations Level 5: I Engage

* * *

To empower your child's sense of free will and agency, I introduce you to the second most powerful word in Sanskrit, *hare* (huh-ray). *Hare* is the source of all energy and the Goddess Mother Radha, the feminine counterpart of Krishna.

For this level, the quality you need to develop is determination (*niscayad*). You'll need a ton of it. By reciting the word *hare* you get energy and determination to complete difficult things like enforcing boundaries with no negativity.

Since *hare* also refers to the original mother, you channel the source of compassion and love. This compassionate side helps you stay loving even while doing difficult things.

In the mantra we call (*nigadita*) on *hara-devi* (Goddess Radha, the source of divine energy). She is the source of deep compassion (*maha-karunya-shalini*).

Like with the other mantras, taking ten minutes a day, reciting it for a set number of times and gradually increasing that number will help you in completing the S.E.R.V.E. process with your child. Your child may also find great energy upon reciting it. You will both be connecting to the source of all energy and compassion.

hare krishna hare, hara devi nigadita, maha karunya salini
he hare, nija seva yogyam mama kuru
Let me show my child how to serve with full detail.
Let me give them a reason for each task.
Let me energize what they already love doing.
Let me establish boundaries with determination and compassion.
Let me kindly give natural consequences.
I am determined. I am compassionate. I engage my child.

PART V

ACCOMPLISH

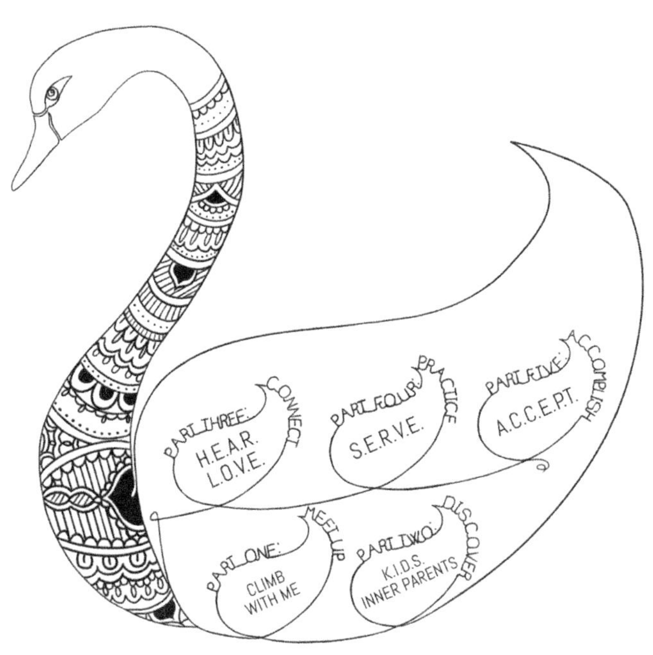

9

WHAT IF THEY MAKE MISTAKES?

"Acceptance makes an incredible fertile soil for the seeds of change."

— STEVE MARABOLI

ACCOMPLISHMENT VS. ACHIEVEMENT

We have reached the accomplishment space where your child's third set of needs – achievement and completion – will be fulfilled. In leadership, achievements are defined differently than accomplishments. Achievements are hitting goals for personal growth, and only benefit the individual. Accomplishments are collaborative tasks that benefit others. Through accomplishments, one can complete many achievements. Companies are usually looking for those interested in accomplishments where everyone wins together – not just their own achievements. Individuals who have that team spirit are more valuable to society than those who are just in it for themselves. And like every other chapter in this book, this requires humility.

While the previous S.E.R.V.E. process starts our child on completing both, the key to ensuring your child will fulfill this third set of needs is to accept that mistakes and obstacles are an integral part of the process. In this chapter, your child will work on their confidence to achieve, by accepting mistakes.

THE CLIMB

While you're working toward your goal of your child's social success, you're going to be faced with many mistakes – your child's and yours. Mistakes are like challenges – they make us want to quit. During this climb, you will want to quit more than ever before. You will feel that your child *still* fights, that the program isn't working, or something is wrong with you. The terrain in accomplishment space is rough, steep, and a difficult climb.

Once, I went for a long hike over a steep climb in El Paso. Out of shape and exhausted, I was struggling to catch my breath. A mother carrying a toddler in a backpack was going faster than me! Another mom with a little baby in a front carrier was doing it as well. Toward the end of the climb, a six-year-old boy was on his way down. He looked at me and said the prophetic words, "It's not about the destination; it's the journey." Smart kid. It kept me going, Slow and steady.

Remember, your child's mistakes and struggles through this are all a part of the journey. You will undoubtedly still experience them fighting with their friends. It won't switch off immediately. You may still feel that your child is too quiet, insecure or reactive, and you may still worry that they don't stand up for themselves. You may start noticing it more than ever before. This is natural at this stage – you've learned to observe, so you'll be surrounded by it at times! This is part of the journey. Don't give up. Today we step into Level 6, the second "E" in EMPOWERMENT.

* * *

Level 6: Embrace Their Mistakes

* * *

As a math teacher for lower elementary students, my job is to lay out math problems for my students. I know that the more problems they do, the better they get at figuring out the solution. Every time your child cries because of a friend issue, see it as an opportunity for them to grow. Only with the problems can they find solutions. We want mistakes; we need mistakes.

But the problem is that we don't like mistakes. We, as eternal spirit souls come from a perfect spiritual world, where there is no stress, and no mistakes. So, mistakes and challenges stretch our comfort zones! They cause very real worry and concern. That's natural.

But you're not alone, remember? The Inner Parents are here with you to hold your hand during these challenges. They know why your child is here, what their purpose is, and which interactions they need to grow and become the amazing leaders they are. Know that there is a plan.

MISTAKES ARE PART OF THE PLAN

When a mistake arises, think what area may need to be fortified. Is your child feeling heard? Did they get R.E.J.E.C.T-ed? Do you need to offer more L.O.V.E. boosts? Do they need to work on specific tasks with their friends?

One day, Angela was sitting on the playground crying. Though her crying has decreased because her mother has implemented the processes in this book, she still has a ways to go. She had already been on the swing for the entire break and another classmate wanted a turn. After arguing loudly with the boy, she retreated and started crying. I can see she's crying because she's not ready to share a turn on the swing.

I walk over to show her some love. I want to tell her to stop making such a big deal over having to share the swing. But that's not helpful so I don't. I drop into H.E.A.R., letting her know she's valuable and validated.

What she said surprised me. She wanted to stay on the swing because her other friend was there. She had finally connected with this girl, and they were discussing all kinds of play experiences while swinging together! What I thought was selfish (her not giving up the swing for another child) actually was not. It was quite the opposite – she didn't want to leave a relationship that is now working well. She didn't want to stop swinging with her new friend. I was glad I hadn't berated her for not sharing, and glad to have just heard.

This problem wasn't in the need for autonomy (I'm not able to do what I want, which is swing on the swing). It was in the need for connection (I want to keep swinging with my friend). Angela is working on her achievement need. How do I achieve that friendships space even if I'm not on the swing?

As soon as I practiced H.E.A.R., literally just a minute later she comes up with her own solution. Wiping her tears, she says, "I know. I can ask my friend if she wants to do something else instead of the swing." That was it. Problem solved.

Angela needed me to not jump to conclusions to realize that she could figure it out. If you continue following H.E.A.R. and think about what needs aren't being met, you'll see similar results. Your child is in the achievement space. Things are getting a whole lot better. Even though they're getting better, they may look worse for a while, because you'll notice the mistakes and issues more. Just trust the process and keep going.

OUT OF MY COMFORT ZONE

One school morning, in class with the middle school students, I noticed a T- chart with the names of two subject teachers: the math/science teacher, Mother Sita, and the language arts teacher, Mother Priya. There are tally marks in both columns.

"What's this about?" I ask. These revered teachers are second generation *bhakti* students like me. A student answers my question, "Oh, that's the teacher's mistakes. We're tracking to see who makes more mistakes."

"What!?" I feel my face getting red with shock. *These middle schoolers are being taught to count the teacher's mistakes?!* As vice principal, it is my responsibility is to encourage the culture of the school, and this is certainly not appropriate. My Asian-ness comes out and I feel a surge of discomfort.

"We could add your name to the chart, if you want and count yours too." Another student says, hoping that I would participate.

Okay, now I'm totally uncomfortable. *Why are they being encouraged to count their teacher's mistakes?! Are we encouraging our children to be offensive to their authorities?!* I try not to show my discomfort, knowing there must be some reason, and try to understand. I don't want to be uncool to these middle schoolers.

A young lady pipes up. "They're teaching us that we shouldn't be scared of mistakes. That mistakes are just a part of life, and if we have one, we just rectify it. We don't get all bogged down by it or invested in it too much; we just acknowledge it and fix it."

Another student chimes in. "They told us that we're going to need to make a lot of mistakes in all our subjects in order to keep going. And that we need to get used to making them and not fear them. That we can just put in the time and the work to fix it."

As she speaks, I'm whisked back to my own childhood. A's and 100's came easily to me in most subjects. The one subject I had difficulty with was Writing – go figure. I had written a beautiful poem where I put my full heart into about Gopinath Krishna, the charmer of the girls. The poem was filled with alliteration, rhyme, and metaphors. When my teacher "edited" it, man, I was so upset. Being a top student, I wasn't used to being corrected, or accepting my mistakes. For a few months, I lost my motivation to write. I wasn't used to feeling like a failure, and it affected me. *But look at these kids – learning that it's okay and to expect it! Interesting.* Their goal wasn't perfection. It was to achieve perfection by being okay with the mistakes.

The conversation ended with a seventh-grade young man sharing his thoughts. I will never forget what he said. "We know there will be mistakes and we know it's okay if we fail. We'll just get up and keep trying and keep working. The process to success counts just as much as the end result."

This practice really worked for them. They had lost their fear of failing, and it showed. That year, even usually low-performing students scored in the top 5 percent in standardized end-of-year tests. As a class, they performed significantly better than the other classes, and compared to the previous year. "That test was so easy," they had said. I was amazed at the transformation.

When I was four, my uncle taught me to ride a bike. He ran alongside me for a few steps and then suddenly let go. It was intense in those moments. I remember my inner panic. I also remember his encouraging words. When he would let go, I would pedal ferociously, but I didn't know to steer so well, so I'd always end up in a tree, with my arms and legs scratched up. My uncle would run over, wipe them down with the palm of his hands, speak reassuringly, and say, "come on, let's get back on the bike."

Although I hesitated, he didn't, and I could feel his confidence in me.

Back on the bike I would go, and he would be by my side holding it up again. He didn't give up. Every time I fell, he got me back up. Within two days, I was flying down the street. I loved it! Because he hadn't been scared of my falls, I conquered my fear as well.

LET THEM STRUGGLE A LITTLE

Fifteen years ago, I had a five-year-old student who had spina bifida and was in a wheelchair. His mom was adamant, "Mother Gopi, please, please don't make it easy on him." He needed to learn how to live in a world all by himself as an adult and his mother wanted him to climb on and off that wheelchair by himself and climb up and down the playground structure on his own. She needed to build his upper body strength.

Her inner willpower was incredible. It was natural for us to want to help him, but tough and resolute, she would remind us strongly, "Mother Gopi, he can do this on his own. Don't help him."

I learned so much from her. She wanted her child to struggle. She knew his physical struggle now meant a good life for him later. *The struggle was vital* to his success.

BUILD RESILIENCE

When our child is faced with mistakes and social challenges, that's when we get those I Quit moments. We decide to cancel playdates. "This is too much drama." We instruct them to stay away from all friends. When you see a mistake or a challenge, you think, "maybe it's a sign; it's not meant to be." Our child feels our cues and quits too. They learn you don't trust them to communicate through it. You lose the chance to teach them resilience, and to push through the yucky feelings, to be validated by you, and to try again.

I have a beautiful student who struggles with dyslexia. For five years, I've seen her sound out words every single day while her classmates are reading full books. For them, it comes easily. But she is so determined. She never cries, never complains, although I'm sure she wants to. It's not easy being in a class full of readers and writers and still sounding out words and needing help. Her struggle in reading has made her excel in every other area of her life. She is intuitive with younger students, she's patient, she knows how to collaborate, how to ask others for help, she's humble. I could go on. It's amazing to watch. Her determination brings me to tears. I learn so much from her.

Adversity will make you stronger. I know this is scary to hear, but you know as well as I do that in leadership, we are faced with a thousand conflicts, a thousand personality types, and difficult conversations. If we are to prepare our children for a life of service and leadership, we must be okay to work with them through their mistakes and allow them to process it. Please, when a mistake arrives, remember that. Accept their mistakes.

I say this from a ton of experience. I've had countless challenges in my life and damn, they keep coming. But every single challenge has made me who I am today. I've been sexually abused for prolonged periods in my childhood; my husband dealt with recurring cancer five times and has limited mobility; I have a son who's had a brain tumor, and yet, we're standing strong as a family. We know our place in the universe and we live in happiness and peace. We know deep in our hearts that all these challenges, all these mistakes of the universe have made us almost invincible, and we will keep going. What doesn't kill you makes you stronger; it's not a cliché quote that makes little sense; it is absolute truth.

Every single challenge, obstacle, event, mistake, or failure, every single tear that your child cries, is a specific part of the puzzle of amazingness that your child learns and will propel them to fulfill that achievement need – the third and final core need of an individual. *They need those tears and conflicts to help them get to the next level.*

GROWTH MINDSET VS. FIXED MINDSET

Growth mindset is the view that I can make mistakes and become better in any or every area of my life. Fixed mindset is thinking that I am the way I am, and mistakes show that I need to stop in that area and redirect my energies.

Let's figure out where you are. By taking the below survey, you'll see how comfortable you are with mistakes and what you can work on so you can thrive in Level 6.

After reading each sentence, write a number from one to five (one being strongly disagree, and 5 being strongly agree) for each statement. Be honest with your mindset.

1. My child is intrinsically born a certain way and they can't change much.
2. My child's ability to self-regulate, or not, is already set, it can't be taught.
3. As soon as my child was born, I could see that they would be difficult.
4. It really makes me want to give up when my child is having difficulties.
5. I like to only have them hang out in easy social environments.
6. My child can learn new things, but they won't be able to change their emotional ups and downs.

7. When my child completes a task, I'm just glad it's done. It doesn't need to be improved.
8. My child has a set social barometer that isn't going to change much.
9. The fear of my child getting upset prevents me from holding boundaries.
10. Only happy children, who are not like my child, will be able to have successful friendships.

TALLYING THE RESULTS

Write the total number of responses and add up the points. How many fives do you have? How many fours? Add up both. What are your results?

Now add up your ones and twos. How many of those do you have?

If you have more fives and fours, you're a fixed mindset and we're going to have to do significant amount of work together (we've got this!). I would recommend you sign up for my coaching now.

If you have more ones and twos, you're a growth mindset, and you're probably already seeing a lot of change in your child by implementing the principles in previous chapters.

When you have a fixed mindset, you believe that your intelligence and abilities do not change much, despite what you do. You believe that your child shouldn't have to work so hard, and if they're struggling in something, it's okay if they forget about it. The fear of failure may prevent you from helping your child start new friendships and persevere. You're just up for the drama/ trauma involved.

With a growth mindset, you're open to the work required. You welcome constructive criticism and can avoid blame when talking to your child. You see mistakes as an opportunity to learn and are not scared of failure. You know you can increase their happiness, intelligence, and success. You know leadership skills arise from these learning opportunities.

I need you to change your mindset to one of growth. It won't happen overnight. Here's the A.C.C.E.P.T. process that will help. Use it for any mistake, challenge and obstacle that happens with your child. Use it for spilled milk, bad grades, lying, broken windows and even friend fights.

A.C.C.E.P.T. PROCESS

The A.C.C.E.P.T. process is a mood to be developed and completed in gradual stages. By accepting your child for the good and the bad, you allow them to grow into who they are meant to be. You acknowledge their mistake, comfort them, cheerlead them, engage with them and practice this repeatedly.

A – Acknowledge Their Mistake

First, say the mistake out loud. Be okay to accept it. Crying kids don't always need to be shushed. Mistakes don't need to be hidden under the carpet. "You're feeling sad because you hurt that child's feelings and they're mad at you!" "You're feeling sad because they yelled at you, and it hurt your feelings."

Even if it's your child's fault, please acknowledge it directly to your child. You accept them. You're not going to punish them for making a mistake. You're going to acknowledge it: "I know that sucks and you wish you didn't do that, but it's okay." And the key phrase here is: "We all make mistakes."

Instead of acknowledging, we frequently respond by getting angry or ignoring it. We may redirect them, correct it, or blow it off with, "Oh, it's not a big deal. Don't worry; stop crying." Remember, mistakes are good for them to accept and acknowledge.

C – Comfort Them

When your child is upset, step into H.E.A.R. Don't find a solution for them. Allow them to feel the discomfort of it and process it on their own. Don't say, "Oh, don't worry, it's not a big deal. Here, take a lollipop."

Accepting means letting your child's tears flow if they need. Yes, their pain may be too much for you to handle but find your own resilience for your child's sake. Uncomfortable spaces are difficult, yes, but that's where your child grows.

Listen, and hold them if need be. Give them your absolute undivided attention and use the sentences required. Let them process this. Let them feel it and let it go. Don't go to the next step until later when they're completely calm and have self-soothed. That may take a few minutes, or it may even be hours or days.

C – Cheerlead

Once their feelings have settled down, cheer them on.
This includes statements like:

- "I know you didn't mean to do that."
- "I know you were really hoping for a different result."
- "I understand that it was a mistake."
- "You've worked so hard up until now."
- "You're really trying. It's natural to be frustrated.
- "You've been showing so much perseverance."

We need to cheerlead the way we cheerlead when a baby is taking their first steps and falls. You know the energy that comes out from everyone in the room when a baby is taking their first steps! You need to be your child's cheerleader. Remember, make sure they've processed their feelings from the previous stage before you step into cheerleading, otherwise it will feel fake.

Self-reflect and think internally: *Okay, I will listen and the lesson will manifest. I will trust that they have all that they need to get through this. I'll ask the right questions and help them find clarity. I'll let them express their needs to me so then they can fix the problem with their friend.*

Cheerleading in Seventh Grade

Not many people know this, but I was a cheerleader for a few months in middle school. Before they accepted me, I thought, *those girls are so perfect, they're flawless, they have all the cool kids looking up to them and they get all the attention. They're so graceful and it looks all so easy.* Because I was horribly made fun of my first year in middle school, my goal was to become like one of them the next year.

But it was far from easy. Not only did I have to master the routines, learn baton twirling, and keep up with their friendships, I had to muster up my courage to dance publicly. On top of it, no matter what was happening on the field, winning or failing, our job was to raise everyone's spirits.

Our school's football team sucked. Even with so many losses, we were expected to show a strong front when we didn't want to. Many girls had boyfriends on the team, and they were just as upset as the players. I still remember the captain, a short little girl Meghan, rallying us all to action, "Come on everyone – let's get out there!" She did it. She reinvigorated our spirits. She packed a punch. She got us moving. Her energy spread and the guys would get up, the audience would get up. Yes, we were failing yet again, but at least we were having a good time.

Dear parent, when your child is down and feeling the weight of mistakes and failure, it's your job to cheer them. Maybe even grab your pom poms if you need. Reinvigorate their spirit.

Remember they have all those leadership qualities you wrote down, and these moments are when they will start emerging. Think: I'm not going to let you give up, because I know deep inside you've got what it takes even if everything sucks right now.

When your child learned to walk, you didn't get on their case or quit when they fell. No! You were a cheerleader because *falling is part of the process,* and you *embrace the mistakes.*

E – Engage with Them

Once they're okay to get back up and try again, start it off with them. You can plan, to revisit the activity or playdate or task and ask them for ideas on how to proceed. "Do you think we should...?" "What would you like to do to...?" Let them share their thoughts to engage themselves in the activity again. It's natural if they're hesitant to get started again, worrying about the failures arising. Doing it *with* them will help. When my son would get a bad grade on his spelling test, he wouldn't want to study the next week's words. Naturally, he didn't want to put effort in something he failed in. I did the practice with him. I helped him overcome that natural hesitation and push past it.

P – Practice the Process

That brings us to practice. Practicing again and again is the process of learning. This process is an integral step in reaching the end goal and meeting the needs of achievement and completion. If you focus only on the end goal (the good grade on the test without studying with your child, the bike-riding without running alongside them, the happy friendships without spending time with your child first), they will have more difficulty reaching that result. They will want to quit more often and feel not good enough. Put more attention to your child's process rather than the end goal.

A six-year-old approaches my desk. He's been fully absorbed in drawing a lion in the middle of a square. He explains to me that it's a lion at the zoo. I ask him open-ended questions, and he decides to add details. When I look over, I see him scribbling all over his picture. I want to admonish him – *why are you scribbling all over your drawing and ruining it?* I pause instead, and ask, "What happened? Are you not happy with the drawing?"

He pauses, looking for the words to explain. He's taking time to develop his thought processes. I will never forget this conversation.

"No, Mother Gopi Gita, I was thinking that if I go to the zoo, and I'm standing here with the lion, I might get very scared. So there needs to be a really big brick wall between me and the lion, so the lion doesn't jump out to eat everyone. This is the brick wall that I'm making."

His "brick wall" is an intense jumble of scribbles made from a black colored pencil with a tip all blunt now. There is even a slight tear in the paper from the intensity of the scribbles. One can only see the silhouette of the lion behind the black crayon, as the lion was drawn with pencil.

This boy was fully absorbed in the process of his story. As an expert artist, he placed himself within the picture and felt fear at being too close to the lion. His "scribbles" were intelligent thought processes making a brick wall to protect himself. The goal here for me as the teacher was not to get on his case for scribbling everything he had drawn. The goal wasn't the end art product. The goal was his process –

the process of thinking, the process of developing fine motor skills in knowing how much pressure to apply and how to color, the process of laying out a story for language arts – "I'm at the zoo. There's a lion. I get scared. Let me make a brick wall to protect myself. "

I continue talking to him. He decides, with my help, that he'll redraw the lion on another page and stick it behind the brick wall so there are two pictures instead of one. If I only reacted to the end product, his work and growth would have been hijacked.

My Daily Jog

When I started jogging again, I found my muscles complaining, my breath unorganized, unable to run even two blocks without getting winded. I would just keep my eye on the streetlamp at the top of the hill, my end goal, and will my body to make it. It was tough.

But with regular practice, how quickly my body adjusted. The more I climbed that same hill, the less my body complained. I just needed the practice. After a few short weeks, I started listening to my music as I made it up the hill. Instead of focusing all my energy on the end goal and whether or not I would make it, I began to enjoy my surroundings. What beautiful, grand trees were on this path; how beautiful the homes were. Now when I jog up that hill, I don't even notice the streetlamp. I'm too absorbed in the feeling of running. I usually pass it without even a thought. Listening to the beat of the music, I feel like I'm dancing, and I love it so much. What a stark contrast to my first few days. Practice strengthened my ability to reach the goal. Not only that, but with practice the streetlamp no longer became my end goal. I found enjoyment in running and now do it for the pleasure of it. Let your children practice. With practice, they will get their mind off the end goal and enjoy the process. The goal will become so easy to reach.

T – Trust

Our last step is trust. In accepting our child for their mistakes, you need to trust that past those mistakes are successes. Trust their ability to work through it, without you rushing to their rescue. I know this isn't easy. Trust them. They *will* find a way. Lean back and let them.

One mother shared an experience with her five-year-old son in the kitchen. He was washing strawberries on a cutting board that was placed across the sink. The water began accumulating on the cutting board and started to spill out of the sink onto the floor. A typical adult response would be to react and jump up to clean up. "OMG, you're making a mess! Here, do it this way!" She however, fully aware of the process in place here, paused. She watched as her son noticed the water spilling on the floor. Instead of reacting and running to help, she saw that he calmly turned off the water and grabbed a towel from the shelf. He patiently wiped up the mess on the floor and went back to washing his strawberries. This time, he shifted the cutting board in such a way that the water no longer fell on the floor when it accumulated on the board but fell into the sink. He saw the mistake. He cleaned up after it. He corrected his process without her saying a word.

By trusting her son, this expert mom empowered him to know what to do when there are mistakes and gave him the chance to "self-correct."

This trust strengthens their needs for achievement and completion and empowers their confidence in ways you can't imagine. In leadership, they will need to accomplish goals, and know how to do so even if there are obstacles. They will need to develop the confidence needed in themselves to endure through failures. When their needs for achievement and completion are met, they can discover their purpose. We'll get there in Chapter 11.

It's important to mention that as parents we frequently do the opposite. When your children make mistakes and fail, do you berate them, shame them, embarrass them, and make them feel way worse? That R.E.J.E.C.T.ion language is much worse than the actual feeling of failure. It is not necessary to shame children into success or yell them into expertise. You do not need to be heavy-handed to get your child to achieve their goals. What you are expected to do is stay with it, calmly and lovingly. "I know you can practice this, and I will do this with you."

If they fall apart, stay peaceful – no need to shame. Let them know that you stand by their ability to succeed so firmly that you will not let them give up. Give them the chance to practice again and again, and then trust them.

TRUST THE INNER PARENTS

Surely you know the poem, "Footprints in the Sand." The weary traveler requests, "God, why is it that you've left me at the times when I most needed you?

And God answers, "No, dear one, it is during these times that I've actually carried you – that is why there is only one set of footprints."

Remember this when you find it difficult to embrace your child's mistakes. Ask your Inner Parents to guide your child through them. Remember, they are carrying you, even if it feels they aren't, especially when it feels they've deserted you. Ask to see their presence. They will respond.

They are waiting for you to connect with them and know precisely what you and your child need to grow. You are both exactly where you need to be. A.C.C.E.P.T. the mistakes along the way. They will help you turn every weakness into strengths.

WEAKNESSES INTO STRENGTHS

Here's an empowering lesson from my leadership courses that I have done with my college class at University of Dallas, Texas. Every time I guide students and adults in this lesson, what they share is so heart-warming. See the mistakes in a different light and help your child with this as well. The fear will subside.

What your child is facing internally when they make mistakes is their own weaknesses and inadequacy. *I'm too slow. I'm not fast enough. I'm not smart enough. I'm not pretty enough. Why does it take me so long to learn? I never finish my to-do list. Why am I so scared? Why don't my friends like me?*

By following the A.C.C.E.P.T. process, you're helping those weaknesses turn into strengths.

Pick your child's three top "weaknesses" from the following list.

- Disorganized
- Inflexible
- Stubborn
- Inconsistent
- Obnoxious
- Emotionless
- Shy
- Irresponsible
- Boring
- Unrealistic
- Negative
- Intimidating
- Weak
- Arrogant
- Indecisive
- Impatient

Think about how these weaknesses manifest. Here are a few examples that clients have shared.

- *Disorganized*: her room is always a mess. She rarely will put her clothes away and she can't find anything if her life depended on it. She forgets her backpack at school, her lunch in the car, her book club novels in the playground, her folders in random classrooms, and I regularly get reports that she's not bringing her homework back. It's not that she doesn't do it; she loves doing the work, and she's responsible to do tasks, but she just is so disorganized that she forgets everything.

- *Unrealistic*: he has too many dreams. He's always making

something, leaving scraps of paper in his wake. He makes these grand plans that no one can seem to understand. He's going to create a whole cake for one of his projects – but he doesn't know how to bake, nor do I know where I'm going to get the time or supplies to help him do that. He is going to have a massive birthday party when he turns seven and he is already talking to all his friends about it, but how and when – his birthday is in the summer, and we may not even be in town? He's dreaming yet again and how unrealistic it can all be.

- *Impatient*: When she's talking and others don't listen, she gets all huffy and puffy. She needs to say something important, and if someone else is talking during that time, she gets all annoyed about and it annoys those around her. She doesn't like to wait for responses to her calls, for meals when she's hungry; she starts just *tantruming* and getting "hangry." She gets all reactive if she has to wait for anything.

Now it's your turn. Think about the behavior and action that comes with your child's top three "weaknesses." Write them down if you want.

FLIPPING IT

Every weakness has an incredible strength that lays just underneath. It just depends on your perspective and the environment you set up for your child. Here are the beautiful leadership qualities that come from the above list of weaknesses.

- Disorganized ---> Creative
- Inflexible ---> Organized
- Stubborn ---> Dedicated
- Inconsistent ---> Flexible

- Obnoxious ---> Enthusiastic
- Emotionless ---> Calm
- Shy ---> Reflective
- Irresponsible ---> Adventurous
- Boring ---> Responsible
- Unrealistic ---> Positive
- Negative ---> Realistic
- Intimidating ---> Assertive
- Weak ---> Humble
- Arrogant ---> Self-Confident
- Indecisive ---> Patient
- Impatient ---> Passionate

Does that change anything for you? At this point in my lessons, my students' eyes are bigger and a full of wonder. It takes time to discover and think about it. Is your impatient child really passionate about things? How does that manifest in a powerful way?

Let's look back at what the clients said in those three examples above, now considering the flip side.

- *Disorganized >> Creative:* Yes, so true! She is very creative. Her room is filled with glitter pens and stickers. She showers everyone with cards. She has creative solutions to problems and tons of innovative ideas. Even though she's so disorganized, because of her creativity, she was chosen to be one of the organizers for the fair!

- *Unrealistic >> Positive:* I never see him complain; there is literally no task that he feels can't be done. He *does* embrace everything with enthusiasm, and he will never give up. A very half-full-cup kinda guy with bright, happy, positive energy.

- *Impatient >> Passionate:* Yes! So passionate! She just jumps right into things she's really excited about, and she wants to

> do, and she brings everyone else along with her. She can convince the whole family of one of her ideas!

Think about your child's correlating weakness and strength and how you will use the A.C.C.E.P.T. process to manifest them. *Embrace your child's mistakes and you'll be on your way.*

THE CRUEL KAZI AND SAINT GAURA

Saint Gaura loved to perform music with his friends, where he would dance and sing Sanskrit poetry and songs with traditional Indian instruments, the two headed drums and delicate cymbal bells. Unfortunately, one of the leaders of the town, the magistrate Kazi, saw that many people were awed by Saint Gaura's singing and dancing. Even the Kazi's own followers wanted to attend the enchanting performances in the streets. The Kazi was of a different religion, and did not approve of Gaura's unitarian approach, inviting all races, castes and creeds to participate in his musical performances. Hearing of Saint Gaura's attractive qualities, and that he was quickly amassing followers more than that of the Kazi's, he became full of envy. He wanted to kill Saint Gaura and his followers.

One day, when Gaura's band was assembling, the Kazi, along with a few of his burly, scary-looking bodyguards, interrupted their set up.

"Leave this place at once! You don't have a permit! You're disturbing the peace!" One of his men smashed a drum to the ground.

In those days, music was sacred, a way to reach the inner most depths of the soul, to connect with Source, Divinity, and the Inner Parents. In the bhakti culture, any instrument is as revered as an embodiment of Divinity and even today bhakti musicians do not touch their feet to the instrument or leave it irreverently on the ground. Smashing the drum was a serious act of violence. Fearing for their lives, the band members fled to Saint Gaura and relayed everything that had transpired. Defiantly, young Gaura immediately called for a large gathering. "This is unacceptable! The message of peace can never be stopped. Gather everyone you know. Bring torches to light the way. We will peacefully march to the Kazi's home and confront him. Let us see what type of Kazi can stop us." That evening, in the very first civil disobedience march in history, Saint Gaura walked with more than 10,000 associates to the Kazi's residence.

As he walked, Saint Gaura, the patron saint of love, full of compassion and mercy considered how to confront the Kazi. Surely this tyrant must be corrected – but how?

When they arrived at the Kazi's house, the peaceful group turned into a mob and began to destroy the Kazi's gardens. Saint Gaura firmly instructed, "No! Stay peaceful. I will speak to him."

Seeing the masses on his front lawn, many with revenge in their eyes, the Kazi hid, his heart overcome with fear. But when his servants told him that young Gaura was alone at the door, unarmed, and actually sitting on the ground at the doorstep, the Kazi was surprised and agreed to speak to him.

Here was an obstacle for Gaura to address; a major mistake committed by the Kazi. It is never okay for a leader to terrorize innocent, peaceful people. But Saint Gaura's mission was to establish love over fear, and love over hate. How was he to do this?

The dialogue that ensued is recorded in bhakti history books as one of the most eye-opening conversations. While the details of the conversation are too esoteric to describe, it is important to see how Saint

Gaura began. He established a personal relationship, calling him the honorific title "uncle." He started by giving him respect and building trust. He said peacefully, "I just have a few questions for you. Is it okay if I ask you these?" His mannerisms were of service, without any anger, and the Kazi was enchanted. He asked, "You are a respectable leader of religious principles. Why do you act with hate and hurt innocent beings?"

By immediately giving this tyrant respect, Saint Gaura called to the Kazi's internal qualities – the soul qualities we wish to discover in each other – and the Kazi immediately opened up to the dialogue.

By getting respect and love, the Kazi was able to respond with respect and love. They discussed common religious principles, quoting their scriptures. Ultimately, the Kazi shared remorse for breaking the drums, having had ferocious nightmares of being attacked by divine beings. Gaura lovingly said, "No, you do not need to fear me." Gaura discussed compassion, and the need for a leader to protect all beings, including the animals. In that short conversation, he convinced the Kazi to become a vegetarian, to protect all beings under his jurisdiction, and to allow the songs of love to be sung everywhere. The Kazi, now filled with inner peace, made a proclamation. "As long as I am magistrate, no one will ever disturb the songs of Saint Gaura." By the strength of his love, Saint Gaura changed the Kazi's aggression into the opposite – compassion. Even today, you can journey to his memorial, a small village in India, where he is glorified for his compassion. Saint Gaura was able to turn his negative quality into a leadership one.

This is what is expected of us, dear parents. We are seekers of soul qualities. With love and acceptance, we turn around our children's weaknesses into their strengths. This is true spiritual leadership.

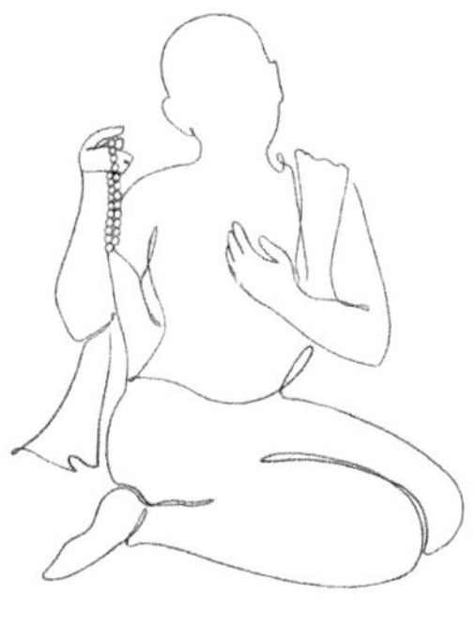

* * *

Mantra Affirmations Level 6: I Accept

* * *

We introduce the third mantra word: *rama*. Rama is the source of strength. This deity manifests as Balarama, the elder brother of Krishna in the transcendental realm of *bhakti*. He is the divine protector and maintainer of all.

The main quality needed for the Accomplishment Space is patience *(dhairyat)*. You will need patience to observe your child's process, to practice with them, to not rush them to completion.

You will also need strength (*rama*) to navigate the intense emotions that come with the mistakes and challenges of your child's interactions. Bhakti texts share that when Krishna and Balarama play with their friends in the forest, many demons come to attack them. Their friends ask to protect them with the following mantra.

The demons represent weaknesses – cruelty, duplicity, brutality, and treachery. When you chant this mantra, these qualities within you and outside of you will be reversed.

Like the other meditations, recite the Sanskrit ten times and the affirmations three times. Completing this with your child makes it more powerful.

Visualize the mistakes your child has experienced – that friendship that they really struggle with, that task they are failing at, that horrible conversation that went all wrong. Ask for the ability to energize your child's strengths. As the spiritual sound of *rama* is murmured through your lips, he enacts a powerful force in your heart and gives you the patience to turn the problem around.

Rama (source of strength), mahabaho (one with spiritual power), na jane tava vikraman (denotes hidden strength.)

rama rama mahabaho, na jane tava vikraman
May I see hidden strengths in my child's mistakes.
May I find patience to engage them in the process.
Let me accept them as they are.
I am patient. I am process-oriented. I strengthen my child.

10

WHEN CAN I TAKE A BREAK?

> *"Self-care is giving the world the best of you, instead of what's left of you."*
>
> — KATIE REED

So far, you've learned so much and implemented as much as you can. You must be just exhausted. Parenting takes its toll. All these tools require strength of mind and body. It's not easy to stay in a non-reactive space when you also want to yell or scream or cry. It's not like raising a child is the only thing you're doing. You're also navigating relationships and the drama of them, work issues, tasks to complete, and more. At this point, you may be wondering, *why are these processes not working for me?*

Here we will take a break and take care of you. For you to continue fortifying your child's third set of needs (achievement and completion), it is vital for you to take time for yourself. Self-care is not just a vital part of getting to our end goals, but also an integral part of parenting. Every time you do self-care, you'll discover something about yourself. Your core needs also need to be fulfilled. You need time to self-reflect, to pause, to nourish yourself.

THE TERRAIN

There are no rocks or steep climbs. We enter a beautiful meadow, where the grass is a carpet bed we can rest on. We will sit peacefully together, listen to the nearby creek that flows and take care of you, and only you. You are vital to this process, and you deserve attention and love.

Let me say first how very proud I am that you've made it this far. I know your life is highly stressful and jam-packed. I can't imagine how much effort it takes to work through your child's needs. Very few make it this far. You have the grit, you're doing it. While you're probably seeing growth in your child, but you may be confused as to why they're not as miraculous as some of the stories in this book. Before we tackle those questions, we step into the next level, a grass-made bed under a large majestic oak tree. This is "R" in EMPOWERMENT.

Level 7: Rest as a Spiritual Practice

REST IS vital to your wellbeing. As a parent, you give up that rest to support your child. Maybe because your motherhood or fatherhood was built on no sleep.

Becoming a parent is a dramatic life-change. Your very identity is tied to another human being. You can't sleep or eat or take a shower without thinking of this other human being who's fully dependent on you. How much time has there been for just you?

The list of to-dos as a parent is crazy long: work, cleaning, cooking, packing meals, spending time with the kids, exercising, shopping, play-dates, taking kids to extracurriculars, and work, and more work. Maybe if there's time, you add in spiritual practice but that too, most likely, is done half-asleep, if at all.

Then some lady named Mother Gopi Gita gives you eleven chapters of things to do. *Umm when, and how?* Even if you have the time, do you have the energy to implement all these things?

This, my dear one, this is when you need to just R.E.S.T. If you feel like you have read the other chapters and stuff doesn't make sense, please allow yourself to R.E.S.T. It is the most important spiritual practice you can do as a parent.

When you're flying in an airplane, they always say, "Put your oxygen mask *before* helping your child." Why? Because you need to be breathing to help your child breathe.

You also need to be peaceful before your child can find peace. You need to be happy to make them happy. You need to be relaxed to relax them. You need to feel whole so you can fill them up. Today, we will fill you up completely with R.E.S.T. Here's what it means.

R – Release Your Guilt

It is absolutely okay and essential for you to take time off and care for yourself. The laundry will get done. The clothes will get folded. The children will get fed. Order pizza! Yes, I know you may only eat home-cooked meals that are organic, without sugar, unprocessed, maybe even only quinoa and veggies. So kudos to living an amazing lifestyle, but hey, (I'm whispering right now), no one is watching! Seriously, no one.

If you take a break and you let up on your solid principles for a bit, you won't damage your child. Go order that damn Domino's pizza and stick the kids in front of a T.V. and eat chips and sour cream and *take a break and release the guilt*. Yes, Mother Gopi Gita, who's a spiritual guide and lives a monastic life of service with two hours of meditation each morning is *giving you permission*: release the guilt.

E – Escape Every Now and Then

Listen, escape means actually getting away from the kids and finding some quiet time. Maybe it's a Starbucks. Maybe it's a movie with friends. Maybe it's the church or temple. Maybe it's going on a walk all by yourself. Maybe it's a bike ride.

I know, that's so much easier said than done. But every single time you step away for self-care, you will maintain your identity and be able to fortify theirs through the processes learned so far.

Here's a whole list of escapes I highly recommend that I did plenty of once I wisened up. My "escapes" were happy, joyful excursions and experiences with friends and were vital to me during my children's early years. Make a plan with your significant other if you're co-parenting. Get a damn good nanny like a family member, or parent or friend you trust. There are some amazing childcare specialists out there as well.

Here are twenty-five beautiful escape ideas. When you read them which one makes you pause and brings a visual image to your mind? That's your needed escape.

1. Read a book in another location.
2. Go to the movies.
3. When the kids are sleeping, make popcorn just for yourself.
4. Surprise a friend with a visit.
5. Write beautiful cards or do any art project.
6. Go to the gym.

7. Go on a bike ride alone or with friends.
8. Take a pottery class.
9. Visit a museum that doesn't allow kids.
10. Eat out at a fancy restaurant with some friends.
11. Get a hotel room with your significant other and make love (*date night*!)
12. Go to the spa (yes, there are amazing spas for guys too!)
13. Get a massage, facial, mani-pedi, either alone or with friends.
14. Take a long bath, with flowers, oils, and candles.
15. Sit in the backyard under the stars with a blanket, book, music or your phone.
16. Watch T.V.
17. Binge period pieces or cool tech shows.
18. Wake early and watch the sunrise.
19. Watch the sunset at the nearby lake.
20. Go to temple early morning or late at night.
21. Go dancing.
22. Go to a concert.
23. Get a hot chocolate.
24. Go shopping without any kids and spend tons of money and then return it all!
25. Get a hotel and sleep for a whole night without any kids, all by yourself.

Even reading that list will make you feel better. Pick three. Now schedule it in. Every week. At first, you'll feel guilty and miss the kids.

That's natural and means you really love them. Dear friends, I learned this the hard way. Up until my kids were five and seven, I tried so hard to just be that perfect mom in every shape and form. I read books; I ate organic and cooked and cleaned, and even though I also had a full-time job, I was always with my kids. I never took space. And then bam, I found such an incredible need for it! It was a prolonged need and I still need my space even though they're both grown up.

It's so important that you allow yourself to have physical and mental space from the all-encompassing work of being with children. Escaping will give you that space. Without it, your judgment and decisions will be clouded by identity crises, and you won't have the ability to work through all the underlying things coming up as you parent.

S – Seek a Spiritual Space

Spiritual spaces will fill you up more than any of the other escapes above. You connect to your Inner Parents and heal. My favorite is spiritual music (*kirtan*), yoga, workshops given by Swamis, and rejuvenating retreats where there are sound baths. What is your favorite spiritual space?

Parents in leadership give and give and give. Dealing with others' conflicts is overwhelming. Your reactivity will increase, your ability to tolerate will lessen, and emotional exhaustion will creep in. At that time (or before it happens!) take that spiritual space.

The difference between spiritual practice and the other escapes is you connect directly to the Inner Parent. You offer all your challenges to them and hear their messages back to you. Who are you and who is your child? What are you meant for? How will you take the next step with so many issues? However those messages come to you, you'll feel empowered, and ready to step up your leadership space. Entering your spiritual space regularly is vital - even ten minutes a day, or twenty-five minutes a week. You decide what works best for you.

Here are ten ways to enter a spiritual space:

1. Quiet meditation
2. Mindfulness during the day
3. Kirtan meditation
4. Visiting your church, temple, mosque
5. Weekend retreats
6. Singing
7. Pranayama breathing exercises
8. Yoga
9. Sound baths
10. And my favorite – mantra meditation

As we move from this chapter into the next level, which is a more difficult level, I'll introduce to you the mantra I practice every day. I've been practicing this for more than three decades now and it is the fastest, most energetic way to balance both our core needs and our children's three core needs.

T – Trust a Mentor

Part of resting means sharing your challenges with someone else and allowing their support to carry you. You don't have to do this alone. Raising another human being amidst all these other responsibilities is not an easy task. It's naturally to feel all alone. You may find yourself overwhelmed with panic attacks, negative self-talk, self-defeating behavior, and more. This is part of adulting and growing up and asking for help is okay. Mental health is as important as physical health. See a therapist if you need to sort it out. Talk to a mentor or a guide. It's part of the resting space.

You can't imagine the difference it makes to have someone who has walked the path you walked hold your hands and say, "Hey, I know what you're going through. I know which steps you need to avoid and which areas you need to thrive in." I have a mentor who guides me every day and it feels so much easier.

My dad is getting older, and we have a tall set of stairs to go to the second level. At the end of his day when he's going back to his room upstairs, my boys help him. They push his back as he walks up the stairs. He gets a major grin and he feels "elevatored" up.

That's what having a mentor feels like. It cuts your work down and releases the pressure on you. You'll be able to share your parenting challenges and have someone to hold you accountable. Sign up for my coaching and I will guide you step-by-step.

UNCOVERING THE LAYERS

When you R.E.S.T, whether through escape or spiritual practice, you give yourself the chance to find out what lies underneath all the layers you have. Each of us wears masks in different environments, showing to others what we feel safe to, and hiding parts of ourselves. Taking time for yourself uncovers your layers one by one. We will see what needs haven't been met and how they're connected to our child's unmet needs.

Know that your child has specific issues to help your own growth. You've been matched as puzzle pieces that fit perfectly, and working through yours will help them, and helping them will help you.

Let's review the processes in the book and think about what is missing. You can take notes here as you go through this list.

Level 1: Envision Your Dream Child

Are you able to see leadership qualities in that dream child you envisioned? as you go about your days? Are you able to treat them with gold-tinted lenses, and as K.I.D.S., or do you drop into low expectations and judgments? Why or why not? What do you feel about this process?

Level 2: Meet the Inner Parent

Are you able to connect internally and accept your own parent personality type? Or do you feel unworthy and not good enough? Have you tried any of the meditative practices and mantras? Do you feel connected to divine source – the Inner Parents? Why or why not? What do you feel about this process?

Level 3: Preserve Their Hearts by Hearing

Are you working on fortifying their first set of core needs of connection and belonging through the H.E.A.R. process? Do you avoid the empathy B.L.O.C.K.S.? Or do you react strongly? Why or why not? What do you feel about this process?

Level 4: Offer a L.O.V.E. Boost

Do you avoid the R.E.J.E.C.T. words? Or do you berate and criticize them easily? Do you see qualities related to the actions they do and verbalize them with the L.O.V.E. boost? How many times have you actually used that? Why or why not? What do you feel about this process?

Level 5: Worship Their Work

In order to fortify their second set of core needs of free will and agency, have you been able to identify tasks that aren't working in your home and use the S.E.R.V.E. process? Have you felt strong to maintain boundaries and enforce consequences? Do you see your child getting a true love for some of these tasks, whether it be work or play?

Level 6: Embrace Their Mistakes

To fortify their third set of core needs of achievement and completion, have you been able to A.C.C.E.P.T. their mistakes and their challenges? Did you focus on the process, and help them practice? Have any of their weaknesses turned into the strengths?

Level 7: Rest as a Spiritual Practice

This is the level we're on right now. If you find that just by reading all the above terms, you're getting totally exhausted and "done," it means you need more rest. Put this aside and go take a break.

YOUR SHINING CHILDHOOD ... OR WAS IT?

Our ability to practice the EMPOWERMENT levels stems from our childhood encounters. Let's travel back in time to when you were little. What was life like as a kid? What positive and negative memories do you have?

Your childhood memories create the foundation with which you view every experience in your entire adult life. Childhood memories form the map for most decisions we will make. Understanding how these memories shape us can help us create healthy and happy childhood memories for our own children. These memories are known as *samskaras*, deep psychological impressions made in the mind, the heart, and even in the body. They come out at the most random times, consciously or not, when we interact with our children.

MEMORIES

In my twenties, I served as a volunteer at a temple's evening Sunday dinner for the public. One of the other volunteers was an elderly priest. After a few months, I noticed something strange during meal distribution. He would stuff his pockets with some of the breads and samosas, thinking no one was watching. I didn't want to embarrass him by asking him about it, so I arranged for to-go boxes for people to take home extra food. I thought this would solve the issue, but he continued stuffing his pockets every Sunday night while we were cleaning up. A few years later, I found out he was raised in a war zone in Europe. As the eldest child in a large family, he needed to forage for food for his siblings during a time of scarcity. He had a deep psychological urge to store food – indeed even as an adult, when he was safe, it was vital for him to replay his childhood responsibilities, bringing home food stuffed in his pockets.

Another friend, Susan, shared how when she was six years old, her parents had gone out one evening and left her with a babysitter who had fallen asleep. She thought she was alone and felt abandoned. Now, even twenty years later, she will not leave her children with anyone during the evenings. It brings up that intense fear of abandonment.

Ryan also shared evening fears from his childhood. His mom worked late nights for a few years. He would stay awake to wait for her to return and feel anxious if she came back after 11:00 p.m. When his children would put off their homework till late at night, he would get reactive and his anxiety would creep in. It took him some time to realize this came from his childhood.

Another young woman Gloria couldn't fathom why she would get angry every time she cleaned the kitchen with her children. If they didn't get completely involved as soon as she asked, she would start barking orders and yelling. After working with me, she remembered that her overworked mom was the same – frustrated at all the housework after a long day of work. The tension, stress and frustration accompanying cleaning a kitchen had come to her through her childhood associations. These emotions were in her very biology, her very blood.

The most powerful childhood impression I have been privileged to hear was one shared by an older client of mine. Her little girl had received a purple bathing suit from a family member as a birthday present. Not knowing why she absolutely despised it, she placed it in the back of her daughter's drawer. When I was mentoring her on other parenting aspects, and we spoke of childhood memories, this suddenly came out. She suddenly remembered the man who had taken her purple panties off and touched her inappropriately when she was a little girl. She hadn't remembered that image for thirty years, and this memory was the beginning of a whole year of healing that accompanied it. After uncovering deep sexual trauma from her childhood, she was able to be more present and attentive with her own young daughter.

Such is the impact of deep impressions created in one's childhood. I tell you these stories, dear reader, because it's not your fault that you struggle to H.E.A.R., L.O.V.E., S.E.R.V.E, and A.C.C.E.P.T. You also have deep unconscious memories that hinder your ability to be present when your child is struggling. You won't even know they're there until you are ready to work through them.

However, not all memories are negative ones. We all know that certain smell of apple pie that whisks us back to our grandma's kitchen (for me, it's rice-eggplant curry). Sounds, tastes, smells from our childhood bring us happy associations. Here are some happy memories.

In our own home, when it's time to read bhakti literature as a family, my husband is warm, loving, happy, and gentle. What are his memories associated with reading as a family? Every night, from the time he was two until a teen, his mom cuddled in the bed with him and his sister and would read Krishna book for a few hours as they all laughed, shared love, and discussed the beautiful stories of Krishna. I was lucky to be raised in a similar environment. Because we both had those happy associations with studying bhakti literature, we wanted to create the same environment with our children.

A father shared that he loved eating salad and was able to transfer that love to his children. Why? When he was a teenager, his friend's mom would prepare a delicious salad for dinner. They would hang out at the table, crack jokes, laugh and have a blast while eating salad. His love for salad lasted him for twenty years. It wasn't even about the salad – it was about how happy he was when he ate it previously. He associates eating salad with warmth and love.

Can you imagine how different your life would be if everything you needed your child to do was wrapped in the love this man felt when he ate salad? Can you see how important it is to make happy memories for your child, full of warmth and love?

SELF-DISCOVERY: UNCOVERING YOUR MEMORIES

You have some difficult work to do now. It's time to uncover your happy and sad childhood memories so you can be fully present for your child. If you see that trauma is coming up, I urge you to seek professional help with a therapist. Just as we see an eye doctor if we can't see, or a cardiologist for heart murmurs, or a podiatrist for feet trouble, it is vital to see a "mind doctor" or therapist for past memories and painful encounters. Your mental health is every bit as important as your physical health. It means you are deeply committing to your self-care.

Put aside some quiet time to think about your childhood memories. Sit in a peaceful place, where there's no disturbance. Put your favorite music on, drink some herbal tea, and pull out your journal. The memories you uncover will help sort out why you struggle with your child.

In my experience, negative memories surface much quicker than positive ones. If that's the case for you, write them down to release them, and try to look for a positive one as well. Let it flow as it comes. You are protected and safe. Say those words to yourself, and you are not alone as you go through this. I am here with you.

These are the questions I would like you to answer when writing your positive and negative memories. Think of these answers in your mind, before you write. Visualize yourself in that memory and think about how it feels.

For the positive memories, imagine a time you felt warm, loved, happy, safe, and even excited. What images do you see?

For the negative memories, imagine a time you felt sad, hurt, scared, lonely, or unloved. What images do you see?

When you begin writing, share as many details as you can. Write in positive present tense: "I am sitting with my grandmother. She is teaching me how to write letters in another language. I feel important, worthy and smart." "I'm hiding in my closet. I can hear the community leader outside my door yelling severely at my father. I feel powerless to help."

In your writing, answer the following questions.

- Who are you with? (e.g., Mom, Dad, brother, sister, cousin, grandparents, friends, teachers, etc.)

- Where are you located? (e.g., countryside, America, Mexico, city, farm, forest, playground, etc.)
- What is the setting? (e.g., my living room, bedroom, park, classroom, the car, on a couch, at the dining table, etc.)
- How do you feel?
- What is happening?

When you have completed this exercise, drink some water to fill your body with refreshing energy from nature. Take a bath or eat some ice cream (or something you love). Sometimes watching a show you enjoy can help your heart get past it, so it doesn't linger and affect the rest of your day (or night).

When the memories surface, you will see the following patterns. For the positive memories, you're probably recreating them effortlessly with your child.

For example, every summer when we would visit Detroit, my uncle would take us to TCBY's for a frozen yogurt sundae as a tradition. I established that as a tradition for my boys as well, and we still love the TCBY's treats at least once a month, if not more.

For the negative ones, there are two responses. You either unconsciously repeat them (do the same negative action done to you), or you strongly reject them (never go near that environment that caused the negativity in you).

For example, Christy became really disturbed when her children wouldn't eat their packed lunches at school. She would force them to eat it upon coming home, even if it was old, crumbly and no longer tasted good. She remembered being forced to eat as a child and was continuing that with her children, though it didn't help them.

On the other hand, James did the opposite from his negative childhood experience. Although his music teacher had told him when he was six that he had a really good voice and should pursue singing, his dad rejected the idea saying it was a waste of time. This negative feeling of his dad's rejection came up during this exercise. He realized that when he had children, as soon as they were old enough to talk, he took them for singing lessons. He hadn't connected the two experiences until we worked together.

Think of the connections between your memories and your present interactions and write them down. Are there any patterns or correlations? As you process this, you'll uncover some powerful realizations. Though it takes time, this is what growth looks like. It is a vital part of your self-care and will enhance your interactions with your child.

I know this isn't easy. When those negative memories surface, a ton of pain and anger will come with them. They will make you want to yell, scream, shout and fight. Call a friend. Go for a run. Pick one of the twenty-five escapes above, or one of the ten spiritual spaces. Find a good therapist. You have a right to say you didn't like what happened to you. Let it all out. You are important. Your childhood is important. You also have the strength to turn this around for your child. You will get through this.

Make a commitment to me that you will do this. Change the narrative for your child. Don't let them experience all those negative encounters you have had to experience. Don't let it become a generational gift. Using the principles of love from the *bhakti* path, please envelop your child in as much as loving memories as possible, so they can lead the world to a better, more peaceful place. Practice H.E.A.R., L.O.V.E., S.E.R.V.E., and A.C.C.E.P.T and turn this around for your child.

SAINT GAURA'S CARE

TAKING care of his associates and friends was the most important priority in Saint Gaura's life. Thousands of people felt that he was their main caretaker. With his gentle smile, he had this ability to remove the distress of anyone he was near – just by his loving attention to them. There are countless stories of little acts of love he did to make others happy. Here's just one of them.

Knowing the importance of rest, Saint Gaura once saw that his followers were working hard promoting an event in their town. They had been going to every door in every street in West Bengal. They were just getting exhausted. Though they never wanted to complain, as they knew the sheer importance of the work they were doing, their energy was depleted, motivation was waning, exhaustion and burn out was creeping in, threatening to take away their mood of service. Sensing this, Saint Gaura asked everyone to meet him for a picnic at a park. He sat together with everyone, asked how they were doing, and listened sweetly, full of gratitude. Was their message being accepted or rejected? Were they feeling successful or it to be a waste of time? "I have come here, just for you. I am here to take care of you. Tell me all that you wish to get off your chest. I will help you." As his associates rested, they felt unburdened just by his presence. So was the magical nature of his love.

As Saint Gaura sat there, he saw a few dried mango seeds right near him. Historians have shared detailed stories explaining what took place next. Without any effort, he dug one of the seeds in the ground. In front of everyone's eyes, the mango seed, now under the soil, broke open slightly and a small little stem peeped out from the soil. As people watched, the stem turned to a sapling, then a small tree. It grew leaves on it and kept growing bigger and bigger. The branches were now covered in leaves, and then flowers. The flowers brought out big, delicious mango fruits. Many people gathered from all around to see this miraculous mango tree sprout up! How was this possible? As everyone watched in awe, Saint Gaura picked out a fully ripe mango and gave it to one of his followers. It is described that the mango was unlike any other; a grape-size pit, very thin edible skin, and full of delicious, otherworldly juicy pulp. He personally picked each mango and handed it to every one of his associates. "Please rest up and please be rejuvenated by this mango. The work you are doing is for the betterment of mankind, and the world needs you."

Whether or not you believe in the miracles of saints, what I want you to know by this story is that the most powerful saintly leaders know the importance of rest. Only through self-care and rest will you find the answers to all the conflict in your parenting experiences.

Remove the guilt and give yourself permission. Go escape, or better yet, immerse yourself in a spiritual space. Your desire to keep going will come as soon as you're rested.

We only have four levels to go. At this point, you will see the results of all your hard work.

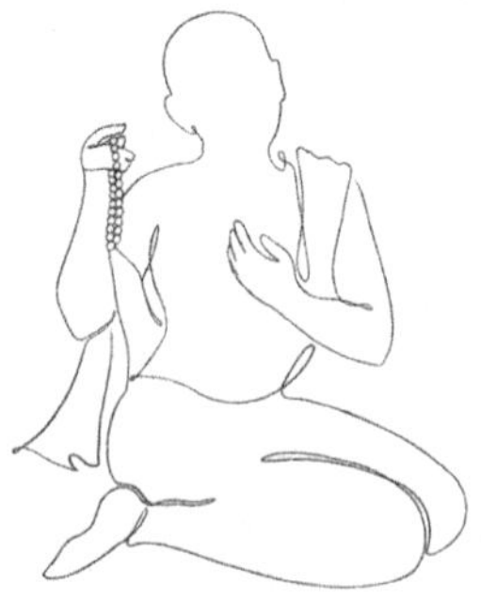

* * *

Mantra Affirmations Level 7: I Rest

* * *

Mantra meditation is the most powerful type of rest. Mantra sounds, if spoken with attention and intention, lift your work off your shoulders and complete them out by divine power. They connect you to your deeper self, and help you navigate all the yuckiness from your childhood. Offer all your past pain to the mantra. Yell, scream, shout if you need as you process. Beg for strength, and recenter yourself.

For Level 7, we continue with the mantra that denotes strength – *rama*. We ask for release from our past demons, and for strength to give our children happy memories.

rama rama (source of strength), *mahabaho* (one with spiritual power), *krishna* (let me connect internally) *dusta nibarhana* (May the demons of my past be removed.)

rama rama mahabaho, krishna dusta nibarhana
Let me take rest as soon as I need to.
Let me connect to my past memories to help my child.
Help me remove my childhood pain.

Let me make only happy memories for my child.
I am rested. I am growing. I am ready.

PART VI

LEAD

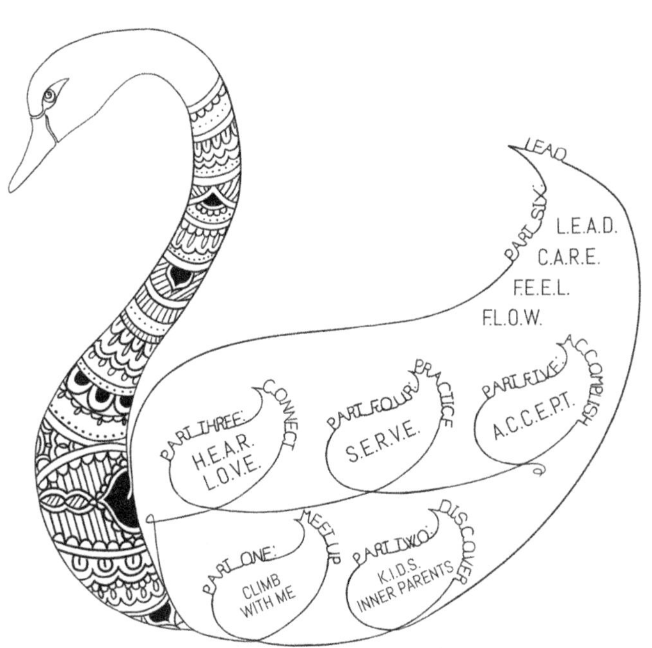
LEAD
PART SIX:
L.E.A.D.
C.A.R.E.
F.E.E.L.
F.L.O.W.
PART THREE:
CONNECT
H.E.A.R.
L.O.V.E.
PART FOUR:
PRACTICE
S.E.R.V.E.
PART FIVE:
ACCOMPLISH
A.C.C.E.P.T.
PART ONE:
MEET UP
CLIMB
WITH ME
PART TWO:
DISCOVER
K.I.D.S.
INNER PARENTS

11

WHERE IS THEIR PLACE?

> "The master in the art of living makes little distinction between his work and his play, his labor and his leisure, his mind and his body, his education and his recreation, his love and his religion. He hardly knows which is which. He simply pursues his vision of excellence at whatever he does, leaving others to decide whether he is working or playing. To him, he is always doing both."
>
> — L.P. JACKS

WHAT AM I MEANT FOR?

Now that you've learned how to fortify all of their core needs, you can help them find their place in the world. *What are they good at? What do they enjoy doing?*

When children see their peers happily engaged in activities, they tend to question their own place. In this chapter, you will help your child discover their purpose.

At a field trip to Klyde Warren Park, six-year-old Isaac approaches me. Usually a happy little boy, today his little body is slumped over with sadness. This boy is such a genius. He can do complicated multiplication in his head, and loves creating innovative patterns with manipulatives in the classroom. But today, something is wrong. He sits near me, and whispers.

"I'm just not as fast as any of them." He says quietly. He wants to keep up with the other boys in the group. Many are older and bigger than him. They're playing tag, with "hot lava" areas.

"Are they not involving you?" I ask.

"No, they're involving me," he says. "They're trying to slow down for me. But I don't want them to have to slow down. I wish I was just faster!"

I stop questioning as I see this young man coming to terms with that which he is not. Like in the chapter of mistakes, he's realizing areas that may not be his level at this moment and that's making him sad. I drop into H.E.A.R. By reflecting and listening, I allow him to process it.

I'm surprised at how connected he is to his feelings. "Why am I not as fast as them? Why am I made this way? Why am I different?" Many children feel this regularly. What they're actually asking is "who am I? What is my purpose?"

Though it's hard, I avoid the empathy B.L.O.C.K.S. I know not to give solutions just yet. I need him to feel it first before I dump a Band-Aid on it, but it's breaking my heart. He's such a gentle, intelligent boy, soft spoken and methodical. I remember my own son going through these questions. I remember when people would make fun of him and when his brother had so many externally shown talents that he would wonder the same things.

Soon, I guide him to look at all the other kids on this magical playground. "Let's figure out what you're good at doing on this playground, Isaac. Look – there's a wooden puzzle structure to climb up. Would you be able to get to the top of it? Look over there, it seems like binoculars looking out over the city. What about that music ensemble with the different colored bells?"

"Find out what you're really good at doing. It doesn't matter what the others are doing or not doing. Maybe if you figure out what you're good at, you can invite them to do it with you! They might get bored of hot lava tag soon."

This sparks something in his eyes, and he goes off to figure out what he's good at. I observe him for the next fifteen to twenty minutes, and his body is no longer slumped. He's keenly enjoying the other activities on the playground. I make a mental note to watch him at school and help develop his sense of purpose. This is his first semester with me in the classroom, so I'm excited to see what develops in this upcoming year. The most incredible experience for me was when I heard him on the school playground a few months later. His friends kept calling for him to play soccer, but full of confidence he said he didn't want to join them. "No, I'm doing 'such and such' right now, and I'm good! You can join me if you want!"

He had gained great confidence in his own abilities, after only a few months. With this confidence, he is comfortable to say no to his friends. He's discovered what he *does* love to do and this discovery fills him with strength in all other areas.

FIVE MISCONCEPTIONS

Isaac's story brings us to the five misconceptions. Remember the ones you had to let go of back in Chapter 2? For us to continue down this path, you need to let go of the same misconceptions but in relation to your child.

Child Misconception #1: Your child needs to have friends and shouldn't play alone.

It's okay if your child doesn't have a ton of friends or playdates and if they play by themselves on the playground. *There is nothing wrong with that.* A child steeped in purpose will be so absorbed they may not be aware of who is around them during their engagement. Don't put ideas in their head that something is wrong with them if they don't have a ton of friends. Let that go.

Child Misconception #2: Your child needs to love doing what other kids are doing.

Nope, wrong again. Your child is an individual and shouldn't be pressured to do something because everyone else is doing it. Let them find what makes them tick, not because other kids are doing it.

Child Misconception #3: Your child needs to be doing it all.

Engaging your child in every activity under the block and expecting that they succeed in all of it is just a manifestation of you thinking you need to be doing it all and isn't fair to them. Don't pack their days with extras every single evening. Piano, soccer, violin, dance, gymnastics – some kids are going until 8:30 p.m., and back up the next day for school all over again. Give them unstructured time to play. Let them discover what they love in free time and engage them in natural household tasks with you in the evening. Give them a break.

Child Misconception #4: If your child cries, they're a failure.

Although we went over this in a previous chapter, it needs to be solidified. It's okay if your child cries! Allow them to express their emotion, without getting it all stuffed up. They won't break or ruin their lives. Let them cry and process using the A.C.C.E.P.T process.

Child Misconception #5: Your child should know how to do things perfectly.

This extension of you thinking you should parent perfectly is also not fair to our kids! As you step into the next level shared in this chapter, it is so important that you not place this idea of perfection on them. The process is just as important as their end goal and releasing the expectation of perfection will help your child discover their place.

THE PATH

Now equipped with a sense of freedom and getting rid of all those misconceptions, it's time to enter into Part 5: the Leadership Space. Here, concepts are a bit harder to understand and implement, but I know you can do it. We cannot reach the following levels by our own strength. They must be accessed through the grace of the Inner Parents. Without our own connection to source and divinity, it will be difficult to proceed. For your child to grow into leadership spaces, meditation is a prerequisite. We will be unable to do this without inner guidance.

Here's an overview of what you've learned so far.

	Leadership Parenting	Child's Feeling	Bhakti Texts	Maslow's Hierarchy	Self Determination	Erik Erikson's Stages
Ch. 6-7	Connection & Belonging	*"I know myself. I trust you."*	*sambandha*	Belonging	Relatedness	Trust vs Mistrust
Ch. 8	Free Will & Agency	*"I can do it."*	*abhidheya*	Freedom	Autonomy	Autonomy vs Shame/Doubt
Ch. 9-10	Achievement & Completion	*"I did it!"*	*prayojana*	Esteem	Competence	Industry vs Inferiority
Ch. 11	All Three Needs Chapter 11	*"I know what I'm meant for."*	*dharma samadhi*	Self-Actualization	Motivation	Identity vs Confusion
Ch. 12	Others' Core Needs	*"I can understand what they need."*	*vadanya*			Intimacy vs Isolation
Ch. 13	Win-Win	*"We can help each other."*	*sanga*			Generativity vs Stagnation
Ch. 14	Win-Win-Win Leadership	*"We can serve everyone together."*	*sankirtan*			

Our first Level in the Leadership Space is the "M" in the EMPOWERMENT process.

* * *

Level 8: Magnify Their Purpose

* * *

Every single being on this planet has a very specific purpose – who they're going to be when they grow up, who they're going to serve, what difference they will make on this planet. Remember your child is a powerful being, and every single one of their qualities are made for a reason. They can feel this purpose even when they're five. This feeling will help them socially. It will ensure they don't feel aimless as teenagers and adults. Finally, they'll be so internally connected that they can begin connecting with others. That is an important step in leadership.

This process of developing one's purpose is pretty simple.

FLOW STATE

Have you ever felt like it was too quiet in the house and wonder where your little one is? As you look for them, you see them so absorbed, they've lost track of time. That is called *flow* or *samadhi.*

Flow is an academic term that describes a state of total absorption, when an individual forgets everything else around them. Their bodies, minds, desires, and tasks are all fully immersed. When children are in a state of flow, they lose the desire to fight, argue, whine, and complain.

In *bhakti* texts, when an individual activates their flow, purpose *(dharma)* can be revealed. *When one is fully absorbed in flow, the goal simultaneously becomes the process and the outcome together.* That means the child isn't doing the activity just for the end result. They're also enjoying the process of it. Picture a little boy stacking cards to make a long tower. Or a girl absorbed in reading a book for hours. Or when a child pulls out her art supplies and her sketchpad. Each of these are engaged in flow. These activities, once developed, become a part of their purpose.

It is time for you to notice flow in your child's actions. For a three-year-old, it can be when they're working hard to put on their shirt or coat, fiddling with the buttons, inside-out or outside-in, taking it on and off to work through it. For a four-year-old, it's when they're having an avid conversation about something they're interested in – showing you exactly what they're doing and why they love it. For a five-year-old, when they're showing another friend something they're excited about. It's such an incredibly beautiful thing to witness a child in flow.

Every one of these moments of flow is just the beginning of them developing their overall purpose. *I want to learn how to put a shirt on by myself. I want to communicate my love of something to someone else.* Purpose just means a reason for doing something. Every time they feel that inner drive, that's purpose coming out.

When you recognize your child's purpose, you will feel supported in your own purpose. You'll feel so satisfied – *wow, I'm doing this parenting thing right.* Both of you will enter that state of flow in your life. I've heard moms say, "I'm doing what I love and you're doing what you love."

When my boys were five and seven, I would work on lesson plans or graphic design on my computer, and they would engage in the things they loved. I would notice their work with a L.O.V.E boost here and there. We would be in the same room, all absorbed in *samadhi* flow, like an enchanting trance. You can have the same experience with your child.

SAMADHI CIRCLES – MEETING THREE NEEDS

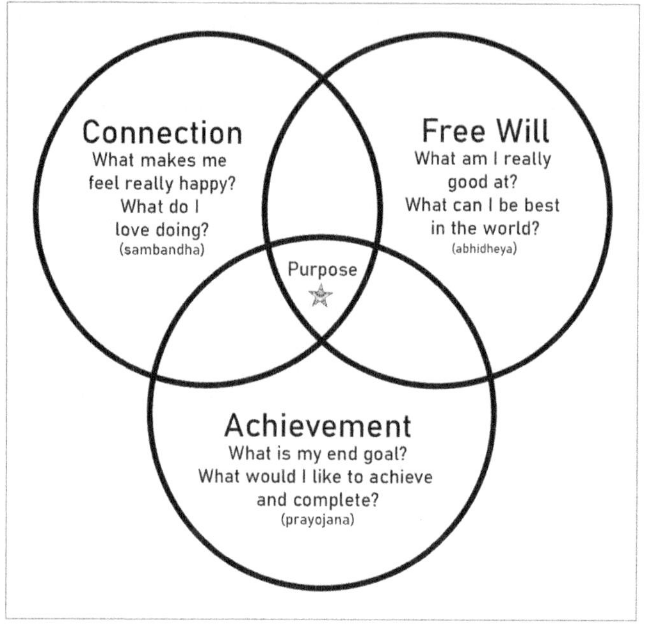

So, let's look at how it all comes together. Flow can emerge when any one of the needs are met. Purpose emerges when all three needs are met.

These are the questions you're looking for answers to.

- Connection: What makes me feel really happy?
- Free Will: What am I the best at doing?
- Achievement: What is my end goal?
- Purpose: What am I intrinsically motivated and rewarded by?

CIRCLE 1: FULFILLING THE CONNECTION NEED

In Chapters 6 and 7, you learned how to fulfill your child's connection need with you. Now you will help them connect to themselves. What makes them the happiest? What do they enjoy doing, more than anything else? What activities to they turn to? What are they deeply satisfied by?

Because you've been following the H.E.A.R. and L.O.V.E. boost processes, you're in tune with your child's feelings. You know what makes them sad. You should also notice what activities bring them joy.

Does your child spend their free time absorbed in a book and love reading? Do they love doing puzzles – big or small? Do they love dressing up and wearing fancy clothes? Do they love building, or art/markers? Even the same item may be used differently by different kids. One child may use markers to color; another may stack the markers and build a robot. A third kid may take it apart and get to the ink tube inside. All three have different likes.

Observe what your child loves doing and make mental notes. For example, instead of getting on their case for using the markers incorrectly, see that your kid loves taking things apart instead of drawing, and find them things to take apart. The goal here is to find out what your child *absolutely loves doing* and increase that.

CIRCLE 2: FULFILLING THE FREE WILL NEED

What are they really good at? What can they be the best in the world at?

Some kids are amazing at playing the piano, even at age two! Their fingers dance on the keys and music pours out without any effort. Some can sing complicated tunes with a powerful voice. Some have detailed fine motor skills where they can pick up scissors easily in their hands and cut paper; others struggle with cutting even in a straight line until eight or nine. Some are really good at working with tiny Lego bricks, while others prefer the larger bricks. Some kids can do headstands and flip and twirl in the living room, while others may be too scared. Each child has their *dharma* purpose, their nature, their unique individual place.

By following the S.E.R.V.E. and A.C.C.E.P.T. processes, you will learn to identify what they're really good at, and what they can be the best at doing. You will also eliminate things they aren't so good at doing. Those processes help build their confidence, and aptitude.

The most important part of that chapter is the process and product part – you want to make sure your child is okay to practice things they are already good at. Sometimes children are naturally good at things, but they don't enjoy doing them. Other times, children love doing something but they're not so good at it. The key to meeting all three needs is first finding activities they love doing, and can be the best at, either automatically, or through practice.

CIRCLE 3: FULFILL THE ACHIEVEMENT NEED

Once you can figure out what your child loves doing, and what they can be really good at, let's add the last circle. What activity gives them a sense of achievement, that they're totally motivated by. Did that puzzle they were working on stay on the kitchen table for some time because they loved looking at the completed piece? Did the markers that they take apart stay open for a while because they were still trying to figure out how to put it back together? Do they love going to the library and keeping their books even after they've finished reading them? Do they love reading the books out loud to you or a sibling? Do they want to show their completed tower of blocks, or Lego creation to you or anyone else ("Take a picture and send it to Grandma!")? Are they able to make money out of the item they've made? Are they called to perform, build, or fix by others? These are some ways to see that their achievement need is being met.

For example, if a child loves to sing, and is really good at it, but shies away from doing it in public – that's an achievement area that needs to be strengthened. If a child loves doing 1000 piece puzzles, and is an expert at finding matching pieces, but doesn't ever finish the puzzle –

that's a missing achievement area. They're not *that* into it – not enough to finish it and enjoy the completed puzzle. You fortify this space by S.E.R.V.E and A.C.C.E.P.T. processes in Chapters 8 and 9.

Intrinsic Motivation versus Extrinsic Motivation

Once you're become aware of the three areas – what is my child satisfied by, what is my child really good at, what is my child's end goal – you can see what they are motivated intrinsically by. Bhakti texts share six areas where humans are naturally motivated.

But before I can teach you those six areas, you need to learn the difference between intrinsic and extrinsic motivation. You will need to stop motivating them extrinsically or they will never find out what they really love doing, what they can be the very best at, and what gives them a sense of achievement. Leadership means finding that space where you're doing it for the sheer pleasure and benefit of doing it, less because of an external reward. John Mackey, the CEO of Whole Foods, and the author of *Conscious Leadership*, himself decided to take only $1 salary because he did the work he did "for the pure joy of it." He understood the meaning of intrinsic motivation and got rid of the extrinsic rewards.

There have been many studies analyzing motivation. In one experiment, college students were asked to solve 3D puzzles, creating a specific shape from smaller shapes. They were given three sessions to "play with" the puzzles. In the first session, they played with the puzzles for as long as they wanted to. Researchers tracked their time, seeing how long they naturally played for.

In the second session, half the participants got $1 for every puzzle they correctly solved. Again, their playing time was tracked. For the final and third session, they were given the puzzles to play with again, but with no reward.

Researchers found that the students who were given $1 for solved puzzles were significantly less interested in playing with the puzzles during the third session. Whereas those that were given no reward showed no change in their interest. By getting the $1 reward, the motivation for playing with the puzzle decreased. They were no longer motivated to solve the puzzle. They wanted the money instead. Extrinsic rewards reduce intrinsic motivation.

Another study by Mark Lepper was with preschool children. The kids were shown a brand-new box of big markers. Half of them were also shown a paper certificate that said, "Good Player Award." "You'll get this award if you play with the markers!" The other kids (the control group) were just given the markers, with no paper reward.

All the kids quickly absorbed themselves in coloring with the markers. They were to draw with the markers for six minutes. After the six minutes, the group who were shown the award got their certificate. The other group just finished and put the markers away. A panel of judges, unaware of who was in the control group, rated the drawings.

The drawings done by children who expected rewards were judged as significantly lower in quality than drawings done by the other kids. Second, surprisingly, a few weeks later, the classroom was observed for marker use, and the children who had received a reward for using markers were uninterested in them this time around. They used them half as much as the other children! By getting a little paper certificate after only six minutes of completing an activity that most six-year-olds love doing, those children lost interest in coloring with the brand-new markers. In her book *Montessori: The Science Behind the Genius,* Angeline Lillard sums up this concept well. "Engaging in a well-liked activity with the expectation of a reward led to reduced creativity during that activity and to decreased voluntary participation in that activity later."

If you want to suck the joy right out of any task, add a reward to it.

In his book, *Breaking into the Heart of Character,* psychologist, cofounder of Heart of Character, and dear friend, David Streight, lays out the best analysis of motivation that I've come across. He shares five circles of motivation, from intrinsic to extrinsic.

David Streight's Motivation Circles

The first circle is "Buy Me Off", where you motivate your child by paying them. Paying kids for tasks in the home, for grades, for being good. "I'll give you a dollar for bringing in the groceries." "For every 100 percent you get, you'll get $10." "You'll get $50 a week if you do your chores."

The second circle is "Ego Protection." Here, the child is motivated by others and recognition. "Do that so your friends will see how cool you are." "All our family members are going to see you so make it good." "Your grades are in the top ten percent of the class! Keep it up!" The message is: Be good at that item so you're better than others, and so others can see your accomplishment. The child isn't necessarily motivated to do the activity without the external ego boost they're getting.

Moving toward intrinsic motivation, the third circle is "This Could Be Useful." In this stage, they're realizing, "Hey wait, maybe I'll do the task because I can see it actually helps me." "Maybe I'll clean my room because my friends are coming over to play board games and we'll need space." "I'll put my toys away so I know where to find them tomorrow." "I'll organize the Lego pieces so I don't lose important parts." "I'll clean my dishes so I don't have to wait to eat." "I'll study that Science text so I can learn cool stuff about animals and space."

The final and most intrinsic circle of motivation is "I love this stuff." This is where flow is activated. This is where your child gets lost in the activity, and where you can discover your child's inner purpose. This is where your child is deeply connected to themselves. A child engaged in this space frequently throughout the day will have very few social issues with other children. They know themselves. Not only that, they can engage others in their flow as well.

Here are a few examples for you to notice with your child.

Tying Shoelaces

- *Buy Me Off*: "I'll give you $1 every time you tie your own shoelaces and don't ask me to do it for you!"

- *Ego Protection*: "Look, kiddo, every one of your friends knows how to tie their shoelaces. You're still struggling with that?"

- *This Could Be Useful*: The child thinks, *I don't want to be dependent on an adult. I better learn how to do this.* Or, the child trips on a loose shoelace and realizes, *Oh wait, I don't want to trip again. Let me learn to tie them.*

- *I Really Love This*: "It's so fun to make bunny ears. And I love tying that knot. I love knowing that I can do it."

I actually heard a little girl say last week that it's really fun to do the bunny ears in tying her shoelaces. At five years old, she was showing another child how to tie shoelaces. Her mom carefully develops her intrinsic motivation in everything she does. Immediately, she was confident to step into a leadership space and teach another, because her motivation for the activity was intrinsic.

Riding a Bike

- *Buy Me Off*: "If you learn how to ride your bike without

training wheels, I'll get you a brand-new bike that's shiny, glittery, and beautiful!"

- *Ego Protection*: "All your friends already know how to ride the bike!" Or "Look how good you are doing that; I'm going to post a picture / video up on Facebook about how amazing you are!"

- *This Could Be Useful*: The child thinks, *I want to go to my friend's house without depending on my mom to take me. I would like to ride my bike with my friends when they're playing and not be left out.*

- *I Really Love This*: "I love the wind in my hair. I love the freedom of bike riding. I love being able to balance it all by myself. I love knowing I can do it! I love learning how to brake and seeing that I'm not going to fall. I love the sense of freedom and achievement. And I love riding my bike with my friends."

Doing the Dishes

Children start life loving to play with soap suds (bubble bath for the dishes); which two-year-old wouldn't like to stand on a step stool and play with a bunch of bubbles and scrub a few dishes in the process? But by the time they're ten-years-old, doing the dishes turns into a horrible chore (I know, I hated doing dishes and very healthily transferred that hate over to my kids!).

- *Buy Me Off*: "I'll give you $10 a week to do the dishes every Wednesday and Friday."

- *Ego Protection*: "I'm going to put you in a time-out if you don't do the dishes. You're going to get your privileges revoked – no computer time. You can only use dishes marked with your name."

- *This Could Be Useful*: The child thinks, *"If I clean the dishes, I'll have my own bowl to get whenever I want a snack, or cereal and milk. If I clean the dishes, I can get to what I really want to do. If I get it over with, my mom will stay happy and I won't have to hear her lecture."*

- *I Really Love This*: "I love the feeling of the hot water on my hands. I love playing with the bubbles. I love having my bowl exactly where I need it. I love having no streaks on my pot and I love that I can get my own cereal and milk in the morning, or yogurt and fruits in the morning when I get up and I don't have to bother my mom."

You see how this works? Avoid the two external circles with your child. Don't give them money tied to tasks or it'll be difficult to find out if that task is tied to their purpose. As much as possible, guide your child to intrinsic motivation and remove the external motivators. If you've only used rewards to motivate your child to follow instructions, this may be hard to do. I'll share how to do that later in this chapter, and you can always sign up with me as a coach to help you in your specific circumstances.

Also, be aware that your child will not develop intrinsic motivation for every activity. Each child has their own nature and areas of motivation. For example, no matter how much I love soapy bubbles and bubble baths, and no matter how much I've tried, I struggle to enjoy cleaning dishes. I'm just not kinesthetic and don't enjoy working with my hands. My mother-in-law, on the other hand, is a jewelry designer and maker. She used to make little clay beads of all types, bake them in the oven, turn them into stunning artistic jewelry pieces and sell them at elite art shows across the country. She loves doing the dishes and sees it as a Zen practice. Just watching her makes me want to join her!

That is an amazing byproduct of a child engaged in something they're intrinsically motivated by. When they're in a state of flow, it attracts others to do it with them. That type of natural leadership, inspiring others authentically, is what we're looking for.

PURPOSE TIED TO SIX MOTIVATORS

Bhakti texts share there are six areas where a human can be motivated, giving an indication of a child's purpose. When you observe your child, see which categories they're motivated by.

Wisdom

Some are motivated by knowledge and wisdom. They love learning new things, watching documentaries, teaching others, memorizing things, like the little kid who can rattle off all the state capitals of the U.S. and beams when he does so. They play with words and language, and love feeling smart. They may win the spelling bee and can answer all those Jeopardy questions. They get upset if they're intellectually bored and haven't learned new things in a while. They will be writers, scientists, researchers, guides, teachers, professors, mentors, and coaches.

Recognition

In this category, people are motivated by being famous and recognized by others. They love being seen and showing others what they've done. They love posing, making YouTube videos, or Facebook lives. They're okay to be in front of the camera and they're the ones who are going to be the beautiful angel dancing around on stage at a community event. "Everyone, look at me." They're people pleasers and like making others happy. They get upset if they're isolated too much, if they aren't around people, or if they've been insulted and criticized by others. They will have a career in administration, be influencers, public figures, actors/ actresses, senators, congressmen, human resource managers, and have public-facing careers.

Physical Strength

Some are motivated by physical acts and strength. One little boy always carried more than everyone else. When it was time to organize chairs for an event, at only six, he took three of the chairs and moved them. Any time you may need help to pick something up, they'll be there. Physical, big motor skills are important to them. They like jumping off high structures, running, soccer or any type of sports; they push themselves to run faster and climb higher, even at a really young age. They love doing gymnastics, flips, headstands, and are always moving. They're motivated by their bodies and like to stay fit, healthy, and young. They run marathons, climb mountains, do 1,000-mile treks, fly aerials, perform circus acts, dance, and more. They will get upset if they have to sit still for long periods of time and have no movement. They will be athletes, builders, wrestlers, martial arts teachers, fitness coaches, soccer or basketball coaches, the trail guides, rangers, geologists, and any career that requires physical stamina.

Beauty and Arts

Others are motivated by beauty and arts; they're the artistic ones. They love playing dress-up, putting on cool hats, making beautiful designs in the margins of their notebooks, using a variety of paints or watercolors to come up with pretty paintings. They love beauty and all aspects of it – art, drama, music. They love the sound of music, and they love creating, designing, and making new things. They're motivated by a finished art piece. They will get upset if they have to follow someone else's ideas frequently and aren't given the chance to create their own pieces. They won't like to wear rough, mismatched or ugly clothes. They will be the world's artists, musicians, designers, sculpturers, innovators, creators, directors, music conductors, make-up artists, actors/ actresses, and any career built on beauty and art.

Riches

They love collecting things, like baseball cards or Pokémon cards, or having a ton of little crafty items, erasers, or *spinny* toys. They'll take the gifts out of other people's party bags at a birthday party and place it in their backpacks or hands; they'll have little toys and gadgets they hang on to. They like shiny things like gems, crystals, chocolate gold, and fake money, and having the more expensive, high-quality dress or fabric. They love soft, luxurious blankets and teddy bears, the latest gadgets, tech gear, dolls, or toys that everyone has. They love shopping for new things and get bored by their existing toys. They will get upset if their toys are old, falling apart, or if they don't get the latest gadgets, and if you throw their valuable collections out. They will be the real-estate agents, accountants, investors, employers, financial analysts, doctors, investment bankers, lawyers, and any career that makes them wealthy.

Renunciation

This is a tricky one to understand but it's basically the opposite of wealth. These are the kids who may not care for their new clothes, who don't care to put them away, who are okay to be alone in a good way, who are proud of how much they don't have or don't need. A little boy once told me, "I have a small bed and I'm happy with it." Their backpacks are sparse; they don't like filling them up with a ton of extras. They're minimalists, neat and tidy, and they don't like to accumulate things. Their areas are usually organized, with just a few things there; they don't like to save things from the past, and they don't like to hold on to stuff, either physical things or emotional mental things. They get upset with clutter and mess, with waste, with their days packed with too much to do. They will be life coaches, developers, human resource managers, spiritual guides and visionaries, and they look beyond the physical.

F.L.O.W.

Do you see your child fitting into a few of the above categories? What areas can you develop? What is your child naturally inclined to and what areas are they motivated by (without the stickers, rewards, and ego boosts)?

Now you will learn the process to help your child discover what they're motivated by, and what their purpose is with the F.L.O.W. process below. It's pretty simple.

The steps are:

- F – Find It
- L – Let Them Be
- O – Offer Opportunities
- W – Witness Wonderful Magic

F – Find It

Watch your child. What are they showing? What are they engrossed in? What do they love doing? What are they really good at doing? What gives them an internal feeling of contentment and competence? Write out your list. Every time you see your child working on something, absorbed in something, make an actual note of it (not just a mental note).

Victoria's mom shared that Victoria's head is always in a science book. At her sixth birthday party, she explained the physics behind the balloons floating down at the end of the day. *Which little kid talks about physics,* Victoria's mom thought. Here was a good observation of her child's proclivities.

My own son Nitai loved taking things apart at age four. He loves working with his hands. All throughout his childhood, he went from mastering card tricks, to origami, to solving all these different types of Rubik's cubes, to building his 3D printer and racing drone when he was thirteen. He is in college now studying to be an electrical engineer, and it makes so much sense! His "purpose" was apparent because of how many *flow* activities he was engaged in as a kid.

Rose's dad shares that she gathers all the shawls, and fancy clothes in the house and stands in front of a mirror. She becomes different characters, using voices and mannerisms of everyone she knows. In front of the world, she's super shy, so you'll never see her doing it outside her bedroom, but her dad's observing, and he notices where she's in *flow*. This will lead to a deeper understanding of her purpose.

Albert is a people person. He brings all his friends together, and loves hanging out. He's always got one arm on a friend, talking, making them feel good. If there's an argument, he'll be right there helping out, fixing the problems. If a friend doesn't come to school, he'll worry. He'll be able to tell you what everyone was up to in class and will always want to hang out with friends. His friends listen to what he's saying, even though he's young. He's going to be a manager or mediator when he grows up.

All these parents found their child's flow states and their purpose being developed. What have you found with your child?

L – Let Them Be

Don't disturb their process when they're right in the middle of it. Don't correct them while they're in the middle of it. If they're struggling a little, lean back, not forward. Let them figure it out and let them discover their strength in this. Be the cheerleader but don't get into correcting it or taking it over. It's okay if it's not perfect.

Don't even jump in to say, "oh wow, good job!" Even a simple "good job" can get them out of flow state and drop them into extrinsically being motivated by "ego protection" as they think: *Oh, I'm being watched, I have to do this better.*

A little boy brought home a science fair project he was working on and upon going home, his mom took one look at it, and decided to redo the whole thing. She bought a new board, and yes, she laid it out very beautifully, but what did the young boy learn? He absolutely loved science, but he learned he wasn't good enough, that his work wasn't memorable. He definitely didn't want to do that cutting and pasting again. That mom was me, and that boy was my older son. He told me a few years later that he didn't appreciate when I redid his whole science board in first grade.

One student in first grade was completing a historical figures project. She cut and pasted all kinds of papers on it, and man, to my adult eyes, it was just one big mess. Pieces were falling off; there was just so much she wanted to place on there and not enough room!

"Why can't she be neater?" her mom asked me.

"Let's just wait," I responded. Sure enough, three years later, she's doing the same massive projects with grand big ideas and tons of paper, but she has learned all by herself, just by practice, to fold them, and glue them, and create masterpieces of cut-paper art. The quality is like night and day. We adults in her life didn't unnecessarily criticize or correct her. Her purpose was being discovered by every movement.

Just leave them alone and let them engage in purpose. If you want to sit with them and do it with them, that's fine but on their time. Don't step in to criticize or correct it. Just let them be.

LIFELONG SEARCH FOR PURPOSE

A decade ago, I met two doctors for dinner. They were gushing, "Oh Gopi, you're so accomplished! You've started schools. You make an actual impact. You're living your dreams and fulfilling your purpose! How did you get there?"

I was surprised to hear this. My field is education, not medicine, and growing up in an Asian family, medicine was more recognized than education. How were these doctors recognizing my accomplishments over theirs? Basically, during my entire childhood, I had many family and community members question me about the type of doctor I was going to be. Though I had been accepted into Duke University School of Medicine, I realized it was only because of societal pressure, and I wanted to be an educator. Luckily my dad supported me. He accepted me for who I was and encouraged me to find my purpose – do what makes you happy.

So, hearing these two accomplished doctors recognize my achievements as an educator was humbling and surprising! One was an accomplished M.D. at a children's hospital; she was the doctor that T.V. news turned to during the pandemic, during any health crises. The other one had opened her own natural health clinic serving the entire Dallas Lakewood area. Both were extremely successful in my eyes.

I decided: *Hmm. Let me ask them about their journeys.* What makes them feel that I'm so accomplished, when clearly, they seem to be so much more than me! I went out on a limb and asked a simple: "You've done years of hard work to get where you are. If you had to do it all again, would you?"

Their answer was strong and powerful. Both of them, immediately, without hesitation, said, "No way."

They are both extremely creative. They felt they lost their twenties in chasing other people's dreams. They were keenly looking for their purpose. They wanted to satisfy that internal need – the middle point of the three circles. Yes, two circles may be met, the one of "doing what you're really good at, and doing something that you feel massive achievement in," but what of the third circle – "do what makes you intrinsically happy?"

The whole conversation was so eye-opening. Help your child discover their purpose earlier and they won't spend their twenties and thirties still trying to figure it out. Give them this gift of time, won't you? Start now. They will be able to fulfill others' needs so much better, if their own need for purpose is fulfilled and identified early on.

O – Offer Opportunities

Once you've found the areas your child is absorbed in, and you're letting them be, start offering them opportunities. This process will go on for a few years. It's easy these days – there's no lack of toys, gadgets, and extracurricular activities – the sky is the limit!

Remember the six motivators? Offer your child opportunities in the areas you see they're attracted by.

Wisdom

Get them science documentaries. *How It's Made* was a favorite in our house. Fill up a few shelves with informative library books or good series to read as they get older. Bring in a science and social studies books, full of facts. Get them science kits, with lab coats and scientific glasses. Teach them how to cook, sew, and knit; basically, these kids just love learning and will eat it all up! Have them make their own how-to videos on things they're learning to do and draw out charts and models for them to implement things to do in the home.

Recognition

Let them make YouTube videos. Take pictures of dressing up. Get them acting on a stage. Have them work with bigger groups and compete in competitions. Place them in positions leading younger siblings or younger friends. When they play, they'll be the teacher, or the mom, or the boss. Take them to work for a day and introduce them to all your colleagues. Talk about them when you're with your colleagues or extended family. Let them give speeches, present songs and poetry publicly, and give them many opportunities to do so.

Beauty & Arts

Buy them soft clothes, luxurious blankets, sets of paints, acrylics, glitter pens, markers, and colored papers. Let them draw/ color beautiful pictures. Let them make crystals and gem sets. They may be interested in knitting, sewing, cross-stitch (even boys!), painting, and more. There's a ton of $5 kits at Michael's for children to engage in. Have a home salon day, where they can put yogurt and oatmeal on their faces. Make a kid's tea party for their friends, where they dress up. Read them stories of kings and queens from bygone eras. Teach them music, singing, and an instrument. Get them to dance, act, play, and laugh a lot.

Strength

Build a tree house with them! Have a climbing gym or playground in your backyard. Put a ladder up against one side of the house and show them how to come down safely. (Even if you don't put that ladder up there, these kids will be climbing up to your roof.) Keep a step ladder in the kitchen when they're young, as they're just going to climb and climb. Have them help you move boxes, have them mow the lawn for the neighbors, and ask them to help you bring the groceries in or the trash out. Take them to Little Gym, Jump Street, Ziplining, let them climb trees, and more. They're physical and they need tons of movement. Most of the time, if they're bugging you, it's because they just need to get that physical energy out. I would stop two blocks away from home when my boys were small, and they would hop out of the car and race me home, on foot, with me driving the car very slow. This was so fun as they would see if they could go faster than each other or faster than me. Kids who love strength are builders and tinkerers. Whether it be their fine motor skills being developed with tubs of Lego blocks, or their gross motor skills with soccer, basketball or tennis, give them plenty of opportunities to develop these physical abilities.

Riches

Get them fake coins and money and teach them the difference between a penny, dime, nickel, and quarter and have them learn to add it up early. Take them to the store with you and have them estimate how much everything will cost. Give them a piggy bank to save up for cool things. Help them open a lemonade stand in the summer (or hot chocolate in the winter). Kids who are motivated by riches will find their own way. One boy was selling fidget spinners to all his neighbors. Another would sell decorated paper cups and spoons in school for 10 cents a piece. Encourage that and give them more opportunities. Buy them luxurious things – soaps, lotions, and candles, and make sure their room looks fluffy and decorated. Teach them how to donate their wealth to others (do a toy drive at Christmas time). Just observe what they're motivated by and give them opportunities to do more of it in a different way.

Renunciation

These kids are minimalists and love nature. They love Ikea! Get them furniture that's clean lined. Get them containers to organize their items in, with labels for everything. Let them play in nature and build things from organic natural materials. Don't overwhelm them at gift time – let them choose their gifts or make their own gifts for others. They like to put things away in the right spot, so encourage them to do that. They don't like to hold on to old clothes so tidy up their drawers every summer and winter. They are self-sustaining – they like to be in control of their environments so give them a snack drawer and let them figure out how to make their own breakfasts and meals if needed. They don't like to be overly dependent on others as internally and externally they're minimalists and don't have that many needs to throw on others.

No Comparisons or Criticisms

As you're offering opportunities, make sure to avoid comparisons or criticisms. The fastest way to reduce a child's inner sense of purpose is to criticize them for something they're doing. I've spoken of this a few times in past chapters, but it is so important that it warrants saying it again. A child who's discovering their purpose in this new space of life is tentatively seeing if that's going to work out. If during that process, we criticize them, or worse still, compare them to another, that's going to suck them right back into not trying to live their fullest. As humans we already have tons of fears of living our best most creative lives – fears delineated so expertly in Elizabeth Gilbert's book *Big Magic*. For you to help your child develop that space of *Big Magic*, of living their full purpose, allow them to surpass those fears. Even if it doesn't make sense to you in that moment, keep encouraging them and giving them opportunities, and it will unfold naturally and automatically.

Every day, every week, every month, every semester, think: is my child doing things they enjoy doing? And are they discovering what they're good at?

Minimize Screen Time

Unfortunately, while screen time does offer powerful educational opportunities, learning through the screen is inferior to learning through actual physical, spatial activities and personal interaction. I don't recommend completely eradicating screens because children do need to be technologically savvy, but it is very important for their growing brains to limit the time spent. It's okay if kids are bored – what they figure out to engage themselves in during their boredom is key to them identifying their purpose. Enforce regulated screen time and limit it as much as possible.

W – Witness Wonderful Magic Every Day

Watching children living in their purpose is beautiful. When a child is so truly in their element, they know who they are in those minutes; they know what they're meant to do, and they confidently go and do it – that is purpose. Perhaps it's not a mind-blowing career at that point of making $160,000 as an adult in purpose would be experiencing, but they have plenty of moments every single day. You, as their parent, need to recognize their moments. Go ahead, witness it, watch it, and feel the wonderful magic of it – and your child will as well.

In the classroom, a little girl whispers in my ears quietly about a little story she has drawn and "written," dictating it to me as I write the words on her drawings. No, they don't look much like the thing she is describing, but oh, how joyous to hear her confidence and sense of accomplishment after a full hour of being absorbed. To her, this story is everything and she's so proud of it.

The six-year-old who has come into the classroom after fall break made a whole book with thirty pages of an ancient story on Krishna. Yes, it was messy, the staples were falling off, the spelling wasn't perfect, but wow, how dedicated he must have been to write that whole thing on his own. He was living in his purpose, and I acknowledge this little author.

These days my teenage boys have been in a state of flow. Because Mommy is busy writing a book, they make their own plans for our dinner. I don't even have to ask. They made pasta and sauce and broccoli today. They attend college full-time. They play music in their downtime. They get side jobs. They do the chores here and there, without me asking. Life is on autopilot; each of us fulfilling our dreams every day, and I get to be the witness. They join me in the areas that align with their purpose, meditation through music and mentoring in our online leadership classes. We all engage in the flow of bhakti and the flow of purpose.

As I'm writing this chapter, I had an interesting experience. I've been stuck on the chapter, playing with the ideas for a while. One Saturday evening, I was listening to music, and trying to push past my writer's block again. My boys, hearing the music from my laptop came to join me on the couch. The twenty-year-old grabbed his guitar, and the seventeen-year-old his flute. Without any words, they began playing music to accompany what I was listening to. As I saw them absorb themselves, entering the state of *flow,* my thoughts automatically began to pour out.

Playing musical instruments and singing is a big part of my life, and I've secretly always wanted my children to play. But they didn't show much interest when they were younger. So I didn't force them to take classes. Now, however, they play just for the sake of it. Not for external recognition, but for the sheer enjoyment of playing. Watching them totally in the zone, playing to the music on my laptop, in a state of flow, on either side of me – was so powerful that this entire chapter emerged from their state of flow. My own flow was discovered while seeing their flow.

Your child will get there. I promise. Just follow these steps and you too will witness this wonderful magic each day.

SAINT GAURA'S PURPOSE

Saint Gaura also showed his life's purpose when he was a child. He incarnated to establish a mantra meditation in the form of song as a means of sharing love. He loved singing and had a powerful voice, which strengthened people's hearts. As an adult, he held concerts all throughout India, bringing millions together. All the Sanskrit mantras I have introduced to you were shared by him. He was expert in playing a variety of instruments and wanted to bring people together through transcendental sound. Today, this singing and dancing is practiced worldwide as "kirtan" a form of *mantra* meditation. When many together celebrate pure love and connect to divinity through mantra songs, it is known as *sankirtan* or collaborative joyous service.

He displayed his mission and purpose throughout his childhood, as you will see your child do as well. When he was a baby, his parents would sing out loud to get him to stop crying. It worked every time. When they would stop singing the *mantra* he would start crying again.

When he was in school, he would take his friends out to the playground, gather them together and make music.

And when at sixteen, he opened his own school, he turned the logic lessons into song, incorporating the mantra hymns and Indian tunes to make them melodious.

A little later, he held music sessions in a friend's home in the evenings and throughout the night. Only a select few were allowed. He sang with his heart, and everyone did as well.

As an adult, he took the song and dance to the streets, creating street parades and festivals with beautiful Sanskrit words floating around for everyone to hear. He spread love (*bhakti*) to all through these outdoor performances. This purpose that he had was always present in different ways in his childhood.

In summary, remember, fortifying your child's purpose means meeting their three needs. It means seeing that they know the answers to these three questions:

- What makes me totally internally connected and happy? (need of connection fulfilled)
- What am I really good at doing? (need of free will fulfilled)
- What can I bring to completion and feel a sense of achievement in? (need of achievement fulfilled)?

Once you start noticing their moments of flow, and you discover their purpose, you'll be impressed by their internal confidence. Because their three needs are met, they can help others develop their purpose. We will learn how they do this in the next chapter. Let's go!

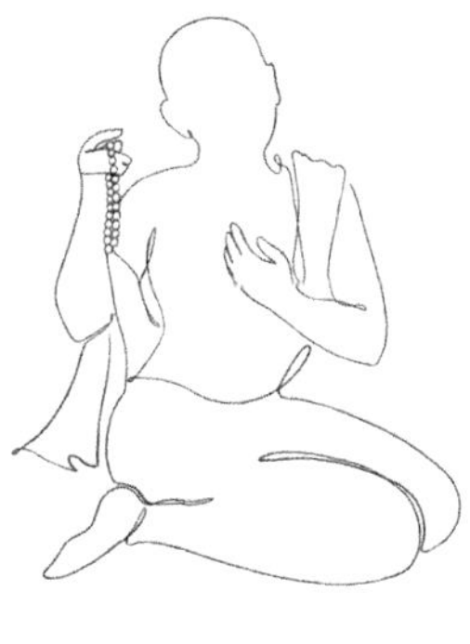

* * *

Mantra Affirmations Level 8: I Motivate

* * *

The primary quality in Part 5: The Leadership Space is humility. It takes humility for you to allow your child's purpose to arise, and not force your idea of who and what they're meant to be, and it will take humility to journey to the next levels until you get to the Garden of Harmony.

The mantra introduced now is a combination of energizing all three needs, as a child in the flow of purpose is activating all three needs: connection, free will, and achievement. Therefore, we use all three energizing mantra words. *Krishna* (energizes connection), *Hare* (energizes free will), and *Rama* (energizes achievement).

The mantra I introduce to you now will be the same mantra used for the rest of the book. It is known as the *maha-mantra* or greatest of all *mantras* and is the most powerful mantra introduced in ancient *bhakti, Vedic* and Hindu texts. You may have even heard of it. It has many meanings when placed in this specific combination. The meaning for today's meditation is, dear Divine Inner Parents, activate within us the purpose of our existence here.

hare krishna hare krishna
krishna krishna hare hare
hare rama hare rama
rama rama hare hare
Let me meet my child's core needs.
Let me find purpose in every one of their activities.
Let their F.L.O.W. manifest in service.
I notice their absorption. I give opportunities. I am excited.
I fulfill my purpose as a leadership parent.

12

HOW CAN THEY FEEL FOR OTHERS?

> *"Leadership is about empathy. It is about having the ability to relate to and connect with people for the purpose of inspiring and empowering their lives."*
>
> — OPRAH WINFREY

Now that your child knows who they are with their flow activities settled, they can start thinking about the needs of others. In this chapter, we climb to the next level of EMPOWERMENT, the third letter "E." You will begin seeing powerful leadership experiences emerge after this chapter.

* * *

Level 9: Encourage Their Empathy

* * *

If a child's needs are not met, and they still display frequent bouts of upset and loneliness and disturbance, it will be difficult to guide them toward empathy, so it's very important that you make sure the other processes in the book are followed first. Their physiological and social needs must be met first because only then can they begin to think of the needs of others. Asking a hungry child to share a popsicle or a piece of pizza isn't fair to them. Asking an angry child to be kind is an unreasonable request. However, a child whose overall communication needs are met, who's feelings are valued, who's given the benefit of the doubt, who's engaged in meaningful tasks, and who's compassionately expected to hold boundaries will begin to show empathy and compassion even in trying circumstances.

I frequently see leadership kids displaying empathy even when they're upset. Though it is not something to be forced upon a child or instructed, it will emerge naturally when their needs are met. Don't say, "Say you're sorry. Take care of their feelings!" As a parent, you do not need to instruct your child to show compassion. Children whose hearts are filled with love will show empathy and kindness to others naturally. Empathy is a natural state of maturity, past the stage of egocentrism. (Many adults haven't even fully entered empathy, so be patient with your child.)

One day in the classroom, little Robert was sitting down at his desk. He was so engrossed in his creative work that he didn't realize that he'd taken over the entire desk, encroaching on Carl's space. A little annoyed, Carl moved his chair into Robert's space, saying "Hey, you're in my spot!" The leg of Carl's chair smashed right on Roberts's foot. Robert yelled, and fell to the floor, holding his foot. As he fell dramatically to the floor, the scissors in his hand flew out and hit Carl in the nose.

As I rushed to help, I noticed there was no blood coming from either of them, but both had hurt feelings and slightly hurt bodies (the handle of the scissors had hit Carl's nose, not the pointy part). Though Robert's screams were literally reverberating throughout the classroom, suddenly he looked up and stopped mid-scream, noticing he hurt Carl too. He paused and said, "Oh, Carl, I'm so sorry. Did you get hurt too?"

There was true and natural empathy, in its most raw state. This boy was six and his empathy softened Carl, who came over to help Robert.

How were they able to do that? I struggle with this even as an adult! This is the beginning of leadership and the process I share in this chapter will help you get there with yours.

The first thing that I must say is that every single one of the processes I've shared so far in this book are vital. Harvard educators stress that a child who lives in an environment of empathy will be able to show empathy to others. If you follow the process of H.E.A.R in Chapter 6, and L.O.V.E in Chapter 7, and avoid like the plague sentences that are R.E.J.E.C.T.I.O.N, and continue on with A.C.C.E.P.T and R.E.S.T, you can be assured that you are raising a child full of empathy. Empathy arises after one's internal needs for connection, free will, and achievement are met. Empathy arises if one feels empathy themselves. Empathy is a required prerequisite for leadership.

If you'd like to continue encouraging direct empathy and love toward others, here are some simple things to be aware of.

THINKING + EMOTION + LOVE = EMPATHY

Bhakti texts define empathy as "feeling the pains and joys of others as your own." Basically, empathy is the Golden Rule, "do unto others as you would have them do unto you." Here I present a simplified understanding of the concept shared in ancient texts.

Beyond our physical body lies the mind, the intelligence, and our core identity – the soul. Each of us are an eternal soul. The soul resides in our heart and experiences pure love with the Inner Parents (*paramatma*) a.k.a. the Universe, God, The Divine, Nature, etc. This spiritual relationship between the soul and the Inner Parents is the source of pure emotion (*bhava*) and pure love (*prema*). It manifests as "I feel, I love." Once a soul experiences true connection with the Inner Parents, that love can be so powerful, that it can spread to all living beings around. Martin Luther King understood this with his firm commitment to brotherhood. "We must all learn to live together as brothers."

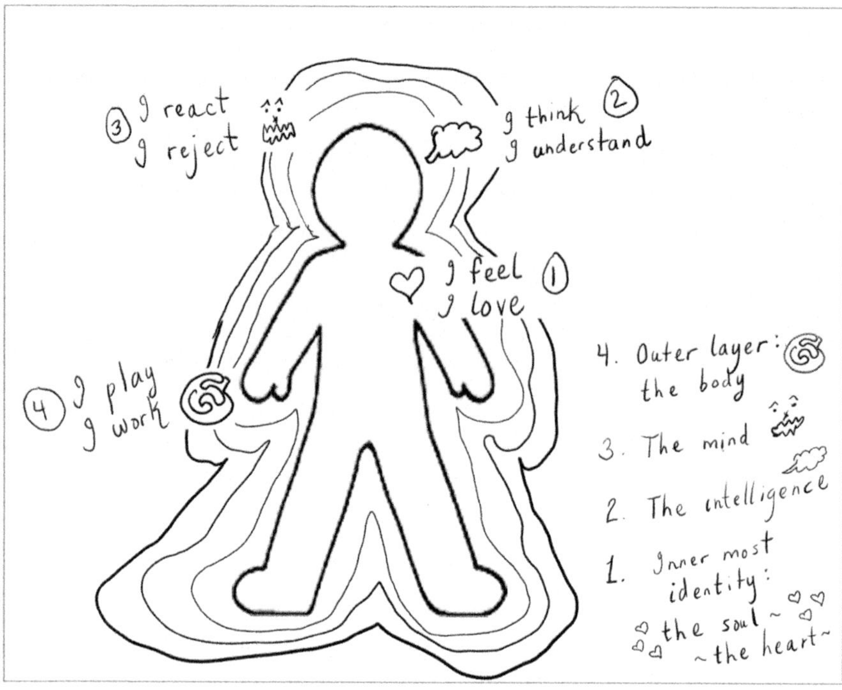

The outer layer around the soul is intelligence. Intelligence translates the feelings and love of the soul into cognition and thoughts. Why do I feel this? How can I experience love in my external spaces?

The layer around the intelligence is the mind. The mind is a machine, programmed by experiences. It tries to make sense of the core feelings of the soul and the thoughts of the intelligence and translates that into behaviors that the body acts on.

Many religious philosophies promote thoughts as more important than emotion, which must be rejected to attain spiritual perfection. However, this couldn't be farther from the truth. On *The Ellen Show* in April of 2022, Brene Brown summed this up expertly, "We so desperately want to believe that we're cognitive thinking beings who on occasion get inconvenienced by emotion. This is not true. We're emotional beings who on occasion think."

Why is this important to know? Because children are more in touch with their emotions and their cognition is developing, they can show and share empathy more easily. This does not mean they are dumb. It means they can be more heart-centered and show care for others easily.

By understanding this, you can learn to reach their thinking spaces, and their deeper emotion spaces. The goal is touching their pure love space, where they can share and show love to everyone. This spiritual space of universal empathy is the very heart of the *bhakti* path. With careful nurturing, children can get there quicker than adults.

You will do this with the F.E.E.L. process:

- F –Fortify their core needs
- E – Encourage their thinking
- E – Encourage emotions that lead to empathy
- L – Love unconditionally

F – FORTIFY THEIR CORE NEEDS

As I mentioned, follow all the previous processes in this book before you jump too quickly into asking your child to show empathy. If there is an altercation and your child needs to see that they're at fault and apologize, make sure you follow the process of H.E.A.R., or A.C.C.E.P.T. before you ask them to apologize. Take time to hear and meet their needs first. I can't stress this enough. A child who's struggling with empathy is one who hasn't experienced empathy enough yet. Then, you can gently encourage empathy in him.

E – ENCOURAGE THEIR THINKING

For a child to become empathetic, they need to know how to think about another's experience. So first, they need to learn how to think about their own experiences and strengthen their cognitive thinking processes. The more you encourage it, they will be able to understand things larger than them.

Start by respecting their thoughts. They love to think, don't they?

Their *why's* can drive us mad. They have such deep questions; they question life, the universes, and even mortality.

Here are some statements to encourage their thinking.

- "That's an interesting way to look at it."
- "Thank you for sharing your perspective."
- "I never thought about it that way."
- "How do you know so much about this topic?"
- "That sounds like something you're really interested in."
- "Sounds like you have come to an understanding of the situation."

When you say these types of sentences, they may respond with another thought. "So, you're figuring it out. You're realizing its deeper than you initially thought." Keep being open to their thoughts.

A simple example: A student kept having to sharpen his pencil every three seconds. An inexperienced adult in the room asked, "Hey, why are you wasting so much time with the sharpener?"

The child came up with a serious problem, "It just keeps breaking."

The inexperienced adult responded, "Are you lying? Are you just trying to distract the other kids or waste time?"

This is a typical response adults give to children. I call the boy over and just state a fact about what he's doing. "You're needing to sharpen your pencil a lot, huh?" He gets a respectful, non-judgmental space to explain what's going on.

He says, "Yes, Mother Gopi Gita, it just keeps breaking! The lead keeps falling out!"

I respond simply with, "Oh that's frustrating. You're having to resharpen it because the pencil lead is breaking?"

I literally just reinforced the thought he had. With my simple sentence, I acknowledge him, his environment, and his thought processes. He responds.

"Maybe I'm pressing too hard when I'm writing. Maybe I have to press less."

Voila, he came up with the solution himself. "That's a good idea," I respond.

There was no need for him to be berated. Fixing it was a simple step: encourage his thoughts.

Each Question and Resulting Thought Is A Gift of Discovery

Another more powerful way to answer their questions is to turn it back to them, lovingly and respectfully. "Why do you think that is so?" Let them know that their thoughts are respected (yes, even when they're asking the same question again and again and it's driving you mad). "Why do *you* think the sky is blue?" When they're stuck, say, "let's look it up." Yes, you may already know the answer but give them a chance to discover the answer themselves.

I see each question a child asks as a delicious gift. Remember at Christmas time, the excitement of unwrapping the gifts? Having someone else unwrap it for you is cool, yes, but nowhere near as if you're discovering it yourself. Having children discover their solutions through their thoughts is like that. They get to feel confident in understanding the world around them. They get to feel empowered as problem solvers.

Dad Asks the Questions

Scott Sampson shares a perfect example of this in his book, *How to Raise a Wild Child*.

"One day while Jade and I were out walking near our home in California, she spotted a tall bird sitting perfectly motionless in a clearing adjacent to the creek. 'What kind of bird is it?' she queried.

"My strong inclination was to blurt out the answer, particularly since it was one of my favorites, a great blue heron. Instead, I turned it back to her. 'What kind of bird do you think it is?' She thought for a moment and came back with, 'Maybe a heron. I'm not sure.'

'Great idea,' was my response. 'Let's sit here and watch it for a while.'

And so we did. 'Why do they have those long beaks?' I asked.

'For catching critters,' was Jade's quick reply.

'So what do you think it's doing now?'

'Maybe hunting,' came her response.

'What do you think it's hunting for?'

'I dunno. Probably rodents.'

Sure enough, within a couple of minutes, the heron performed its classic slow-motion head bow, as if in solemn prayer, followed by a lightning-strike jab at the ground. When it rose up again, it held some kind of small mammal firmly in its beak.

'I was right. It's got a rodent!'

We watched as the giant bird skillfully maneuvered its prey within the jaws and then swallowed it whole, the neck contorting as the animal passed down the gullet. Fascinated, we stayed long enough to watch two repeat performances, as the heron depleted the clearing of its rodent population. When we got home, Jade immediately grabbed one of the bird books and paged through it until she found the correct entry. 'Look, Daddy, that bird *was* a heron. A great blue heron!'"

E – ENCOURAGE EMOTIONS THAT LEAD TO EMPATHY

The H.E.A.R. process you've already learned helps your child wade past the superficiality of blame, accusations, and mind-emotions and brings them deeper to their needs. You also learned the importance of compassionate boundaries (Chapter 8) where even if they're expressing their emotions, the standards and expectations you have set do not change. You can compassionately accept them while staying firm on what is expected. In Chapter 9, you learned the A.C.C.E.P.T. process, how to work with a child through mistakes (theirs and yours). All of these processes bring out their empathy. We will add to them with I Statements.

I Statements

Teach your child to communicate their feelings directly through I statements. Instead of "You did this. They did that!" teach them to say, "I feel." Identifying how they feel takes away the blame on others and gives them control of the environment.

- Instead of "That kid stole my stuff," say "I can't find my things."
- Instead of "You hurt me," they can say, "I feel hurt by *the action that caused it*."
- Instead of "I hate you!" say "I need some space right now."
- Instead of "They're horrible and mean," they can say, "I'm feeling really hurt by them."
- Instead of "You're never coming to my house again!" they can say, "I need some space from you!"

Stepping into Empathy

Empathy is called "perspective-taking" in psychology, literally seeing the world from someone else's perspective. When you read together, watch stuff, or interact in the world, ask these kinds of questions to get your child to see other's perspectives.

- If you were that person, what would you do? How would you feel?
- How do you think they feel about this?

- If someone wanted to help, what do you think could help them?
- Would you do something different in that situation?
- Even ask about the antagonists, the bad characters, the criminals in the news story, the angry vengeful hateful people: Why do you think they're acting that way? What could be wrong for them?

Sometimes there's an altercation and your child is at fault, and yet isn't able to see that. In this scenario, make sure you listen plenty to the full story. After your child has been heard and understood, when they have calmed down, you can start leading them to think of the other person or people in the scenario. If you try to bring in the other person's perspective too soon, in an attempt to force empathy on your child, it's not fair. Remember, your child *is* naturally an empathetic soul, and their friend is too, and hold this conversation with respect.

This conversation might sound like: "Your feelings are important. Your feelings are natural and normal. I accept you." (Once the child has calmed down and feels totally loved), "Can we take a minute to think of the other person's feelings? Why do you think they are acting that way?" Or, "You know you really love that friend, and they hurt you bad. Do you know why they may have acted like that – because I know you really do like them."

Remember, empathy is walking in another's shoes. Have these conversations every single day with your child. Let them think of the world in a lens that includes everyone and not just themselves.

Importance of Diversity

It is important to place our children in environments where not everyone is like them so they can develop their empathy. Different cultures have different styles of communication – sometimes completely opposite to our own! For example, in collectivistic cultures, being precisely on time to social functions is seen as rude, whereas in many individualistic cultures, being late is considered rude! In some cultures, looking right at a person when they're talking is expected, but in others it's considered too direct and disrespectful. It is so important that our children know that their way of doing something isn't the only way. One amazing perk of living in America is how many races, colors, creeds, nationalities and genders there are. By having your child just hang out with friends of the same race, you're limiting their ability for empathy.

A friend of mine placed her child in a school where deaf children also learned side by side. I found that eye-opening. Her whole cohort of doctors at the local hospital placed their children in this school. Seeing other children who didn't look or act exactly like them opened them up to accepting differences and seeing it as a norm. My own sons were blessed by a friend who had spina bifida and was wheelchair-bound. Their own father (my husband) was wheelchair bound for many years and struggled with cancer and neuropathy; when my son's own hospital time came, they weren't shaken by it. They saw different ways of living early on. This deepened their empathy.

It is natural to seek out those who are just like yourself, to want to spend time with those who are similar to you. There's nothing wrong with it. But if we are to encourage leaders, we must be okay to go out of our comfort zone and our children must learn to understand and empathize with those who are different than them.

Saint Gaura and the "Untouchables"

In the fifteenth and sixteenth centuries in Southeast Asia, the caste system was firmly established and in place in India. Saint Gaura did not appreciate the distinction between humans as high and low, rich and poor, kings and paupers. He promoted the eternal philosophy of love – all humans are equal. The spirit soul is equal to every other spirit soul. Just because each human has a different set of circumstances than others, doesn't mean that one is better than the other. Indeed, did you know that those who live most modestly in the country of Bangladesh are considered the happiest, even compared to rich Americans? Money or luxury or social prosperity does not equate happiness, and likewise – it does not make someone better than another.

Saint Gaura preached so vehemently against discrimination. This philosophy was highly controversial, and he was rejected by strict priests but he continued preaching his important message of universal brotherhood.

There is a very famous ancient temple in Orissa where the Deity Lord Jagannath is worshipped. Even to this day, non-Hindus are not allowed to enter. Saint Gaura fought against this standard. Right outside the temple he welcomed the street sweepers, the cleaners, the maids – the class in India known as the untouchables. He derided this term given to a whole class of society. Pure love is shared for all, and he eagerly, personally interacted with and embraced them, speaking to them, sharing love and eating at their homes.

So rigid were the rules of his time that those who were considered outcastes but were taking up "higher class" statuses because of their empowerment by Saint Gaura were severely tortured. One of his followers was beaten in thirty-two marketplaces; one was thrown in jail. Still, they believed so firmly in Saint Gaura's philosophy of universal brotherhood that they stayed strong. Saint Gaura protected them and predicted an international society where every town and village in the world would be swept with universal brotherhood and love.

If you, dear parent, who are already serving in leadership, are to make a real impact in your life and with your child, encouraging your child to look beyond the externals and reach for friendships with all, you will need to place your child in a diverse environment to increase their empathy.

Now we reach the last step of the F.E.E.L. process.

L – LOVE UNCONDITIONALLY

Feeling empathy for another means expressing love – pure, unselfish, unadulterated love for others, beyond the love we can experience ourselves. Love is not just a feeling. Love is an action word. Your child needs to see that your love is action – not just a word or a thought. We, parents express love in many ways, and all of that fortifies their ability to empathize. You probably make their breakfast in the morning, their bagged lunches, comb their hair, do their laundry, fold their clothes, clean out their backpacks, make their beds, buy them new clothes, and organize their toys. All these activities are acts of love that a child sees every day. These acts can be done with a smile, with a beautiful thought of your child engaging with all the items, without the frustration and tiredness that accompanies parenthood as we have to do all these chores.

Spend undivided attention with them few minutes a day or longer a few times a week. My first teacher had a boarding school, with students living with her. Although she was so busy – running a school, writing, a mom, and more – she spent at least thirty minutes of undivided attention with each child in her care. I remember being in awe about that.

Make your time with your children fun! It doesn't have to be productive. Cuddle, playfight, pillow fight, sing songs, dance throughout the house, play hide-and-seek, read, go on walks, and more. You'll find that the more time you spend with them happy, their sadness will go away quicker when it comes. They'll remember your presence when they get in a fight and you're not around, and they'll be able to think about another's feelings more quickly.

Let them learn that love is an action. We hold the door open for people, we cook for our family, we work hard for the people we love. We sacrifice for those we love. Show it. Give them water. Lay in bed with them. Put them to sleep. Write thank you notes. Get presents for their friend with them. Cook together. Basically, do things as actions together to show love.

Spiritual Love

At five, I was taken to the temple each morning. At the temple there were all kinds of worship ceremonies taking place. I could feel the superior beings and their divine presence in the temple room. I loved singing Sanskrit hymns, really long ones that talked of the nature of the spiritual kingdom and all its magical beings and angels, and I loved knowing that I was one of them, only temporarily covered by the material sphere. A young child can very easily feel the strength of divinity. How easily they fall in love with even fictional characters – Santa Claus, the tooth fairy, Superman. Why not attach them to true reality, unending powerful absolute truth: the beings who have created this entire universe, who protect and maintain, who give us the light of the Moon, the stars in the sky, the waves in the ocean, and the perfect whorl and scent of a rose.

Love means reaching that spiritual place and connecting with the Inner Parents. You can do this through mantra meditation with your child. Make your spiritual practice with your child as important as brushing your teeth or eating as a family. With these spiritual practices, you want your child to feel that they are never alone. If – God forbid – something were to happen to you, or to someone around them, give them the fortitude that they are spiritual beings, guided and taken care of by a higher power than you, and that they will be safe and okay. These fortifying meditative practices will help their emotional state.

Here's a list of twenty other activities that can encourage your child's empathy.

Activities that Encourage Empathy

- Having adult friends over for family dinners
- Having your child's friends over for playdates
- Serving meals regularly at a soup kitchen, shelter, or event
- Volunteering at a shelter that serves the homeless and underserved
- Traveling out of state to other cities, states, and countries
- Visiting and living in a third world country for some time
- Volunteering at a church, mosque, temple, community center
- Being a coach for soccer, football, basketball
- Bringing cookies or baked goods for your child's classroom friends and teachers
- Organizing and celebrating events for others – graduations, birthday parties, anniversaries, etc.
- Visiting a farm with protected animals – cows, chickens, pigs, etc.
- Taking care of an injured animal – bird, squirrel, opossum, cat, dog, etc.
- Volunteering at a farm or nature reserve

- Owning and caring for a pet
- Being a soothing ear for a friend who's crying
- Watering plants and feeding fish
- Helping around the house
- Bringing groceries in
- Holding the door open for others

You get the idea. Make empathy a part of the family lifestyle.

SAINT NITAI SHARING LOVE WHILE BLEEDING

In the beginning, Saint Gaura wouldn't sing the *mantras* in public, only behind closed doors. One day, his brother Saint Nitai was accosted by two gang leaders, Jagai and Madhai, as he was out and about in town. They were feared and notorious for hurting the neighborhood residents and pitched their tents close to Gaura and Nitai's part of town. They were usually drunk and stoned and got violent when under the influence. Women were requested to not go out alone, and definitely not at night, as they would be raped or molested. Even men would only travel in groups.

So sinful were these two, they accosted Saint Nitai. However, he felt great empathy for them. He felt deeply sad to see their suffering and how they were hurting others. He decided he wanted to change their hearts and bring them to spiritual consciousness. That evening, in the middle of Gaura's concert, he shared his heart to his brother.

"What is the point of all our spiritual hymns if we are unable to help those sinners who are truly suffering?"

Saint Gaura, seeing his compassion, responded, "Because a saint like you has already wished their deliverance, surely God will hear your prayers and save them. Today, we will sing outside, and proceed to their residence. Bring every follower of bhakti. Let our combined voices and magical *mantras* bring love to the hearts of even the gangsters."

Saint Nitai, beaming with gratitude, took a handful of people with him, but many cancelled out of fear. Nitai approached the gangsters. "Dear brothers, look, we're having a beautiful concert, why don't you join us." But the brothers felt that Nitai was being rude, – preaching his religion of bhakti, and *didn't he know who they were*. Angered, they threw a piece of a clay pot toward his face, which cut Nitai on the forehead, causing a severe gash. Blood began pouring from Nitai's head, and Jagai threatened to kill him. "How dare you disturb us! Who do you think you are?" They were about to hurt him further, but Saint Gaura heard the commotion and rushed there immediately.

It is described that peaceful Saint Gaura was so angered, the heavens indeed started thundering. He invoked the divine *chakra* – the disc weapon of fire, said to have only been used by the Gods. Gaura was ready to kill both gangsters right on the spot. The peaceful procession had turned into a bloodbath about to happen, with Saint Nitai on the ground holding his head in pain. On the one side were Jagai and Madhai with their band of gangsters brandishing weapons. On the other side, Saint Gaura with his arm raised holding the *chakra* weapon.

Feeling severe heat from the weapon and scared of this incredible show of might from Gaura, Jagai and Madhai realized it was stronger than all their weapons, and knelt to the ground in surrender, asking for forgiveness. They had met their match. But Saint Gaura didn't relent. He was fuming, about to release the *chakra* disk and decapitate them.

Nitai saw what his brother was about to do and very loudly, yelled,

"No! Show mercy, please!" He grabbed Gaura's hand and begged him to please stop. Saint Gaura wouldn't budge.

The discussion that ensued between Saint Nitai, with blood pouring out of his forehead and Saint Gaura, fuming in rage, is one of the most powerful conversations in the history of bhakti. It has been told and retold by hundreds of scholars and sung at festivals as a testament of grace. The way Jesus prayed for those who tied him up at the cross, "Forgive them, Father, they know not what they do." These were the exact words spoken by Saint Nitai in sweet Bengali language.

"They know not what they do, dear Gaura. Please don't punish them. Don't be angry. This incarnation of yours is to give love, no matter who the person, no matter what their sins. Not to punish sinners, but to redeem them with your love. Please be kind to them." For love, the principle of deep love, is always higher than fear, is always stronger than hate. And Saint Nitai was on a mission to prove this to the world, regardless of the personal sacrifice required.

After some time, Gaura was pacified. Jagai and Madhai were so surprised at this conversation – *how is this man who we were about to kill, looking out for our welfare?* They were touched deep within their hearts and decided to learn more about the bhakti faith. Soon, they too were singing with the saints, and considered saints themselves. Saint Nitai's desire had been fulfilled.

THIS WORLD NEEDS YOUR CHILD'S EMPATHY

Empathy, dear reader, is not only thinking of another's welfare when everything is fine and dandy. Empathy is taking pleasure in another's happiness and feeling sad when another is sad. Empathy is placing aside one's ego to take care of another. Someone with true empathy can think about others' pain even if they themselves are hurt. Because their self-confidence is beyond the mental and physical limitations of the body, they can care for other living beings, despite personal difficulties.

This type of empathy is required for leadership. Many leaders have exemplified this: Jesus Christ, St. Francis of Assisi, and more recently

Gandhi, Martin Luther King, and Mother Theresa. They led powerful movements of change and affected revolutions on a massive scale, while continuing to practice only love and nonviolence even to those who would hurt them.

You can cause this type of revolution through your child when they feel supported in their identities, their feelings, and feel deep spiritual love. You are the medium to bring them to that space. Surely, you have experienced putting others' needs in front of yours as part of your leadership responsibilities. You can impart those experiences to your child and bring out their empathy. When the child can care for those around them, they will become qualified for leadership.

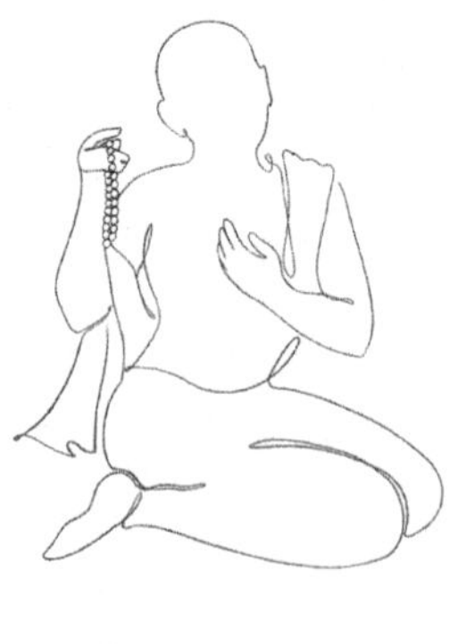

* * *

Mantra Affirmations Level 9: I Encourage

* * *

I'M WELL aware of how difficult it is for even us, as adults, to practice empathy in trying circumstances. *Think of someone else's pain when I'm in pain? Be like Martin Luther King?* What to speak of guiding our child in this, we ourselves may feel these expectations of leadership to be downright impossible.

For this reason, it is vital to add a meditation aspect to one's practice. Without the help of the Universe, Source, the Divine, God – or whatever you want to call the Supreme – it will be difficult to maintain true empathy for others.

The Inner Parents are the source of empathy. Here we meditate upon them to activate a child's emotions and thoughts and reach the core heart space where deep universal empathy resides. With a heart full of humility, you will recite the same *maha mantra* introduced earlier. This *maha mantra* will be our guide all the way to the Garden of Harmony.

You can recite it ten times. As you feel more connected to spiritual energy, you can increase your repetitions. Many clients at this stage recite it fifty-four times and try to do a full round of mantra meditation, which is 108 times.

hare krishna hare krishna
krishna krishna hare hare
hare rama hare rama
rama rama hare hare
Let me encourage my child's thoughts.
Allow me to encourage their internal empathy.
Let their empathy manifest love for all other beings.
I listen. I love. I guide them in leadership.

13

WHAT ABOUT THE CONFLICTS?

> "What the world needs for true happiness is a shift from exploitation to service, arrogance to humility, selfish cruelty to compassion and hatred to love. Preserving loving relationships in this world requires forgiveness, tolerance, patience, gratitude and humility."
>
> — RADHANATH SWAMI

At this stage, you're undoubtedly starting to see many positive interactions with your child and others. When my clients are with me at this stage in personal coaching, they share all the changes they see and the delightful encounters taking place. It is really enjoyable and exciting for me to be a part of the transformation.

In this chapter, continue energizing their leadership qualities from the beginning with L.O.V.E. boost. With your gold-tinted glasses, you'll start seeing them one after another. This is just the beginning.

As we get closer to the Garden of Harmony, you will see children working together for their common goals. You may see groups engaged in conversation, individuals physically creating, lots of discussions, and even arguments. They're figuring out their personal dynamics and getting ready to make magic happen.

EMPOWERED MOMENTS

When children become fulfilled in activities that empower their purpose, and when they start understanding through empathy other children's needs, they begin engaging together really well with their friends.

Little Johnny absolutely loves creating little books and cards. He will spend a full afternoon of writer's workshop folding paper, writing mini stories, drawing pictures, sticking on different colors and shapes, and creating handmade cards. One Monday, he comes in extremely excited. He has made a new type of a pop-up card and it has a beautiful message on it for me. He's only six and he's writing so prolifically already. His creativity is contagious.

His other little friends look at all the cards he's made. Soon, they all decide to make their own cards, collecting lined paper, construction paper, scissors, glue sticks, stickers, shapes, and more. The whole group of young boys is engaged in writing, editing, folding, creating and making handmade cards. They're asking Johnny questions, "How did you do that part?" "What do you think about this part?" They're fully immersed.

Since this is naturally motivated language arts, I observe excitedly. I can't wait to read all the letters and messages they're creating. The workspace isn't quiet; it's bustling with conversations. It's flow in action, a daily goal for my classroom. They don't want to go out for break.

Johnny has shown me a perfect example of leadership. Because he was so absorbed in his work, others got inspired to do it as well. He guides them and works together with them, each child also becoming absorbed.

I've seen personally and heard of many examples of this from my clients. The girl who starts her lemonade stand and soon you see three or four lemonade stands pop up in neighborhoods around the school, because the other kids love the idea! The young boy who designs origami creations and starts selling them to his soccer friends and YMCA friends and school friends, and suddenly a whole little group of kids are selling origami to their friends. The young man who has decided to put on a show for his upcoming birthday party and gathers many friends who want to act in the drama. When children are encouraged in their sense of purpose, they gather other children who have a similar interest, and they lead the group to common goals.

STORMING AND FIGHTING

Invariably, because any social activity is going to have its disagreements, you will also see issues arise. Are you familiar with the phases of team development: forming, storming, norming, and performing? Forming is when children meet each other, become best friends quickly, and engage in creating things with each other.

Usually pretty quickly, children enter the storming phase. Sometimes, the storming can also break the relationship apart. What is important for you to know is that storming is *completely normal and natural*. It is a required stage of team development in leadership spaces. A child who can work through this will be able to strengthen their social and leadership skills.

During this stage you hear statements like, "I never want to go to their house again! You're not my friend! I'm not going to invite you to my birthday party!" The intensity of the emotions that arise at this time are only because their attachment and love to that friend was also just as intense.

If you have done the previous work of H.E.A.R., L.O.V.E., S.E.R.V.E., A.C.C.E.P.T. and more, you will see storming behaviors lessen. But still, these storming experiences and fights are vital for your child to develop social and leadership empowerment. In the next level, the "N" in EMPOWERMENT, you will learn how to neutralize those.

* * *

Level 10: Neutralize Their Conflicts

* * *

Wow, neutralize is a powerful word. Is it even possible to completely neutralize your child's conflicts? Yes, it is, dear parent, it is. Hundreds of thousands of teams in thousands of companies, with members from completely different backgrounds, can get past the storming phase into performing amazingly. Guided by expert leadership, companies like Google, Apple, Whole Foods, Walmart, Sony, and more are successfully enhancing our lives. Teaching impressionable, naturally happy five- and six-year-olds, is much easier.

All the processes you've been following has entered their subconscious, and they will naturally follow these processes with others.

CONFLICT RESOLUTION WITH C.A.R.E.

Here's a powerful process you can use to resolve conflicts for kids aged three to nine. I've used it many times a day for years. The more you follow the practices in the book, the more powerfully this strategy will work.

Johnny and all his friends were having such a magical time creating those cards and writing messages. Suddenly, he notices one of his cards torn apart and in the trash can. "Oh no!" he yells, "Who did this?" He's now on the floor in a puddle of tears. Without realizing, his friend Aaron had scrunched it up and thrown it in the trash. As they begin arguing, voices and emotions rise, and I see I need to guide them through this.

Parents and adults don't usually know what to do when two kids are fighting intensely. *Do I let it play out? Do I ask everyone to say sorry?* Typically, adults jump into fight-flight, or attack-avoidance scenarios. I'm sure you know this well. Two kids fighting can be intense.

Typical responses can fall in a variety of categories.

Avoidance

- Figure it out.
- It's not that big of a deal; I'm sure you can manage it.
- Okay, well, then just don't play with that friend.
- Why do you need to always come up with problems?
- Look, you're doing the best you can, maybe you can just find someone else to play with.

Attacking

- How dare they do that to you!
- I'm going to talk to them right now.
- I can't believe they're acting like that!
- I'm going to talk to their parents right this minute.
- Hit them back. Show them who's boss!

Ring a bell? I know this because it happens to me as well, still! It helps to have an alternative. Reach for the C.A.R.E. process:

- C – Call the children to talk to each other
- A – Acknowledge and accept feelings

- R – Request positive action
- E – Engage together

C – CALL THE CHILDREN TO TALK TO EACH OTHER

Teach your child to trust the person they are fighting with and decide to fix it together. In *Dare to Lead,* Brene Brown teaches about the importance of vulnerability, that leaders who are vulnerable are better managers. When a child is upset at another, they can trust their friend and tell them. They can trust that their friend will help them get through it.

When a child can open up to a friend and say a simple feeling without automatically assuming the worst or feeling insecure, dramatic, or overwhelmed, that builds a powerful foundation of trust that many adults even struggle with. Sometimes children have a hard time doing this. They may drop into intense feelings like, "no one cares about me, the world sucks, I hate everyone."

It's your job to remind them again that they are worthy, and their friend still loves them even if it doesn't seem like it right now. You can also remind the other friend that we're going to help settle your child's feelings. Friends love to help other friends feel better. I was at a farm recently and a little girl was crying. Even the pet dog on the farm came up and was cuddling with the girl who was crying, like even the little puppy wanted to make the little girl feel better. It's a natural tendency of any living being to want harmony. Call both children together and remind them that they are friends who can work this out.

A – ACKNOWLEDGE AND ACCEPT FEELINGS

Win-Win Scripts

This is how the children will communicate with each other. I call these *Win-Win Scripts* as both children have their feelings heard, validated and get to fix the discord that caused the fight. This dialogue needs to be directed by you. After a few encounters, it will become natural.

Hurt Friend: "I feel ___________ because ___________ happened."

Listening Friend: (*repeats back what Hurt Friend has shared. Can do it in their own words as long as they don't change the gist of what the friend says)*

"You feel ___________ because ___________. Is that right?"

Parent: "Did Listening Friend understand you, Hurt Friend?" Usually, the Hurt Friend says yes.

If not, Hurt Friend can continue sharing: "I also felt ___________ because ___________."

Listening Friend is guided to repeat back in their own words what Hurt Friend has said. "Hurt Friend is feeling ___________ because of ___________."

R – REQUEST POSITIVE ACTION

Parent: "OK, thank you. Great communication here. Now that your feelings are accepted, can you tell Listening Friend what you would like them to do differently in the future?" You need to say this as a positive action, like, "I want you do to such and such," not as, "please *don't* do such and such."

When Hurt Friend communicates what they want to happen in the positive for the next time, this process gets rid of the blame and accusations that may be in their heart. They have to activate the principle of generosity, as they have to stop seeing their friend as someone who's out to get them or make them upset, but they have to see their friend as someone who can help them feel better. It's a very powerful process that happens in a child's mind, and it brings about trust.

Hurt Friend: "Next time, I would prefer that you please ___________ instead."

Listening Friend again repeats back: "Okay, so next time you are hoping that I would do this ___________ instead."

Parent: "Looks like you've understood really well. Hurt Friend, are you feeling better?"

E – ENGAGE TOGETHER

At this point, most of the time the kids are ready to go back to their working together and playing. You as a parent need to make sure they go back to engaging together happily and the feelings are all resolved. Sometimes the Listening Friend also has a ton of feelings to share and it comes out after a few minutes of playing. The same script can be used with the opposite roles. It is okay if they spend time on this. Once their feelings are heard, validated, and completely let go of, they can peacefully play together again. As the adult, check on them a few times to see how to engage them again. "Do you want to keep making cards, or would you like to go play with the Legos?"

Here are a few examples.

The Torn-Up Card

Let's think back to Johnny and Aaron. Mother Gopi Gita (MGG) calls both children together.

MGG: "Hey, Johnny and Aaron, please come here. Let's work through this. Both of your needs are important.

"Johnny, I can see you really upset. Go ahead and tell Aaron exactly what you're feeling, and which action happened that made you feel that way. Say it like this: 'I feel ___________ because ___________.'"

Johnny: "I feel really sad and upset because my beautiful card that I worked so hard on was totally thrown in the trash and you didn't even care about it!"

MGG: "I understand that you feel really upset but we're going to avoid any sentence that says you in it because we don't want to make assumptions that Aaron didn't care about it, right? Let's try that again."

Johnny: "I feel really sad and upset because my beautiful card that I worked so hard was totally crumpled up and thrown in the trash!"

MGG: "That was powerful. Thank you so much for being vulnerable and sharing your feelings."

"Aaron, now you're going to say exactly what Johnny just said to you. Repeat it back in your words – but don't change any of his feelings and you no need to defend yourself either."

This takes some time for Aaron to do because he's a bit on the defensive. He tries to argue or defend himself...

MGG: "Aaron, your thoughts are really important, too. But right now, we're taking care of Johnny's thoughts, then I promise you'll have your turn. Please just let Johnny know that he's been heard by repeating back in your own words exactly what he said. We want to make sure that Johnny sees that you heard what he said, and you understood it."

Aaron: "Johnny, you're feeling really sad and upset because your paper was just crumpled up and thrown in the garbage. But I didn't do it on purpose – I didn't know!" *Johnny starts responding and blaming a bit.*

MGG stops both of the boy from arguing. The script needs to be followed exactly otherwise very quickly the arguing will escalate into a fight.

MGG: "I understand, Aaron, you also have strong feelings about this! But remember. Right now, it's just time to repeat to Johnny to make sure that Johnny very clearly understands that you hear his feelings and accept them. Can we try that one more time?"

Aaron: "Yes, of course I understand them. Johnny, you're feeling really upset that your beautiful card was all crumpled up in the trash can."

MGG: "Thank you. That was very clear. Johnny, do you feel like Aaron understood your feelings?"

Johnny: "Yeah."

MGG: "Okay, Johnny, now please tell Aaron what you would like him to do differently next time." *(Request positive action)*.

Johnny has to think about this a bit. He has to jump out of the blame space and has to bring out the goodness in his heart about Aaron. He does love Aaron as a friend, and he has to be generous in his thoughts of Aaron in order to ask him to do something next time. He has to release the blame in his mind in order to do this.

Johnny: "Aaron, maybe next time you could ask me or ask one of us if it's important or if we are ready to throw it away?"

MGG: "Okay, Aaron, can you repeat back what Johnny wants you to do next time?"

Aaron: "Yeah, he said he wants me to ask next time before I throw something away."

MGG: "Great, do you think you could do that?"

Aaron: "Yes, of course."

MGG: "Looks like we've settled your feelings, Johnny. Do you feel understood and like the problem was solved?" Johnny nods yes. "Aaron, do you want to share any of your feelings?"

Aaron is thinking. Earlier he was about to share that it wasn't his fault, and that he didn't like that Johnny just blamed him, but because Johnny requested positive action, this is no longer something Aaron is worried about. Aaron decides he's fine, that it's all better.

MGG then requests both go continue working on their cards (*engage together*). To ensure that both will reengage themselves in working on the cards, she picks up the cards, asks them about some details, watches them interact, perhaps makes a cut or two and leaves when both are fully immersed again. The kids have communicated, they have solved the problem, and both are back in friendship space. Disaster averted; storming solved.

This C.A.R.E. process can be used every day, any time there's a fight or feelings. Children should be expected to use their words, "I feel such and such when this happens. Can you do this next time instead?" After a few times, you'll see them working through this on their own and they won't need your guidance. I have seen children in the preschool and lower elementary classes who have gotten really good at this. Empower your child with the tools to work together, hear another's feelings, and get back to the important work they're doing.

Pass the Ball

For leadership to emerge, you want to teach your child that working with others to achieve a common goal is superior to working independently. This means they need to look beyond their own feelings and think about the needs of the group. Stephen Covey calls this synergy, "Synergy is when two or more people work together to create a better solution than either could alone."

Leadership calls for sacrifice and an unselfish existence. By supporting a friend or teammate's needs, they will find even greater sense of pleasure as "everyone wins." Expect your child to rise to this. Sean Covey shares this story in his book *The Seven Habits of Highly Effective Teens*. While it is a story for teenagers, it is helpful for kids at all ages.

> "In high school, I played on the girls' basketball team. I was pretty good for my age and tall enough to be starter on the varsity team even though I was just a sophomore. My friend Pam, another sophomore, was also moved up to be a starter on the varsity squad. I had a sweet little shot I could hit quite regularly from ten feet out. Seriously, it worked every time. I began making four or five of those shots a game and began getting recognized for it. Pam, obviously, didn't like all the attention I was getting and decided, consciously or not, to keep the ball from me. It didn't matter how open I was for the shot, Pam flat out stopped passing the ball to me. One night, after playing a terrible game in which Pam kept the ball from me most of the game, I was as mad as I had ever been. I spent many hours talking with my dad, going over everything, and expressing my anger toward my friend-turned-enemy, Pam.
>
> "After a long discussion, my dad told me that the best thing he could

think of would be to give Pam the ball every time I got it. Every time. I thought it was literally the stupidest thing he had ever told me. He simply told me it would work and left me at the kitchen table to think about it. But I didn't. I knew it wouldn't work and put it aside as silly fatherly advice. At the next game I was determined to beat Pam at her own game. I planned and plotted and came out with a mission to ruin Pam's game. On my first possession of the ball, I heard my dad above the crowd. He had a booming voice, and though I shut out everything around me while playing basketball, I could always hear Dad's deep voice. At the moment I caught the ball, he yelled out, 'Give her the ball!' I hesitated for one second and then did what I knew was right.

Although I was open for a shot, I found Pam and passed her the ball. She was shocked for a moment, then turned and shot, sinking the ball for two points. As I ran down the court to play defense, I got a feeling I'd never felt before: true joy for the success of another person. And, even more, I realized that it put us ahead in the game. It felt good to be winning. I continued to give her the ball every time I got it in the first half. Every time. In the second half, I did the same, only shooting if it was a designated play or if I was wide open for a shot. We won that game, and in the games that followed, Pam began to pass me the ball as much as I passed it to her. Our teamwork was getting way stronger, and so was our friendship. We won the majority of our games that year and became kind of legendary at school. The local paper even did a write-up on our ability to pass to each other and sense each other's presence. Overall, I scored more points than ever before. You see, Win-Win always creates more."

I was floored the first time I read this. What an incredible experience! She literally was having to pass the ball to make up for her friend's internal feelings of unworthiness or jealousy. She didn't want to, but look at the result! If your child learns how to "pass the ball," and create a collaborative space, the sky is the limit for them.

What does this look like for a five-year-old? They can give the swing for a few minutes instead of fighting over it. They can let the other kid go down the slide first, and they'll enjoy the slide more afterward, because they won't have someone bugging them for it behind them, and they'll see the happiness of the child who went before them. If someone is asking for their markers, they can let them use the markers. All these small acts of "passing the ball" will give your child a sense of positivity.

Read this story to your child. Ask them if they would be able to pass the ball, and how? A five- or six-year-old is very smart. You may be surprised by their answers.

DON'T TOLERATE BULLYING

The next question may arise: how does a child work with other children who have hurt them but who are not their friends, and who may even be bullies?

Bullying is when your child is being physically or emotionally hurt and is very uncomfortable for a child. Bullying does cause trauma in a child's psyche, especially if it is ongoing. If your child is being teased, being disrespected, made fun of, or being left out, it needs to be addressed as quickly as possible. *Bullying shouldn't be tolerated in any form.*

Sometimes good-natured teasing by friends can be a type of bullying. Ask your child how they feel about it. Sometimes they can feel pressured to pretend like it doesn't bother them, but internally they're not happy about it. At ages five, six, or seven, they shouldn't have to think that being a friend means tolerating when someone makes fun of you. I've seen little ones who will stop eating their lunch because their friends make fun of what's in it (calling the raisins ants, etc.). I've seen a little girl stop hugging her big brother because her friends made fun of it. This type of bullying should also not be allowed.

When you're not with your child at school, you may feel worried that you don't know what's going on. Keep healthy communication open and remember the A.C.C.E.P.T. process. If you're not judgy and critical, your child will reveal more. If it makes sense and you're not too busy, involve yourself in the school or classroom so you're around and the other kids see it. If your child tells you they're being bullied, contact the school administration and teachers immediately and request a face-to-face conversation. If your administration doesn't do anything about the bully, I recommend you change schools. Your five- or six-year-old child shouldn't be at the whims of those who will attack them. At this age, it can adversely affect them for years.

While writing this chapter, I surveyed over fifty teens in my youth leadership classes. Ninety-two percent of them were bullied at some point in their life, from good-natured teasing to full-on physical altercations. Eighty-six percent of the ones who were bullied communicated that ignoring and avoiding the bully helped them. The other 14 percent stated that it was bad enough that their parents had to do something. One of the students actually left the school and went to another one because of it. I asked them if they felt that the bullying had caused serious harm to their psyches. Replies were along the lines of, "Not really. You're always going to find people that don't like you for some reason or another, and that are going to end up wanting to hurt you. You have to figure out how to avoid them and stay confident." I was proud of these youth leaders. They showed me that they were confident enough to stand up to the bullies or tolerate it.

YOU NEED NOT HURT ANYONE

How do you help your child navigate bully type relationships without always needing to step in? In the *Secret of the Peaceful Warrior,* Dan Millman shares a powerful story. I recommend actually reading this story to your child. (There's an audio narration of it on YouTube.)

In this book, a young boy named Danny is dealing with an older boy named Carl who is physically bullying him, pushing him over, taking his lunch money, and hurting him. Danny learns that Carl's parents don't live with him anymore, that Carl lives with an uncle who's never home, and that Carl rarely has anyone taking care of him. This is why he's bullying and trying to get negative attention.

He meets an older mentor, Socrates, who teaches him self-defense, learning to use the strength of Carl against him. "The secret to courage is to act brave even if you don't feel like it. Running isn't the answer. Neither is fighting. If you hurt someone else, it only makes you the bully. The true warrior is a peaceful warrior."

Danny questions, "But what if someone attacks me first?

"No one has the right to hurt you. You have a right to defend yourself."

"But how can I defend myself without hurting someone," asks Danny.

Socrates pointed to a small tree bending in the wind. "That tree knows the warrior's secret. If it resists, it may break, so it bends with the force. Never resist someone's force, Danny. Use it. They pull, you push. If they push, you pull. And remember if a railroad train is coming your way, get off the tracks. Deal with whatever happens this way and your life will be easier."

Socrates strengthens Danny physically by giving him physical exercises. This guidance helps Danny get stronger. As he's walking to school one day, Carl accosts him once again. Danny remembers, "Don't run and don't fight." Just as Carl grabs him, Danny evades him and pulls on his sleeve. Carl went tumbling to the ground, surprised at Danny's confidence. Danny realized that Carl was actually not as scary as he looked. With this newfound confidence, Danny turned back and offered Carl his hand to help the bully up. He had defeated the bully.

The next day at lunch time, he realized that Carl had no money for lunch. He buys an extra lemonade for Carl and offers it to him. You can imagine how Carl must have felt. Danny continued trying to connect with Carl, and finally the two boys played basketball together and became friends. The story ends beautifully with the former bully playing with Danny and his friends, no longer alone, no longer hurting others.

This is a powerful story to share with children. I recommend you buy it. The power of empathy coupled with internal confidence and strong boundaries is no match for any bully.

Any time you have a conversation with your child about why things are happening in their world, it will empower them. "Why is that kid bugging you? What sorts of things are going on with him? Why do bullies act the way they act?" Your child will recognize that it's actually a form of deep weakness and insecurities and a lack of love. This knowledge will bring compassion into their hearts. Compassion, empathy, and love are qualities so powerful that they build up the confidence of those who feel it. This will strengthen your child.

Of course, just a reminder, conversations are all fine and dandy. But do address it. Do speak to your child's teacher or school administrator. And if it continues, take them out of the school.

THE REJECTION OF PRINCE DHRUVA

Prince Dhruva, a renowned, young five-year-old in ancient bhakti texts, was playing with his younger brother, Uttama, near his father's throne. They played happily, roughhoused, and laughed. Suddenly, his father, the king, arrived, being announced by the doorkeepers. With the King was his stepmother, the cruel Suruchi. She despised Dhruva because he was the eldest son and heir to the throne. She only wanted her son

Uttama to become king. As she walked by, she picked up her little son Uttama, carrying him with affection.

When the king sat down on the throne, Suruchi placed Uttama on it. Seeing this, Dhruva also wanted to sit on his father's lap. As he clambered up the steps to the throne, and tried to climb on his father's lap, his stepmother cruelly pulled him off and threw him onto the floor. Down all the steps he rolled, his delicate little body hurting, shocked.

"You are not fit to sit on the throne or your father's lap young boy! Because you did not take your birth from my womb, you do not deserve to. Go find God who can give you the chance to be born from my womb." She spoke harshly, sarcastically, her scathing words piercing the young prince's heart. Abusively, she threw him out of the assembly hall.

Struck by the harsh behavior of his stepmother and the silence of his dear father, the king, Dhruva became enraged. He began to breathe heavily in anger and raced to his portion of the palace where his mother, Suniti, lived. Although she was the first wife of the king, she was neglected. When she heard from palace residents what had happened, she shook in pain like a leaf shaking in a tempest, her gentle lotus-like face covered in tears.

Seeing her son, the true heir to the throne, the eldest of all the princes and princesses, being bullied and rejected in his own home was more than she could bear. Not knowing what to do or even what to say, she held Dhruva in her arms. In deep pain and with no other hope, Queen Suniti spoke immortal words of wisdom.

"My dear boy, I know how intensely you have been hurt. I can see you are so angry. Anyone who inflicts pains upon others suffers himself from that pain. So do not wish for pain to come to them. The words of your stepmother are true, dear one. Your father does not even consider me to be his wife, and you have been borne of such an unfortunate woman as myself.

"The only remedy is to follow the words of your stepmother and to search for the Divine. Find out the source of your being and your purpose in this world. Follow the path of the saints who spend their days connecting in meditation on God, the Inner Parents, and you will find peace. That is the only way I know to help you."

Queen Suniti spoke mystically and yet did not clearly even know that her son would take her so seriously. That evening, five-year-old Dhruva left the palace, unbeknownst to his family. He sought out the sages and his story is told in *bhakti* histories. He met the Divine, learned what he needed to support humanity as a king, and returned home years later. Although his younger brother was killed by a neighboring ruler, Dhruva took care of his aging stepmother and father and ruled the kingdom powerfully for many years. During his final meditations, he prayed that his mother, who had first guided him to be compassionate and not vengeful, attain the spiritual destination along with him.

SHIFTING THE PARADIGM: WIN-WIN-WIN

If you, as a leadership parent, can guide your child compassionately the way Queen Suniti had, if you can instruct your child to not be vengeful the way Socrates had in Danny's story, you will empower them to a state of leadership so powerful their names will be commemorated in history. John Mackey, the CEO of Whole Foods and author of *Conscious Leadership,* explains this type of empowerment: "Win-win-win thinking is a deeply satisfying approach to our business relationships in part because it represents the essence of the golden rule – do unto others as you would have them do unto you. It's a triple victory – good for me, good for you, good for all of us."

How did Pocahontas mediate between warring Native Americans and English Settlers? How did little orphan Pollyanna turn a bunch of old grumpy adults in her life into happy loving caretakers? How did Martin Luther King Jr. be the force to turn a whole country around that had embraced slavery, and did this non-violently, with strength and empathy for those he was up against? How did Jesus Christ forgive those that hurt him? How did Saint Nitai wish well for Jagai and Madhai as blood was literally pouring down from his head?

All these personalities were empowered internally. They were stronger than those who attacked them. They were seeped in compassion, knowing that truly nothing can hurt the individual soul but oneself. They worried for others, more than for themselves, and they were called to leadership in powerful ways. You and your child are also being called to leadership. You may have already dealt with your own variety of conflicts in your work environment, and you can use that knowledge gained to help your child – not just with bullies, but in any necessary social environment. You can find the strength within yourself to look deep at what soul qualities are being tested in your child during these difficult moments of social conflict, and which soul qualities are being tested within you. Expect your child to rise to strength and confidence.

> *"An individual has not started living until he can rise above the narrow confines of his individualistic concerns to the broader concerns of all humanity. Darkness cannot drive out darkness; only light can do that. Hate cannot drive out hate; only love can do that. Man must evolve for all human conflict a method which rejects revenge, aggression, and retaliation. The foundation of such a method is love."*
>
> — MARTIN LUTHER KING JR.

The bhakti path is one of pure love, and love alone. Having been now equipped with all the processes needed to instill leadership in your child, you are at your destination. It has been a long journey, with many new concepts and experiences behind you. You are with your child, and it is time for us to step into the Garden of Harmony.

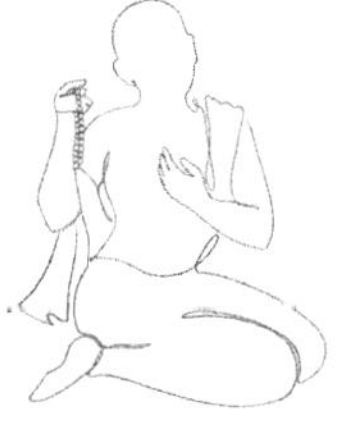

* * *

Mantra Affirmations Level 10: I Guide

* * *

You have worked very hard to get here. You are staying the path, climbing from level to level to level. We are almost there. These mantra affirmations that you have been reciting with me keep you centered and focused. In this space today, you need to find the strength to work through when your child has social issues. Even after so much work, social problems will still come your way. Give your pain and your child's discomfort to the mantra as you recite it.

The Inner Parents know the reasons behind these disturbing interactions. They will sit in your heart and help you walk your child through the "Win-Win" Scripts. They will infuse your C.A.R.E. process with their own care for you. Trust them.

We continue the *maha-mantra* from before. You're doing so well. Reciting this *mantra* today, and during this period, as you're cementing the C.A.R.E. process for your child, despite all their social conflicts, will open the gates to the Garden of Harmony. You have just about arrived. My heart is filled with pride for you.

hare krishna hare krishna
krishna krishna hare hare
hare rama hare rama
rama rama hare hare

Let me C.A.R.E. for my child and their friends.
Let me help them be vulnerable and trust their friends.
Let me guide them properly through the words they need to say.
Let them feel heard. Let them hear others. Let them meet other's needs
I am centered. I am amazed. My child is resilient.
I am a Leadership Parent.

14

THE GARDEN OF HARMONY, SRI MAYAPUR

"To be a leader means to have humility, to have respect and to serve the people we are leading. And that type of character, that type of integrity not only brings real fulfillment to our own hearts, but also has a great effect on the lives of all the people around us."

— RADHANATH SWAMI

We are about to enter the Garden of Harmony, Sri Mayapur. You've made it! I'm so proud of you. I can see your eyes filled with emotion and my heart is bursting with pride. It has been a long, long journey and you have done it.

When you step into this garden, feel the beauty of all that has changed for you. You came to me, lost, scared, and hopeless. How will your child be empowered? How will they feel comfortable in their social dynamics? Leadership was far from your mind. I'm certain now that you will never get back to that space of fear again.

There is an ornate gate at this garden. It opens from the inside when you are ready to enter. If you still doubt that you will see your child engaged in full leadership, you are more than welcome to go back and read any of the processes at any of the previous levels. Close your eyes, and envision your dream child, as you have been doing with me all along. That vision, that dream, is no longer just a dream. As soon as this gate opens, that dream will be a reality.

In reality, in your home, I know you've already been seeing so many interactions of leadership. I'm so excited for you. I'm so blessed to have worked with you so long. We have a little more work to do as we navigate this Garden of Harmony. Once you walk through the different aspects, you will be ready to continue living in this space with your child for a decade more, nay a lifetime.

You are ready. When you recite the *maha-mantra*, the gate opens automatically from within the garden.

You look around. You see grand, mystical trees engraved with the names of all the leadership kids who live here. Birds chirp in song all around us. Musical flute sounds whistle through the bamboo branches, the leaves whisper to the wind. The roots going deep in the ground are even longer than the branches, and together they have reached out to hug the roots of other trees, creating a network of support for the entire path. You see animals around, each engaged in busy tasks from ants, to beavers, to swans, to peacocks. Each single living being exists in harmony, creating, building, communicating – full of love, full of support, and providing for the community.

As you walk, you notice that the pathway is encrusted with rubies and precious gems, glittering in the rays of the sun. Busy animals scurry over to see who has entered. Green parrots fly toward us. They call out the names of Saints Gaura and Nitai, who are on their way to meet us.

Close your eyes and feel the peace of this beautiful garden. Feel the beauty that overwhelms all your senses. Hear the soft droning of *mantras* being chanted, like waves of love they enter our ears.

As we continue to walk, we see groups of children clustered here and there. Some are planting, placing seeds, placing flowers in rows. Some are picking the flowers, playing with them, making garlands and bracelets. Some are planting veggies, some are taking care of the animals, some are playing in the water. Some children are building natural play structures. Some are investigating the earth and trees around them. Some are bent over large drawings in the ground – blueprints for innovations needed on Earth. Others are sitting on tree stumps, deep in conversations about conflicts arising and how to resolve them. They glance at us, curious for a few minutes, but adult activities and thoughts do not disturb them, so they get right back to their full absorption.

There are so many beautiful, bright young children here, the children of leadership parents all over the Earth Planet. They are of all races, genders, and colors on this Earth. Though they speak many languages, they speak one universal language – the language of transcendental sound. These children are powerful, empowered beings. They have been carefully, painstakingly nurtured with great sacrifice from their parents. They have now been chosen to usher in the Golden Age, to eradicate the effects of the Dark Age Kali, the Age of Quarrel, and bring pure love – bhakti – to every single home on Earth. These are your children, my children, and the children of every leader on this planet.

You are scanning each set of children, wondering where your child is. Who are their friends? What are they doing?

DISCOVERING YOUR CHILD'S LEADERSHIP TYPE

As you scan the environment, you notice that there are four leadership types. These types are categories from ancient bhakti times and are called *varnas*. Soon, you will discover what your child's leadership type is. What are they motivated by, and what is their purpose? Who will they serve?

Remember, way back at the beginning, when you placed your gold tinted glasses on and you learned about your kids being royalty and transcendental aristocrats. Here you will see them in their full glory. The four leadership types (*varnas*) are:

- K – Kings and Queens
- I – Intellectuals
- D – Demigods
- S – Sages

Kings and Queens

The first leadership type you see are the Kings and Queens. These children are royalty leaders. They like to protect the environment they're in, immediately stepping in without being asked when there is a problem. Even if they are working on something, they will stop their work to check on what others are doing. Sometimes people think they're nosy or annoying. They will be aware of others' conversations, wanting to make sure things go well for everyone – not just themselves. This selfless mood of service is so they can become managers and caretakers when they get older.

Because they're naturally compassionate, they love to care for others' needs. They're people-oriented, get embarrassed easily, and their reputation and image are important to them. Don't insult them, or they will either get angry or lose their confidence. In a dispute, they will be the mediators; in a game, the scorekeeper or the umpire. They are steady and aware of the entire picture. When there's a class project, they'll most likely organize the tasks. They can be loud or quiet, in the front or in the back. When they grow up, they will be the administrators, the directors, the CEOs, the community leaders, the governors, senators, and presidents. They will be aware of the trials and tribulations of their people and will know how to help everyone under their care simultaneously. Their predecessors are the likes of King Arjuna, Queen Draupadi, Cleopatra, Martin Luther King, and John F. Kennedy.

Intellectuals

The second leadership type you see are the intellectuals. They are the wisdom leaders. They love to learn, discuss, debate, and philosophize.

They can give expert advice on a variety of topics. As kids, they are like know-it-alls and can tell you so many cool facts about basically any subject that interests them. They love science experiments, jeopardy, and the library. Learning and sharing their learning are their passions. They are also righteous. They don't like friends who cheat in games, and they internally feel a sense of ethics and morality to be high values. They get really upset if rules change or things don't seem to be fair.

When they play make-believe, they love to play being the teacher and work with all their friends to go to school. They love to tell others what the best way to do a task is, or to teach difficult school concepts, or to help their classmates in that math problems. They love to share their knowledge and wisdom, because they just know so much, and they can also memorize and explain many higher-level concepts. When they grow up, they will be life coaches, strategists, consultants, mentors, guides, professors, educators, and gurus. People will go to them for advice and guidance in how to live their lives in a variety of areas. Their predecessors are of the likes of King Yudhisthira, Henry David Thoreau, Maria Theresa of Austria, and the Dalai Lama.

Demigods

The third leadership type you will see are the demigod leaders. They are lavish businessmen and women as children, engaged in negotiations, creations, and arts. They are interested in creating heavenly environments around them, so they spend much time in creative endeavors and making profit from those endeavors. They're passionate, with tons of enthusiasm, and can get others excited about something. They're usually the artistically inclined: the dancers, the actors, the artists. They're motivated by beauty. You may see them making things in your home and selling them at school. You'll notice them playing dress-up, drawing, singing, acting, sculpting, and more.

They love collecting things. By the time they're teenagers, they'll most likely have started a small business and made money. Because of their passion for beauty and their strong creative drive, they are inventors. Their go-get-em spirit is contagious, and they can promote and market their ideas to everyone. When they get older, they will be the leaders who create beautiful environments for others. They will take care of other's hearts and create a life of ease and luxury for hard workers. They will remind others to experience joy and love and profit from it. They will increase other's finances, and they will lead people to experience pleasure. Their predecessors are of the likes of King Indra, Queen Victoria, Steve Jobs, Bridget "Bidy" Mason, Elizabeth Arden, and Elon Musk.

Sages

The fourth leadership type you will see are the sage leaders. These young leaders are builders and promote stability in their environments. They are consistent, steady, and responsible. They don't skip out on their chores much, and they like to take care of parents' and siblings' work. They lead by example. They work hard. They're determined and they complete what needs to be done without much complaining. They are generally organized and don't necessarily like to be around a ton of people unless work is getting done. You can count on them.

They can also be very innovative, creating infrastructure and giving ideas on how to fix larger problems at home or school. They're efficient and because they're not scared of hard work, they know how to get things done. But they don't need the fanfare or the recognition – just the simple act of doing the task is rewarding enough. When they get older, they will guide others in stability. They will promote infrastructure that is long-lasting, grounded, and can support many at once. They will always pull up their sleeves to help, never shying away from hard work. They will support individuals, families, communities, and help others feel secure. Their predecessor's guides are of the likes of King Vidura, Jane Addams, Franklin D. Roosevelt, and Mother Theresa.

MEETING YOUR LITTLE LEADER

As you scan the Garden of Harmony for where your child is, you may find them working in more than one of those leadership type areas. Close your eyes right now and tell me, where will they be? You know your child best.

As we journey together to the area where your child is at, your heart beats stronger. You see them. You hold them. You give them a big, long hug. Hold them as long as you need.

Now we will all together step into Level 11, our last level. This level is a little higher ground in the garden. From here we can see the entire garden, with all the children in it. From here, you will be able to see what the future holds. We are the last "T" of the EMPOWERMENT process.

* * *

Level 11: Transform Your Child's Leadership Skills

* * *

YES, it has been quite a journey to arrive here to the Garden of Harmony, but this is only the beginning. In order to continue the empowerment, it is vital that you transform those leadership qualities you have been working on up until now.

Recognize and Verbalize Their Leadership Qualities

Remember the dream child activity we did back at Level 1? Those leadership qualities should be noticed and recognized throughout the process. Continue that. Here are a few examples.

- "I see that you're showing Raj how to specifically fold that square pattern you made. You're showing me that you have so much patience!"
- "Look how hot it is outside, and you, kiddos, are still determined to give lemonade to the passersby. That's showing me resilience and determination!"
- "I can see that you just worked through a big argument about the decision but you came to an agreement – that shows me collaboration!"

Use the L.O.V.E. boost process from Chapter 7 to specifically note actions that show your child's leadership qualities. Do that every single day. Energizing your child's leadership qualities continues to help them see themselves as leaders.

When you as a parent recognize and energize leadership qualities in your child, you are recognizing the glory of the Inner Parents within them. You are allowing your child to manifest a quality that is present for them to help humankind. Our individual qualities are really all just a spark of universal splendor. Be witness to these transformational qualities and mention them.

Just as the apple seed already has a full-blown beautiful apple tree within it, full of leaves and flowers and big, delicious Fuji apples, your child already has within them everything they need to lead a large group of individuals, and to make a massive difference in this world. In a very short time, you will see that. Keep energizing, keep following the practices in this book, and you will experience what I am experiencing every single day.

Give Them Plenty of Opportunities to Lead

How do you encourage a child to hone their leadership skills?

Leadership is supporting humanity. On a very practical level, leadership is finding a problem that affects a group, and working with that group to solve that problem.

In our online leadership classes for youth, youth leaders find problems in their communities they can solve. They assemble teams, set up clear systems for interpersonal dynamics, make plans, and accomplish their goals.

Here's a basic process for little kids. This L.E.A.D. process immediately establishes your child as a leader in their space. They get practice on skills they will use again and again as they get older.

THE L.E.A.D. PROCESS FOR KIDS

Learn About It

Kids talk about problems a lot. "Be a problem-solver" is one of my favorite mottos. Very easily, you can ask them to come up with solutions to the problems. Work it out with your friends and find the solution.

Usually this requires research, talking to anyone involved, listing the possible solutions, and discussing it.

Empathize with People Involved

In that discussion, so many communication skills are at play. They'll need to learn to listen to each other, to truly understand what the issues are in the scenario and how it can be solved. They will be responsible for properly understanding each person's needs, whether in looking at the problem and who its affecting or discussing what is important to their group members. They will use the H.E.A.R. process when talking to others to identify the problem.

Assign Tasks, Roles, and Dates

Each member of the group should know what their tasks are, what role they play, and when it needs to be done by. It is so exciting to watch a group of children come up with this simple list. It creates simplicity and easy discussions, with less arguments.

Do It, Again and Again

Once all the planning has been completed, just lean back and watch your kids solve the problems. Voila, your child has led a group to success.

Of course, as a leader yourself you know this process is much easier said than done. But you can follow it for simple initiatives around the home. Start small, and the children will get more and more comfortable with it.

L.E.A.D. IN ACTION

There are so many areas your children can L.E.A.D. in: decisions regarding meals, chores, cleaning, clothing, vacations, schedules, schoolwork, home organization, even house décor. In no time, both my boys were doing many of the processes themselves, involving each other, me and their dad, and even their friends.

Example: Toys

Do your children argue about their toys a lot? Follow the L.E.A.D. process and ask them to come up with solutions to the problems. Ask them to talk it through and come up with solutions together. Let them assign who's doing what by when and watch the system they choose work well. If it starts falling apart again, and there are arguments or issues, just start again, "Hey, I totally know you can come up with a solution. Let me know how it goes." It's so exciting watching them stick with the decisions they've made together. If they don't have a sibling, they can involve you or their other friends.

Example: Getting Ready

What about problems surrounding getting to school on time? Follow the L.E.A.D. process. My children came up with a chart that had the time they needed to be done with morning tasks. They loved running over to the refrigerator where they kept the list and saying how much time they had left to eat to get to school on time. They also came up with a list of which clothes to wear at which temperatures that also needed my input, because we spent too much time arguing in the morning about which clothes to wear when. "Put your socks on!" "No, I'm not cold!"

With this chart, they would look at the temperature, wear socks or long-sleeve shirts or sweaters or not. They needed to make sure I was on board, and they were on board with all the decisions that were made. They had to serve three people's needs and come up with a "Win-Win-Win." We had some amusing moments of me saying, "Put your socks on!" And my older one saying, "Mommy, look at the temperature. The chart says we don't have to at this temperature." I had to abide by the chart. They loved it!

Example: Mealtime

Involve your child this way for most of the important activities in your home. Mealtime is a great start. Do they always eat what you cook? Do they help with meal prep or clean up? Talk about it as a problem and ask them to solve it using the above method. "Do you like the meals that are being made? I need a bit more help in the mornings to get out of the house on time. Can we discuss our meals? Can you help figure out some solutions with everyone involved?" Make sure they have tasks, roles and dates assigned and you'll see them step up in a big way.

LET THEM LEAD YOU

As they get better at coming up with solutions that help everyone, in a variety of smaller activities, dear parents, you will start realizing how much you can depend on them. Little children are so intuitive and love being helpers. They love to serve. Ask them for advice on a variety of things. Ask them to help you come up with solutions.

"Hey, I'm really tired and the sink is full of your dishes every night. Can you help me figure out a way to solve this? Who all is involved? Who needs to do what by when? Can you take the lead on this one? I'll help you."

Your child is not an ordinary child. Your child is immersed now in the Garden of Harmony and is empowered to help serve the world at a massive level. You may not see that in this moment, but you can start seeing little bits of it, and bringing that out in them. Whether they're kings and queens, intellectuals, demigods, or sages, they will change the face of this world. And you will be totally in awe as you watch them do it.

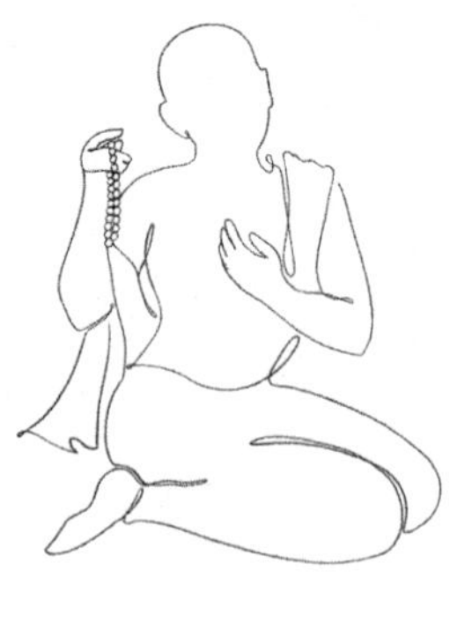

* * *

Final Mantra Meditation Level 11: I Transform

* * *

You have completed this journey today. Congratulations!

Because the body and relationships based on the body are ultimately temporary, it is vital for our children to be connected internally to the Inner Parents. Friendships may come and go. Relationships, like straws of grass in a pond, will come together and drift apart as the waves of time pass them by, only to come together again. Throughout that, the relationships with the Inner Parents stays constant. One day, your child may be in your home; in two decades, they may be living elsewhere. What will always keep you connected is the time you spend together connecting with the Inner Parents.

Through this final meditation, your child can connect to all the future individuals they will be serving with and leading. The connection to the Inner Parents is a most powerful one, and may the Inner Parents continue to guide you and your child on this beautiful trek of leadership parenting. If you recite this mantra, I am 100 percent certain that you will be connected to me, and to all other leadership parents who are reciting this in their daily meditations. This mantra will ensure that your child never leaves the Garden of Harmony. I'm excited for what the future holds.

hare krishna hare krishna
krishna krishna hare hare
hare rama hare rama
rama rama hare hare
Let me continue Leadership Parenting.
I am grateful for all the opportunities.
I am grateful for all the lessons.
I stay connected. I let my child lead. I offer my child to service.

15

YOU GOT THIS

> "The meek shall inherit the earth; and shall delight themselves in the abundance of peace."
>
> — PSALMS 37.11

YOU DID IT!

You made it this far. You started by seeing your child differently than you had before, placing on those gold-tinted glasses, and envisioning their powerful leadership qualities. You accepted your own parent personality and met the Inner Parents, connecting with them throughout with *mantra* meditations. You learned how to H.E.A.R. your children's feelings, and how to avoid R.E.J.E.C.T statements. That's no easy task. You empowered them with L.O.V.E. boosts, and A.C.C.E.P.T.-ed them when they struggled and showed mistakes. Finally, you took R.E.S.T. when you needed it. After your rest, you learned to empower their purpose with F.L.O.W.! You taught them F.E.E.L. to encourage their empathy, and C.A.R.E. to work through social conflicts! Finally, you see them L.E.A.D. in the Garden of Harmony.

All of this was you. You did this. Not me, not your friend, not that mom who was complaining about your child or that teacher who was at their wits' end about your kid and sending you emails. You did it. Give yourself a great big applause and imagine the world of children in the Garden of Harmony looking to you with adoration in their eyes. I know I am.

I know personally how very difficult it is to get this far. I just celebrated my younger son's eighteenth birthday. Every single picture from his childhood from the past eighteen years has memories of struggle pouring in. When the cake fell in the car on the way to the party, when his eye was gashed three days before one, when he was in a major fight with his brother, when he was frustrated because of a math test. Every image we have of our happy children also comes with struggle. You made it here despite all the struggles. You took on your own struggles and their struggles and empowered leadership within them, no matter what.

You will continue this. Know that it's not necessarily going to get easier! They still have a long life ahead of them. At five and six, they have another twelve years in school at least! And more friendships to make, more accomplishments to achieve. Fight against your desire to drop back into old paradigms and responses, and stay strong in this leadership space, the Garden of Harmony.

Always know, you can reach the Saints Gaura and Nitai and the Inner

Parents through the mantra meditation I have taught you. And you can always reach me as well.

Not only can you reach me, but if you've made it this far, I want to hear from you! Share with me your challenges and your successes! Share how these processes have helped you and let me know all about your amazing child. Email me at gopi@gopigita.com or go to my website at gopigita.com and contact me. I can't wait to hear about your journey.

And if you're still feeling stuck and want personal applications for your leadership parenting journey, sign up with me for coaching and you'll definitely get what you're looking for. Look out for the companion class, the webinars and the courses that are being created. And stay tuned for a second book for when your child is in second and third grade to help empower their academics in school.

Have a beautiful time empowering your child.

Love and blessings,

Your well-wisher,

Mother Gopi Gita

FOR THE BHAKTI YOGIS

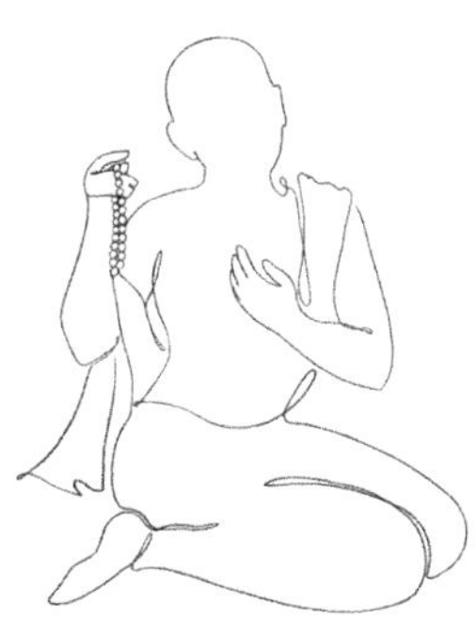

Dear Bhakti Yogis,

You are rare in this world. You are on a path of grace and connection, directly empowering others in spiritual leadership through every one of your devotional practices. Thank you for reading this book.

Leadership parenting is the most natural form of bhakti practice, as the parent acts as a guru to their child. The struggle required automatically enhances your dependence on the Inner Parent – Sri Hare Krishna. Here I will outline your bhakti path as you journey through this book.

In Part One: Meet Up, we meet together, ordained by the Supreme Personality of Godhead. It is no coincidence that you have picked up this book. The *bhakti* practice begins with faith *adau shraddha.* In Chapters 1 and 2, faith is established in me as the author, by hearing my story, and understanding that I do indeed relate to you and understand your pain. As Srila Sanatan Goswami asked Lord Gaura *ke ami, kene amaya jare tapa traya (CC Madhya 20.102),* so you have arrived to ask why your child is suffering in social environments, and who they are. In Chapter 3, you will meet the divine lords and saints *Sri Sri Gaura Nitai.* Giving this book, where They reside, a respectable place on the shelf is equal to worshipping them, as stated by Srila Prabhupada. You will see your path ahead and your destination – the Garden of Harmony, *Sri Mayapur Dham* where They reside with Their devotees.

In Part Two: Discover, you'll establish your identities. In Chapter 4, you are guided to see your child as an eternal spiritual entity *sat-cid-ananda,* beyond the constraints of time. You step into Level 1 where you envision your dream child, a *Vaikuntha* child, already present with spiritual leadership qualities, as described in the Gita (*sucinam srimatam gehe (BG 6.41)*). In Chapter 5, you become empowered to become a *guru* to your child, personally chosen by the Supreme Personality of Godhead. (*guror na sa syat, sva jano na sa syat, pita na sa syan janani na sa syat (SB 5.5.18)*).

Fully fortified, you step up to Level 2, where you meet the Inner Parents, (*Paramatma, the Universal Form,* or *Sri Hare Krishna*), depending on your personal relationship with the divine. Each of you will connect with divinity according to your proclivity (*ye yatha mam prapadyante (BG 4.11)*), and the *mantras* introduced will guide you internally.

Once your faith in your identities is fortified, you can now start on the path of *bhakti yoga. (Adau sraddha tata sadhu sanga).* We enter Part Three: Connect – *sambandha* – and fulfill needs of connection and belonging. You and your child learn how to practice *sadhu sanga* connection with each other, and with their friendships. Establishing these relationships begins with hearing (*sravanam*), the first of the devotional practices. In

Level 3, you are taught to preserve your child's heart through the H.E.A.R. empathic communications process and learn how to hear the messages coming from the Inner Parents through your child. You must be open to receive these messages for daily growth with enthusiasm *(utsahan)*. From here, *kirtanam* begins. You will be taught the word *krishna* in *mantra* meditation, and introduced to a simple *kirtan, krishna krishna krishna he*. You are also shown how to not cause offenses by avoiding the R.E.J.E.C.T. statements. Because your child is a spiritual being, hurting them will cause adverse effects for you (*hathi matha* – the elephant offense). In Level 4, you learn to offer them L.O.V.E. boosts instead, empowering their actions and connecting them to the leadership qualities you envisioned. This service to your *vaishnava* child is most powerful and is a form of *kirtanam,* glorifying the devotee of the Lord. Your *mantra* meditations continue with the sound *krishna*.

From here, you step into the Part Four: Practice – *abhidheya* – and fulfill the core needs of free will and agency. On our *bhakti* journey, we move from *sadhu sanga to bhajana-kriya,* engaging in devotional practices together. In Level 5, you learn how to worship their work, which is transcendental devotional service, and engage in the S.E.R.V.E. process together. Principles of *karma yoga* are taught, engaging one's child in activities according to their proclivities (*BG Ch. 3*), and teaching them about action and reaction – natural consequences and boundaries – in a gentle but firm way. Determination *(niscayad)* is required for this space. Srimati Radharani is your guide during this time, through Her transcendental name *hare*. As the mother of the universe, and the origin of *bhakti-devi,* she gives divine energy to engage in all the work you need to do with your child, and the compassion to enforce consequences and boundaries lovingly. Calling her name through *mantra* helps you get to the next level.

Part Five: Accomplish – *prayojana* – comes next, where you will fill your child's core needs of achievement and completion. On the *bhakti* journey, you move into *anartha-nivritti,* purifying the obstacles. You step into Level 6, where you learn how to embrace their mistakes – not easy to do, but an integral part of the *anartha nivritti* process! Because you are accepted for all your mistakes, you learn how to A.C.C.E.P.T. your child for their mistakes, and to use practice to help them achieve their goals. You need patience *(dhairyat)* and you are given the transcendental name of *rama* denoting Lord Balarama, the source of strength. Strength also means knowing when to take rest, which is Level 7, where you will be encouraged to rest through short escapes and spiritual practices. There may be some past memories to sort through, and this can be painful as well and is part of the *anartha nivritti* space. Sri Balarama will be by your side, as you recite His name through the *mantras* given from the Srimad Bhagavatam.

You have completed the EMPOWER process. The next space is the most complicated one, but it takes you straight to the spiritual realm of the Garden of Harmony, Sridham Mayapur. It is the Part Six: Lead - *sankirtan samadhi.* You begin to see qualities of *nistha and ruci* in your child, step into Level 8 where you develop your child's purpose. You learn to activate their F.L.O.W. *samadhi* at a young age and learn about intrinsic motivation *ruci.* The six motivators come from the six opulences of *Bhagavan.*

In Level 9, you develop magnanimity *(vadanya)* in your child – encouraging their spiritual emotion *(bhava)* and their empathy *(kripa)*, at a very rudimentary state by the F.E.E.L process. In Level 10, you encourage your child in collaborative service *(sankirtan)* despite obstacles, showing C.A.R.E. for each other, even if hurting. Lord Nitai guides us *(maar kheye prema dey)* Thus, equipped and with tons of practice, you are ready to arrive at Sri Mayapur Dham, the Garden of Harmony. The gate is opened by the Lords inside, only by Their blessings, and here you step up to the last Level 11, where you see your child empowered as leaders in one of the four *varnas*. The process of L.E.A.D. teaches you how to practically engage your child naturally. To stay in this Garden of Harmony with your child, the daily meditation of the *maha-mantra* is a must.

I pray you relish your journey, even the difficult spaces. If you ever need personal guidance, I am ready to serve you. Please email me and I will be excited to coach you personally. If these processes have helped your child, send me your success stories as well. *Hare Krishna.*

Yours in service,
Gopi Gita devi dasi

ACKNOWLEDGMENTS

How can I begin to repay the debt I owe to all the individuals who have taught me how to live the principles in this book? I have also been mentored by a community of leaders, gurus, parents, teachers, and children. Here are a few of them.

I begin by offering my humble respects to my gurus. My first *guru, Srila Virabahu Prabhu,* guided us in our early parenthood with hours of hearing and connecting to us, though surely, he had many disciples to attend to. My humble respects to *Srila Giriraj Swami* for checking on my spiritual practices regularly. Continued respects to *Srila Rtadhvaja Swami, Srila Indradyumna Swami, Srila Radhanath Swami, Srila Bir Krishna Maharaj, and Srila Hrdayananda Swami* whose lectures and loving example guide me every day.

My respects to my Mati, *Mother Bir Mala,* an early daughter of Srila Prabhupada. Her steadfast loving faith in him despite so many trials, and her commitment to ISKCON's children, lasting fifty years has been a guiding torch for our family. As I wrote this book, she enchanted me with her book about personal encounters with Srila Prabhupada that brought me to tears every time I read them. My love to *Kunjesvari devi,* our big sister who saves the day quietly whenever needed.

Lastly, I offer my full respects to His Grace Param Prabhu, whose incredible strength has brought the *maha mantra* far and wide, all across the globe, and who has uplifted and created my little sister Gaura Mani into a super star. His stellar example of leadership parenting is one for the world to follow. Big obeisances and love to my brother Gopal Trivedi, who was always there, and to little Gaurangi who was technically the first baby I parented. Tons of love to my Youth Leaders, Kishori and Nimai Rathore, Kana Das and Radhe Devi, who have sent me encouraging comments during this journey and love me on all sides.

Deep gratitude to my writing genius coach and publisher, Dr. Angela Lauria, for being my mentor for over a decade and knowing exactly what to say to bring deep spiritual realizations in this writing process. To my amazing editor Madeline for her encouraging comments and patience, I'm so grateful to have worked with you. You led me through every step of this process for six long months. To my proofreader Natasha and the entire Author Incubator team, thank you for empowering me to make a difference.

To my OG writers' club, Krishna Priya and Naveen Jani, to Ryan Figueroa and Devika Rao for encouraging me to write for years.

THE INTRODUCTION: WHY LEADERSHIP PARENTING IS DEDICATED TO:

- Norma Robinson (Jayanti d), former principal at TKG Academy, who taught me humility, "that the tree laden with the most fruits bows the lowest;"
- Noa Neighbors (Nrtya Kisori d), principal of TKG Academy, who lives the essence of collaborative decision-making;
- Seth Spellman (Sesa Das), ISKCON's Minister of Education, who taught me the importance of hearing others;
- Vinod Patel (Nityananda Das), ISKCON Dallas Temple

President, who led my boys through leadership classes and taught me, "A true leader makes more leaders."

CHAPTER 1: YOU ARE NOT ALONE IS DEDICATED TO:

- All the parents who contacted me personally, looking for help with their children, and who have faithfully followed these processes. I share their stories with their names hidden, but I'm grateful that they teach others through their examples.

CHAPTER 2: THE BRAIN TUMOR IS DEDICATED TO:

- My dear family: Pramodraya and Anandi Trivedi; Shivshanker and Chandubaa Joshi; Jagdhish and Paru Trivedi (Jagadguru and Sri Radha ps); Neeta (Nivedita d.) and Virendra Pandya; Dineshkaka, Motamama, Dilipmama, Hemantmama; and all Masis
- My dear cousins Prashantbhai (Premkishor d) and Snehaben who lead a community; Sheelaben (Devahuti d.), Ketanbhai, Chiragbhai, Sameerbhai, Leenaben, Jigneshbhai, Pintuben, Svetaben, Amarbhai, Joybhai, Gargi and Meghaben and so many more who all cared for me as a parent would.

CHAPTER 3: THE CLIMB IS DEDICATED TO:

- The senior leaders at TKG Academy who I'm fortunate to be serving with, and who have laid out the leadership path for an entire community of children: Kalpana Patel (Manjuali d.), Charles (Chaitanya Chandra d) and Nila Young (Nila Madhava d), Padma Tsang, Danny Thomas (Durasaya d), Ron Robinson (Rupanuga d.) Mike Meyers (Mathuranath d), Lila Meyers, Shalagram Das, Lynda Van Nus, Mother Chandravali, Anna

Penate (Laxmi d), Stacy Ross-Mirahmatov (Savitri d), Gita Mani, Darsie Malynn (Vrinda Priya d) and Atul and Ritika Vohra.

CHAPTER 4: ENVISION YOUR DREAM CHILD IS DEDICATED TO:

- International Mentor Dr. Edith Best (Urmila d) who envisioned the best in me as a child and taught me how to teach with the Law of Expectations;
- Community Director Ananda Bloch (Ananda Vrindavan D) who taught me how to empower soul qualities in a child.

CHAPTER 5: MEET THE INNER PARENTS IS DEDICATED TO:

- Dr. Angela Lauria, Founder of the Author Incubator, who taught me how to connect with my Inner Author, who showed me They were my Inner Parents;
- Leadership Parent Meaghan Bhat, (Manjari d) who was a constant cheerleader empowering me to be a guru mentor.

CHAPTER 6: PRESERVE THEIR HEARTS THROUGH HEARING IS DEDICATED TO:

- World-renowned Guru Bir Krishna Goswami, who taught me empathy through his beautiful book and classes;
- Community Director Vraj Vihari Das, who gave me my first empathic communications course in 1996;
- School Directors David and Vrinda Aguilera, from the Bhaktivedanta Academy, to whom empathic communication just flows naturally;

- Principal Laura Baibourine (Audarya d) who expertly hears the needs of her community.

CHAPTER 7: OFFER A L.O.V.E. BOOST IS DEDICATED TO:

- Authors Jaya Sila and Vimala Howie for teaching me the Nurtured Heart Approach;
- Educators Gopika and Aksh Sharma, Vishnupriya Desai, Krishnaa Henderson, and Madhavi Mangu who empower their students across North America
- Shabnam Modjarred for boosting our children with empowering yoga meditations.

CHAPTER 8: WORSHIP THEIR WORK IS DEDICATED TO:

- Teachers Yashoda Parmar, Ishwari Kumari, & Dipti Naik (Devi Radha d) for practicing S.E.R.V.E with our Lower Elementary students excellently in the classroom;Youth Leader Anandini Plotkin for being steady and consistent in her service;
- Our Bhakti Leadership Academy students who are graduating after two years of hard work: Mahi Patel, Saysha Mahadevan, Dhruv Domakonda, Krishnam Goel, Bhavya Agrawal, Darshini Raghavendra, Ishika Jaryal, Ram Palaniappan, Sukanya Khandelwal, Swadha Sharma. Though I've haven't met most of them in person, they expertly led other teams to S.E.R.V.E.;
- Principal Shabashini Lind (Shubra d) who juggles a ton of work for her students;
- Directors Jay Sri Radhe dd and Manorama das for engaging a youth empire for decades.

CHAPTER 9: EMBRACE THEIR MISTAKES IS DEDICATED TO:

- Leadership Parent Ananda Bailey, a dear friend and sister, who showed me through her personal example to accept challenges in life;
- Teacher Aleena Sita Figueroa who taught being comfortable with making mistakes as an important part of education. She taught me so much through her expert instruction;
- Teacher Krishna Priya Jani who taught my children the importance of practice by writing an essay a week in middle school;
- Dear friend Heather Colson (Vilas Manjari d) who embraced my parenting friendship mistakes and loved me regardless.

CHAPTER 10: REST AS A SPIRITUAL PRACTICE IS DEDICATED TO:

- Leadership parent and my dear friend Hari Chan, who taught me how to rest and escape when my children were young and who helped me work through intense childhood traumas. His sound leadership advice empowered me for over a decade.

CHAPTER 11: MAGNIFY THEIR PURPOSE IS DEDICATED TO:

- Dr. David Streight who magnified my purpose and taught me all about motivation;
- Teacher Melissa Flores who taught me about the state of flow;
- Dr. Devika Rao who magnifies her children's daily purpose;
- Dr. Jayshri Chasmawala who only lived her purpose in all her spheres;
- Leadership parents Todd (Tukaram d) & Radhika Garvey,

Manish & Aarti Soni, Atul (Balaram d.) & Sarika Srivatsava (Siddhesvari d), Hrishikesh (Rasaraj d) & Aarti Shinde (Rasakeli d), Daru Krishna & Melanie Kelley, Navin Shyam & Krishna Priya Jani, Yogi & Rachel Brown, Devadeva & Chitravasini Cater, Dharma & Urjesvari Bearden, Dwarka & Chitra Iyengar, Priti & Sam Patel, Subra (Rupamrta d), Geetha (Madhurya d), & Sunita Narayan, Pankaj (Prem d) & Sunita Dwivedi (Supriya d), Sukumar (Devadarshan d) & Sukanya Natarajan (Rasarani d), Sarvesh & Manita Mahajan (Manjuali d), Chetan (Caitya d) & Vedapriya Patel, Kapil & Kalindi Patel, Ricardo (Nama d) & Gayatri Pena (Gopi d), Sanjay (Sridhar d) & Lalita Sakhi Gupta, Manish (Madan Kd) & Vrushali Raikundalia (Vrajamanjari d), Sanjay (Sarvajaya d) & Sapna Singhania (Sadhvi d), Kalpesh (Kinkara d) & Shital Patel (Sriji d), Jay Gauranga & Tulasi Berger, Anilkumar & Archana Uttarker (Aradhya d) & Sucharya devi, Prema Caru & Gopivallabhi Sabharwal for nurturing our communities of children and magnifying their purpose for over a decade.

CHAPTER 12: ENCOURAGE THEIR EMPATHY IS DEDICATED TO:

- Youth Leaders Radha (Kanchana) Kunda Young and Sri Rupa (Nrsimha Rupa) Tansey for showing natural empathy to everyone they meet;
- Leadership Parents Melanie Kelley, a nurturing friend, and Daru Krishna Kelley for guiding communities and knowing when I need empathy.

CHAPTER 13: NEUTRALIZE THEIR SOCIAL CONFLICTS IS DEDICATED TO:

- Leadership Parents and childhood friends Campaka

Fiorentino, & Pancha Priya Darling, who's commitment to children inspires me;

- Teacher Diane Alex (Divya lila d) who helped me combine Dan Millman's story with a *bhakti* story and turn it into a beautiful drama on social empowerment, The Mystical Forest;
- Youth Leaders Arjuna and Gandiva Penate, and Lila Wanty who brought the Mystical Forest drama to the world two years in a row;
- Teacher Kalindi Patel who inspired the C.A.R.E. process with her Montessori Peace Flower scripts.

CHAPTER 14: TRANSFORM THEIR LEADERSHIP SKILLS IS DEDICATED TO:

- To all my leadership students at TKG Academy, past, present and future, who play beautifully in our garden of harmony, and who I have been privileged to learn from every single day;
- To these older students who taught me by their leadership examples: Giri, Sakshi, Nrsimha, Chakra, Raaja, Dhruv, Abhay, Krishna N, Ava, Padayatra, Bala, Rasalila, Brinda, Gopal, Chakrika, Krishna C, Priyatama, Yovana, and Madhava;
- To these younger students who showed me a sheer love for service and purpose in every one of their movements and who have spent years with me every day: Radhe, Vara, Kanai, Gandharvika, Kirtida, Devaki, Gaurangi, Saumya, Aurav, Aradhya, Gaurang, Vrajaraj, Veda, Parth, Braj, Kavachi, Adi, Raghav, Kairava, Ishaan, Leila, and Daisy.

CHAPTER 15: YOU GOT THIS IS DEDICATED TO:

- Bhakti Singers Jahnavi Harrison, Gaura Vani, Madi Brinkmann, the Mayapuris, Acyuta Gopi, the Kirtaniyas, and my Gaura Mani Devi Ji, whose melodious *kirtans* provided constant inspiration and melody as the words flowed through me

- All the leadership parents in the making who are reading this book now and starting this journey. Contact me as soon as you need and join the growing leadership parenting community

ABOUT THE AUTHOR

Mother Gopi Gita is the founder of Leadership Parenting, parent coach and educational consultant for the ISKCON Ministry of Education. She serves as the Vice Principal of a private school in Dallas, TKG Academy. She's also the founder of Bhakti Leadership Academy, where she and her team mentor teenagers around North America in leadership principles. In the past twenty years, she has served more than 1,000 children, mentored more than 500 parents, and personally guided over 100 educators. She's been trained in Waldorf and Montessori Education and has a degree in Child Psychology.

Her favorite meditation is observing the little ones on the playground at school. She empowers them with communication strategies, and loves watching them build collaborative spaces. She uses all that she learns to help parents authentically connect with their children. She will see your child as a mother does and her techniques can be implemented immediately. Parents in leadership who have worked with her feel simultaneously validated and challenged to change their mindsets to help their kids. They also use the principles for their own leadership empowerment.

She grew up in temples in America and has practiced *bhakti yoga* since childhood. She practices daily mantra meditation with her two grown sons and husband in Dallas. She loves singing, bingeing Netflix shows, cooking, and drawing henna designs. She is grateful for every dramatic kid fight because that's how she practices empowering each child to leadership in every challenging interaction.

You can connect with her at:

- Website: www.gopigita.com/parent
- Email: gopi@gopigita.com
- Instagram: www.instagram.com/leadershipparenting
- Facebook: www.facebook.com/gopigita7

OTHER BOOKS BY DIFFERENCE PRESS

The Father, the Son, and the Aha Moment: Tools for Helping You and Your Child Develop a Path to Happiness by Steve & Spencer Barton

The Scholarship Playbook for Parents of Student-Athletes: Stop Fouling Out and Start Scoring Money for College by Dr. Simoné Edwards

Lose the Weight: Create Your Healthy State by Oliveyah Fisch

Transformational Leadership in Healthcare: The Roadmap to Cultivating a Results-Driven Management Team by Dr. Dorine Fobi-Takusi

Grow Your Recruiting Business: The First 3-Part Blueprint to Create Predictable Profits, Reliable Growth, and Business Freedom by Mike Gionta

Find Your Soulmate: The Keys to Ending Your Toxic Relationship Cycle by Sarah E. Healy

When Marriage Needs a Miracle: The Modern Woman's Guide to Figure out the Future of Your Relationship by Shari Kubinec

The Speed of Passion: How Relationship-Based Leadership Drives Innovation by Carol Ann Langford

Be Happier Now!: Life Is Short. Live Your Dreams. by Angela E. Lauria

The $7-Trillion Shock Wave: 401K Investing Strategies with a Positive Impact in Our Shared Climate Future by Seann Stoner

Understanding the Profiles in Human Design: The Facilitator's Guide to Unleashing Potential by Robin Winn, MFT

GIFT FOR THE READER

It has been such a sweet journey with you. I'm so honored that you took my hand through this energizing process of EMPOWERMENT. You've been walking with me for a while now! Do you feel like you want to keep going and don't want to leave my side? I feel the same way. I want to meet you and your beautiful little leader. I want to hear your parenting stories, struggles and successes! I can't wait to envision their qualities with you and help you manifest them every day.

If you're ready to take this seriously, you can connect with me right away online. You'll get a bonus gift at www.gopigita.com/bookgift

This free gift will help us both decide if you're ready to work with me directly, join the Leadership Parenting community and empower your child!

I honestly can't wait to see what difference your child will make in this world, and how they will be energized in their purpose, their flow, their empathy, their collaborative skills and their leadership spaces.

Take care of yourself and make sure you get plenty of rest. Talk soon!

Lots of love and blessings,

Mother Gopi Gita

Printed in Great Britain
by Amazon